THE THERAPEUTIC RELATIONSHIP IN SYSTEMIC THERAPY

Other titles in the
Systemic Thinking and Practice Series
edited by David Campbell & Ros Draper
published and distributed by Karnac Books

Bentovim, A. *Trauma-Organized Systems. Systemic Understanding of Family Violence: Physical and Sexual Abuse*
Bor, R., & Miller, R. *Internal Consultation in Health Care Settings*
Boscolo, L., & Paolo, B. *Systemic Therapy with Individuals*
Burck, C., & Daniel, G. *Gender and Family Therapy*
Campbell, D., Draper, R., & Huffington, C. *Second Thoughts on the Theory and Practice of the Milan Approach to Family Therapy*
Campbell, D., Draper, R., & Huffington, C. *Teaching Systemic Thinking*
Cecchin, G., Lane, G., & Ray, W. A. *The Cybernetics of Prejudices in the Practice of Psychotherapy*
Cecchin, G., Lane, G., & Ray, W. A. *Irreverence: A Strategy for Therapists' Survival*
Dallos, R. *Interacting Stories: Narratives, Family Beliefs, and Therapy*
Draper, R., Gower, M., & Huffington, C. *Teaching Family Therapy*
Farmer, C. *Psychodrama and Systemic Therapy*
Fruggeri, L., et al. *New Systemic Ideas from the Italian Mental Health Movement*
Hoffman, L. *Exchanging Voices: A Collaborative Approach to Family Therapy*
Inger, I., & Inger, J. *Co-Constructing Therapeutic Conversations: A Consultation of Restraint*
Inger, I., & Inger, J. *Creating an Ethical Position in Family Therapy*
Jones, E. *Working with Adult Survivors of Child Sexual Abuse*
Mason, B. *Handing Over: Developing Consistency across Shifts in Residential and Health Settings*
Ray, W. A., & Keeney, B. P. *Resource-Focused Therapy*
Smith, G. *Systemic Approaches to Training in Child Protection*

Work with Organizations
Campbell, D. *Learning Consultation: A Systemic Framework*
Campbell, D., Coldicott, T., & Kinsella, K. *Systemic Work with Organizations: A New Model for Managers and Change Agents*
Campbell, D., Draper, R., & Huffington, C. *A Systemic Approach to Consultation*
Huffington, C., & Brunning, H. *Internal Consultancy in the Public Sector: Case Studies*
McCaughan, N., & Palmer, B. *Systems Thinking for Harassed Managers*

Credit Card orders, Tel: 0171-584-3303; Fax: 0171-823-7743

THE THERAPEUTIC RELATIONSHIP IN SYSTEMIC THERAPY

edited by
Carmel Flaskas and Amaryll Perlesz

Foreword by
Eleanor S. Wertheim

Systemic Thinking and Practice Series
Series Editors
David Campbell & Ros Draper

London
KARNAC BOOKS

First published in 1996 by
H. Karnac (Books) Ltd.
58 Gloucester Road
London SW7 4QY

Foreword copyright © 1996 by Eleanor S. Wertheim. Introduction copyright © 1996 by Carmel Flaskas and Amaryll Perlesz. Chapter 1 copyright © 1996 by Tom Paterson. Chapter 2 copyright © 1996 by Carmel Flaskas. Chapter 3 copyright © 1996 by Edwin Harari. Chapter 4 copyright © 1996 by Vivien Hardham. Chapter 5 copyright © 1996 by Paul Gibney. Discussion paper I copyright © 1996 by Bebe Speed. Chapter 6 copyright © 1996 by Peter Cantwell and Brian Stagoll. Chapter 7 copyright © 1996 by Amaryll Perlesz and Mark Furlong. Chapter 8 copyright © 1996 by Catherine Sanders. Chapter 9 copyright © 1996 by Mark Furlong. Chapter 10 copyright © 1996 by Banu Moloney and Lawrie Moloney. Discussion paper II copyright © 1996 by Elsa Jones.

The rights of the contributors to be identified as authors of this work have been asserted in accordance with §§ 77 and 78 of the Copyright Design and Patents Act 1988.

All rights reserved. No part of this publication may be reproduced, stored in a retrieval system, or transmitted in any form or by any means, electronic, mechanical, photocopying, recording or otherwise, without the prior written permission of the publisher.

British Library Cataloguing in Publication Data

The therapeutic relationship in systemic therapy. —
(Systemic thinking and practice series)
1. Psychology 2. Psychotherapy
I. Flaskas, Carmel II. Perlesz, Amaryll
150

ISBN 1-85575-096-1

Edited, designed, and produced by Communication Crafts

10 9 8 7 6 5 4 3 2 1

Printed in Great Britain by Polestar AUP Aberdeen Limited

CONTENTS

ABOUT THE CONTRIBUTORS ix

EDITORS' FOREWORD xi

FOREWORD Eleanor S. Wertheim xiii

Introduction
The return of the therapeutic relationship
in systemic therapy
Carmel Flaskas and Amaryll Perlesz 1

PART I
New explorations—mainly theory

Chapter 1
Leaving well alone:
a systemic perspective on the therapeutic relationship
Tom Paterson 15

Chapter 2
Understanding the therapeutic relationship:
using psychoanalytic ideas in the systemic context
  Carmel Flaskas   34

Chapter 3
Empathy and the therapeutic relationship
in systemic-oriented therapies:
a historical and clinical overview
  Edwin Harari   53

Chapter 4
Embedded and embodied in
the therapeutic relationship:
understanding the therapist's use of self systemically
  Vivien Hardham   71

Chapter 5
To embrace paradox (once more, with feeling):
a commentary on narrative/conversational therapies
and the therapeutic relationship
  Paul Gibney   90

Discussion paper I
You cannot not relate
  Bebe Speed   108

PART II
New explorations—mainly practice

Chapter 6
The therapeutic moment:
a double-sided drama
  Peter Cantwell and Brian Stagoll   125

Chapter 7
A systemic therapy unravelled:
in through the out door
    *Amaryll Perlesz, Mark Furlong,
    and the "D" family*   142

Chapter 8
From both sides now:
the therapeutic relationship from the viewpoint
of therapist and client
    Catherine Sanders   158

Chapter 9
Cross-purposes:
relationship patterns in public welfare
    Mark Furlong   176

Chapter 10
Personal relationships in systemic supervision
    Banu Moloney and Lawrie Moloney   195

Discussion paper II
Changing systemic constructions
of therapeutic relationships
    Elsa Jones   215

INDEX   227

ABOUT THE CONTRIBUTORS

PETER CANTWELL, a psychologist, is coordinator of training at the Williams Road Family Therapy Centre in Melbourne. He supervises therapists for professional accreditations and has a private practice for individuals, couples, and families.

MEMBERS OF THE "D" FAMILY have shared some of their own experiences of being in family therapy, in Chapter 7, "A Systemic Therapy Unravelled: In Through the Out Door".

CARMEL FLASKAS is a lecturer in the School of Social Work at the University of New South Wales, Sydney, where she convenes the postgraduate programme in couple and family therapy. She also has a private practice in therapy and supervision.

MARK FURLONG is a lecturer in the graduate School of Social Work at La Trobe University, Melbourne. He was most recently Deputy Director at Bouverie Family Therapy Centre.

PAUL GIBNEY has a social-work background and is currently in private practice in Brisbane as a therapist, trainer, and consultant.

EDWIN HARARI is a consultant psychiatrist at St Vincent's Hospital in Melbourne and also has a private practice. He teaches and supervises in individual and family therapy.

VIVIEN HARDHAM is a psychologist/family therapist working as a therapist and supervisor in rural New South Wales and Victoria.

ELSA JONES is a clinical psychologist and systemic therapist who works independently as a therapist, trainer, and consultant in Cardiff.

BANU MOLONEY is a Melbourne psychologist and social worker who co-ordinates training at Bouverie Family Therapy Centre, teaches and supervises in the Masters in Family Therapy programme at La Trobe University, Melbourne, as well as teaching, supervising, and consulting privately.

LAWRIE MOLONEY is a clinical psychologist, currently working as a senior lecturer in the Social Sciences Faculty at La Trobe University, Melbourne.

TOM PATERSON has a social work background and is currently a senior lecturer in the Graduate Diploma and Masters in Family Therapy programmes at LaTrobe University, Melbourne. He also has a private therapy practice.

AMARYLL PERLESZ is a clinical psychologist who teaches and supervises in the Masters in Family Therapy programme at La Trobe University, Melbourne. She is currently on study leave from Bouverie Family Therapy Centre, completing her PhD.

CATHERINE SANDERS is a clinical psychologist and co-director of Bower Place, a therapy and training centre in Adelaide.

BEBE SPEED trained in psychiatric social work and psychotherapy before working for ten years at the Family Institute, Cardiff. She moved to Birmingham in 1989, where she now combines a private practice with teaching and co-editing the *Journal of Family Therapy*.

BRIAN STAGOLL is a psychiatrist, and co-director of Williams Road Family Therapy Centre, a therapy and training organization in Melbourne.

EDITORS' FOREWORD

Anyone following the recent developments of systemic thinking will be aware that activity has not been restricted to Europe and America. Systemic therapists and writers from both Australia and New Zealand are now making a major impact on the field, particularly in the way they explore therapy as an exchange between "real" people; with gender and with ethical values; and embedded within specific cultural experiences. These people are challenging the traditional way we see clients and the context of therapy. Over the years, systemic therapists have theorized extensively about the client family as a system and have more recently addressed the use of self in therapy, but there has been very little attention paid to the therapeutic relationship between the two.

Flaskas and Perlesz recognized this gap in the field, and they have assembled here a collection of papers that all focus on this central theme. The *Systemic Thinking and Practice Series* is committed to books that focus on one central theme; this is usually best accomplished by a single author or a few co-authors, but in this case we were eager to publish this collection from a range of authors because of the importance of this topic for the field, and we are confident the reader will find that each paper clearly addresses the central theme. It is also a pleasure for us to be able to introduce new authors to our readership.

As the Series Editors, we are aware of the coalescence of different conceptual models of therapy. Practitioners now put ideas and techniques together to tackle particular therapeutic dilemmas in ways that would have been frowned on in the past. There is always the danger in so doing that concepts are simply borrowed and attached to a new model, without sufficient examination of what the concept means in its own context and how its difference can be utilized to build new knowledge. Flaskas and Perlesz, as authors in their own right, have explored the connections between systemic and psychoanalytic models of conceptualizing, and in this volume they show repeatedly that the two models can be used in a complementary way to elucidate the relationship between the inner world and the interactional world and the way these come together in the therapeutic relationship. The book, taken as a whole, represents an advance in our thinking about therapy. It is no longer sufficient just to conceptualize the therapist as "embedded" in an external context, but we must combine this view with an understanding of our own and our client's experience as it is "embodied" in the individual. The interplay between the two leads to greater understanding of the therapeutic relationship.

David Campbell
Ros Draper
London,
April 1996

FOREWORD

Eleanor S. Wertheim

I welcome the Editors' initiative in bringing the issue of the therapeutic relationship in family systems therapy into focus. The therapeutic relationship was given no attention at the inception of family systems therapy and has remained its Cinderella since. This neglect has to be seen in the wider historical context in which systems-based therapy had its beginnings, and in the more immediate context of its own short history.

Family systems therapy was born at a time when a large-scale, profound philosophical and scientific revolution had begun to challenge the established, mechanistic view of the world, dominant in the West until then. An emerging systems paradigm, embodied in a meta-theoretical General System Theory (GST), was demanding a radical change in thinking and a new understanding of how the world at large works. The GST was a body of evolving ideas, theories, and sub-theories, including the theory of open (living) systems. In the light of the GST, accepted mechanistic concepts of reality, objectivity, stability and change, and many others had to be fundamentally revised. Seen through the mechanistic prism, the world consisted of discrete "things", whose "true" nature could be discovered by an objective observer ("objective perspective"). This was a stable world. Change required the application of an external force. Seen through the prism of the theory of open systems, the world was in a flux, as interconnected elements (themselves in a temporary state of stable equilibrium) were organizing and reorganizing themselves into hierarchically[1] arranged systems and sub-systems of varying complexity, more complex systems providing a context (environment) for less complex sub-systems (i.e. the principle of "wholeness"). The observer, as one of the shifting elements, was always part of the system under observation and could only view it from this "relational perspective". The observer was able to change positions in the system, move in and out of it, and so view the system from multiple perspectives but, by definition, could never step out of a relational perspective altogether. In this dynamic vision of the world, change was internally generated in the system through self-corrective or self-organizing processes. The environment (context) provided only the "wherewithal" for the change.

A "system" was not a concrete entity but a conceptual tool providing general principles for organizing "reality" and experience, and for speaking about them at a meta-theoretical level. This generality gave the "system" conceptual power in theorizing across all domains: for example, about an ecological habitat, the human society, the family or an individual. The systemic framework had to be translated into a discipline-specific theory or model and given content at this level by reference to discipline-specific theoretical and practical knowledge. Such lower-order theories or models had to be compatible with basic, meta-theoretical, systemic premises (e.g. "wholeness" principle, non-linear, relational perspective, multi-causality, etc.). For example, a therapeutic model that emphasizes intersubjective generation and sharing of meanings (narratives) can be accommodated within a systemic paradigm. A therapeutic model based on a theory implying linear causality (e.g. the stimulus–response model) would be incompatible with it.

By contrast with the wide-ranging open-system theory, dealing with interactive processes between systems and their environments, the cybernetic feedback model was narrowly focused on control mechanisms in homeostatically regulated systems. The model was more concerned with the underlying structure of systemic processes than with the processes themselves, and its original concept of "feedback" was, strictly speaking, reactive rather than interactive.

The major, initial development of family systems theory and therapy occurred in the United States. Except for Gregory Bateson, a systems theorist, most pioneers of this form of therapy were clinicians with a prior analytic orientation. Challenged by the apparent stability of "pathology" in their psychiatric patients, they had a primary interest in the pragmatic utility of the "system" concept. Their main aim was instrumental: how to become more effective in dealing with clinical problems and achieve results in much less time than was usual in analytic treatment.

The pioneers made a theoretical and practical quantum leap in shifting the therapeutic focus from the individual seen in isolation, to the individual considered in the family context—that is, to the family "system". However, contrary to the "wholeness" principle of open-system theory, they selectively conceptualized the family as a "system". The other, closely inter-related components of the immediate therapeutic field—the individual, as a system in its own right (e.g. the single therapist, individual family members), and the contextual "therapeutic system", constituted by multi-level,[2] sequential, non-linear processes of interaction between the therapist and the family, and between the therapist and individual family members—were not considered.[3] The family system itself was conceptualized in terms of the narrow, cybernetic feedback model requiring an environmental stimulus to which the system responds in a mechanistic cycle of action and reaction.[4] The failure to conceptualize the "therapeutic system", of which the observer–therapist is an integral part, left in place the old mechanistic ideas about the objective, external observer, and about change requiring the application of an external force. The model of the therapist having to remain detached and act on the family as an external agent of change conforms to these ideas. The different versions of family systems theory, on which family systems therapy was based, reflected the lack of an integrated, overall systemic vision and the underlying epistemological confusion. A theory and practice that aspired to being "systemic" incorporated incompatible systemic and mechanistic concepts. The complexity of the contextual therapeutic relationship did not enter into the existing theoretical framework and was outside its pragmatic focus.

In the last fifteen years or so, the field of family systems therapy has experienced a number of theoretical "perturbations"—for example, "second-order cybernetics", a call for the inclusion of aesthetic considerations in therapeutic practice, and others. The former inspired a new methodology based on a systemic rationale (e.g. circular questioning). This methodology was merely put to use in the service of the pragmatic, therapeutic stance. Despite the intellectual recognition that therapists were part of the therapeutic field, the perturbations did not seem to have had significant impact on mainstream theory and practice in regard to the therapeutic relationship.

A look at how family systems therapy evolved over time throws further light on its attachment to the mechanistic model and the associated neglect of the therapeutic relationship.

Importantly, an early theoretical and methodological consolidation of several, "closed-shop" models of family therapy fostered conformity to the oversimplified, clinical theories of family systems and to a range of limited, pragmatic strategies and techniques. The trend was reinforced by a rapid gain in the popularity of family therapy amongst clinical workers, and only a short theoretical and practical preparation of the growing number of aspiring family therapists. This produced a rank-and-file generation of therapists primarily interested in the "how to do" of therapy. Many learnt to use systems jargon without a proper conceptual grasp of the espoused theory, with no knowledge of the meta-theoretical open-system paradigm, of the mechanistic paradigm, and of the difference between the two. Even after training opportunities increased, the available courses often had a narrow knowledge base. Students were required to become familiar with one or more of the theoretical models of family systems therapy and to acquire corresponding technical competence. They had no exposure to the meta-theoretical systems paradigm and its cross-disciplinary literature and were unable to evaluate their practice critically from a general "systems" point of view. Those interested in enlarging their knowledge base and therapeutic understanding mostly turned to non-systemic literature. This was a valuable exercise, allowing for multiple perspectives, but it still left them without a broader, unifying framework for thinking about a more comprehensive, theoretically consistent, systems-based clinical model of therapy. It is not surprising, therefore, that the more recent upsurge of interest in the therapeutic relationship was stimulated not by theoretical concerns, but by individual therapists' dissatisfaction with the accepted pragmatic stance belying their personal therapeutic experience and by a suspicion that common therapeutic difficulties (e.g. "getting stuck") and failures were related to this stance.

Various papers in the present volume reflect the current tension over the place of the immediate therapeutic relationship in family therapy and the need to consider the wider, relevant social contexts in which this relationship is embedded. By voicing their concerns and proposing different, often creative, theoretical and practical solutions, the authors are introducing new perturbations into the field. May these be more effective than the earlier, theoretically inspired perturbations in triggering a much needed transformation of family therapy theory and practice.

It is to be hoped that, in the end, a theoretically better integrated clinical systems theory will emerge to inform a more genuine, intellectually rigorous, and effective therapeutic practice that does justice to the complexity of personal and social human experience.

NOTES

1. In the restricted meta-theoretical language of systems, "hierarchy" denotes organizational complexity. This content-free use of the term should not be confused, as it often is, with its every-day usage implying social status as related to "power".

2. The by definition inter-related, simultaneously occurring interactions

have to be defined at the discipline-specific level. This requires a concept of how human individuals are organized as systems.

3. These two levels of interaction are related but distinct.

4. Influenced by Bateson's ideas, the Milan school reconceptualized "feedback" in systemic terms but only as applied to intra-familial dynamics.

THE THERAPEUTIC RELATIONSHIP IN SYSTEMIC THERAPY

INTRODUCTION

The return of the therapeutic relationship in systemic therapy

Carmel Flaskas and Amaryll Perlesz

Systemic therapy has as its central focus an interactional perspective, and its theory has developed recursive ways of understanding patterns in relationships. The failure, then, to theorize the therapeutic relationship itself seems very ironic. However, recently there has been a tentative renewal of interest in the topic, and this collection of papers is devoted to extending thinking about the therapeutic relationship in systemic therapy. We would like to use the introduction to map the absence and then re-emergence of an interest in the therapeutic relationship, as well as to introduce our editorial project and the papers themselves.

THE THERAPEUTIC RELATIONSHIP IN SYSTEMIC THERAPY—SOME HISTORY

Though a potted historical review is a foolhardy venture that easily slips into simplistic generalization, this is nonetheless where we intend to start! The history of systemic therapy has been documented and "storied" in various ways, but we want to begin here by noting the emergence of systemic therapy in the context of a struggle to generate theory and practices that could more fruitfully meet the demands of therapy with families. This struggle occurred in the context of a therapy field dominated by individual (and more specifically, intra-psychic) therapies. Some of the more conservative ideas of the 1950s versions of systems theory were applied as a dominant metaphor to guide the early conceptualization of patterns of relationships within families, and to force a theory and practice attention on human systems of relationships. At this point, the new systemic thinking in therapy was being forged in opposition to the de facto thinking of families as being simply the sum and layering of individual psyches.

It is perhaps not so surprising, then, that concerns that had traditionally been central to individual therapies became marginalized in the early project of systemic therapy, which saw the development of the structural and strategic models of family therapy. In the search for patterns and systems metaphors, the language and accepted thinking of systemic therapy became "de-individualized". This de-individualization was accompanied by, amongst other things, a de-focusing of emotions and feelings, a de-valuing of the therapist's self in the process of therapy, and a failure to attend to the therapeutic relationship as the venue for the therapy process. And so within two paragraphs we find ourselves making this rather sweeping claim, which we believe to be true, and yet, having made it, we realize immediately that it needs to be qualified.

For while it may be true enough that these concerns were left off the agenda of theory development and the discourse developing within systemic therapy (and indeed this could be evidenced by a review of the content of the major systemic journals and seminal textbooks from the 1960s through to the late 1980s), it is very difficult to believe that these topics could really ever have fallen off the practice agendas of systemic therapists. And though we may have often chosen in systemic therapy to describe therapy primarily in terms of techniques and selected biological and mechanistic metaphors, clients, thank goodness, are stubborn in their consistency in experiencing therapy as a very human endeavour, and indeed in experiencing therapists very much as people in relationship with them.[1] So we could look at the different models of systemic therapy and see evidence of this essential concern for the therapeutic relationship "built into" different techniques, and yet at the same time a lack of labelling of this concern at the level of theory or in "public" discussion in the field of family therapy.

Having made the distinction, then, between the level of theory and the implicit effect of practices, it becomes important to note the dangers to which an absence of theorizing about the therapeutic relationship exposes us. For while all the systemic therapies may have some attention to the therapeutic relationship built into their techniques, failure and impasse in the therapeutic relationship finds us without theory ideas or a way of public discussion. Indeed, it may prevent us even coming to *name* failure and impasse in the therapeutic relationship. This absence also becomes a problem in training, as trainee systemic therapists are often left with a privatized struggle in making sense of the therapeutic relationship and their own use of self as a therapist. And because there is a subtle (if at times erratic!) relationship between theory and practice in therapy, a persistent failure to theorize the therapeutic relationship ultimately restricts the flexibility of our development of practices that sensitize and extend our use of the therapeutic relationship in systemic therapy.

So far, we have wanted to draw the broad context of the absence of attention to the therapeutic relationship in systemic therapy, to pinpoint that the absence has been first and foremost at the level of theory and "public" discussion, and to make some points about the dangers of this absence. But we are aiming to track the re-emergence of the interest in the therapeutic relationship in systemic therapy, which is, of course, the immediate context of this book, and to do this we need to pick up again on the potted historical review.

For though it may not be surprising that the earlier (first-order) models of systemic therapy gave little space to theorizing the therapeutic relationship, second-order ideas which began to be very influential from 1980 begged the question of the therapeutic relationship. Of course, the shift to second-order ideas involved, amongst other things, a major re-conceptualization of the relationship of the therapist to the process of therapy. The shift was from the first-order view of the therapist being "outside" the process of therapy, "acting on" and "intervening in" the family system, to the idea of the therapist being necessarily and inextricably part of the therapist–family system. To follow this idea through, therapeutic change could then be seen as occurring in the space created within this therapist/family system or, if you like, in the space between the therapist and family/client. On the face of it, then, it seems quite paradoxical that this major shift in emphasis with second-order ideas did not bring about renewed attention to the therapeutic relationship.

However, despite the shift in the early 1980s from the strategic and behavioural strategies of the earlier first-order models to the meaning interventions of the Milan ideas and the advent of the practices of the reflecting team, there continued to be very little space given to the topics of emotion, or the self, or the therapeutic relationship. This paradox probably reflects quite complex factors. The move to second-order ideas was tied to a rigorous attempt to place some of the later ideas of the biologist Gregory Bateson as foundational in systemic therapy, and the brief flourishing of the "new epistemology" in the early 1980s, and the even briefer flirtation with the biological theories of constructivism of Maturana and Varela in the mid-1980s, were part of this "foundational project".

It may be that the very language of the biological metaphor was at the one time too general and too limiting to embrace and describe the distinctively human topics of emotions, the self, and the therapeutic relationship, and a number of writers have made this argument very cogently (Falzer, 1986; Luepnitz, 1988). But political factors were perhaps also at work, for one of the momenta of any foundational endeavour is the censorship of topics that are seen to be in opposition to the principles that are being privileged as foundational (Flaskas, 1990). Part of the paradox, then, may simply have been that the topic of the therapeutic relationship was assumed to be "unsystemic", and so the invitation to theorize it in ways that are harmonious with the project of systemic therapy simply disappeared.

Of course, this is all in the realm of interested speculation. Regardless of the precise reasons of the paradox of second-order ideas failing to embrace the topic of the therapeutic relationship, it has now become more possible to respond to the invitation. We would argue that this is in part a result of the freeing influence of feminist critiques, and in part a result of the belated arrival of postmodernist and social constructionist ideas in systemic therapy.

Though the feminist critiques in the 1980s largely targeted the failure of systemic therapy to acknowledge, account for, and understand gender and power relationships, the very effectiveness of this challenge has had the "ripple effect" of allowing the space for other kinds of challenges to be made to some of the historical censorships in systemic therapy. Moreover, concerns with emotions, intimacy, and the experience of the self traditionally have been given credibility in feminist politics, and a reawakening of interest in these topics goes hand-in-hand with an interest in the therapeutic relationship.

The second freeing strand has been the recent engagement of systemic therapy with postmodernist and social constructionist ideas. As Doherty has noted, postmodernist ideas have been used in systemic therapy to give permission for eclecticism (Doherty, 1991). The project of foundationalism, resting as it does in modernist aspirations for secure and universalizing foundations of knowledge, has largely fallen away. Moreover, though social constructionist ideas have been used in different ways, especially in developing the narrative therapies[2], in general the sociological emphasis on meaning provides a far more hospitable environment than the biological frame for pursuing interests in emotions, intimacy, and the therapeutic relationship.

And so, within the past five years, it has become possible to be interested again in discussing and theorizing some of the central topics of therapy that may never have left our practice agendas. Writing has begun to appear that offers systemic discussions of intimacy (James & Kirkland, 1993; Weingarten, 1991, 1992), of empathy (Perry, 1993; Wilkinson, 1992), of emotion (Flaskas, 1989; Krause, 1993; Smith, Osman, & Goding, 1990), of the therapist's use of self (Real, 1990), of the therapist's position

(Anderson & Goolishian, 1992; Hoffman, 1993), and of other issues surrounding the therapeutic relationship and the therapist–family system (Andersen, 1992; Andolphi & Angelo, 1988; Cecchin, Lane, & Ray, 1993; Flaskas, 1994; Gibney, 1991; MacKinnon, 1993).

OUR EDITORIAL PROJECT

We would like to locate our book in the context of this emerging literature in systemic therapy, and indeed our project has been to take hold of the current environment of greater freedom with both hands, and to pursue actively the goal of discussing and theorizing the therapeutic relationship in systemic therapy.

In approaching this goal as editors, we decided against attempting a programmatic "laying out" of the topic of the therapeutic relationship. At a pragmatic level, the very undertheorization of the topic makes any programmatic goal premature, and an approach that encourages different intersections seemed potentially more fruitful of new ideas. At a philosophical level, we were also committed to allowing different ideas to sit side-by-side, and to allowing the space for the enrichment of differences in perspectives and interests in systemic therapy. If you like, we had in mind an edited collection of papers which could stand as a kind of symposium.

Thus, we simply invited Australian colleagues who, we knew, had a special theory and/or practice interest in the therapeutic relationship to write papers on their current ideas, and we wanted them to feel free to pursue the intersections they were finding most interesting and/or helpful. As it happened, the general focus of the different papers fell fairly easily into the "mainly theory" and "mainly practice" categories, and so we have divided the book into two main parts. In some ways though, of course, this is an arbitrary split, as all the papers move across theory and practice—and we are optimistic enough to think that in the enterprise of therapy, good theory ideas are always edifying for practice, and vice-versa! As well, in the spirit of opening out ideas and discussions, we invited discussion papers from two British colleagues: Bebe Speed has contributed the discussion paper for Part I, and Elsa Jones has contributed the Part II discussion paper.

THE PAPERS

Having laid out our own editorial project and the structure of the book, we would also like to give readers a little information on each of the papers. Part 1 ("New Explorations—Mainly Theory") consists of five quite different papers. Tom Paterson's paper considers how different domains of therapy invite a different theorizing of the therapeutic relationship. In the process of making a distinction between the autonomous and relational self, he concludes that within the systemic domain the therapist may at times need to be less intimate and less focused on emotional aspects—indeed, to "leave well enough alone". The next paper, by Carmel Flaskas, chooses to consider directly the potential value of some psychoanalytic ideas in the systemic context of therapy, and specifically the concepts of transference, countertransference, and projective identification are discussed in terms of their helpfulness for extending systemic ideas around engagement and sequences.

Edwin Harari takes a historical perspective in overviewing the ways in which the different systemic-oriented therapies have all sustained the space for empathy in the therapeutic relationship, despite their different practice concerns and techniques. The paper by Vivien Hardham was motivated by her own desire to think about the self of the therapist in systemic ways, and she extends some systemic thinking to incorporate the ideas of the therapist being both embodied and embedded in the therapeutic relationship. The final paper in Part I is by Paul Gibney, and in it he reviews the recent shift to the narrative/conversational therapies in the systemic field. He argues that though this shift is a rejection of the earlier claims to certainty, the failure to construe emotions and the therapeutic relationship remains—and that we would do better embracing the paradoxes of mature practice and theorizing, including the paradox of love and power in the therapeutic relationship

Part II ("New Explorations—Mainly Practice") begins with a paper by Peter Cantwell and Brian Stagoll, whose project is to hold the idea of therapy as being "a double-sided drama" of therapist and clients, alongside the ideas of collaborative therapy and the ethics of participation which have been re-emerging in systemic practice. Amaryll Perlesz, Mark Furlong, and the "D" family write of their experiences of the therapeutic relationship in their joint involvement in a particular therapy. Their description is an integration of the diverse and multiple perspectives of family members and therapist. In her paper, Catherine Sanders chooses to explore themes in the systemic literature concerning the therapeutic relationship. She asks some women who had been in longer-term individual systemic therapy with her to comment on their experience of these themes, and then comments herself on her experience of these themes as the therapist.

Mark Furlong uses a wider lens to consider the social context of the therapeutic relationship, and, rather than doing this in the abstract, he chooses the particular example of public welfare practice to analyse the relationship patterns within which the therapist is so often embroiled. The final paper is by Banu Moloney and Lawrie Moloney. Here the topic is supervision, and they consider the personal and emotional involvements of both therapist and supervisor in the relationship dilemmas that are presented by clients, and they explore the richness of these involvements at both a theory and practice level.

Across the collection as a whole, recurring interests are tackled from different angles—especially the issues of emotional experience, relationship patterns, the therapist's position, understandings of the self, use of the self, and personal involvement, all crop up in different papers with different intersections being made. In some papers, contributors are interested in exploring "outside" theory and ideas to further systemic understandings, while other papers push and extend systemic theory itself to address the therapeutic relationship. Practice leads to theory and theory to practice, though not always in a neat way. There is a lot of common ground for discussion, and certainly some food for debate.

We hope we will not be pre-empting readers' own assessments of these convergences and debates by highlighting in particular the tensions and balances both within and across different papers concerning the use of "outside" theory and critique. For example, a point for debate exists between the first two papers, by Tom Paterson (Chapter 1) and Carmel Flaskas (Chapter 2), as to whether and how psychoanalytic ideas may be useful in the systemic context. Tom argues that the systemic emphasis needs to be more on the relational self rather than the autonomous self, and that many psychoanalytic ideas presuppose an intimacy in the therapeutic relationship which is often neither needed nor appropriate in systemic work. Carmel, on the other hand, argues that analytic ideas are very valuable in the project of understanding the therapeutic relationships, provided that the different environments of psychoanalytic and systemic therapies are held in mind.

In many ways, Tom Paterson's paper prioritizes extending ideas within the systemic frame in the development of new theory, and Vivien Hardham (Chapter 4) also chooses this commitment in her paper but takes quite a different track to Tom in developing the ideas of the therapist as embodied and embedded in the therapeutic relationship. This contrasts to the position that Edwin Harari (Chapter 3) takes in his project of reviewing the practices of systemic models with respect to empathy and the therapeutic relationship, for his choice of a pragmatic and historical analysis means that there is no friction between the use of "outside" theory versus systemic theory.

However, like Carmel Flaskas, Paul Gibney (Chapter 5) also chooses to make a "foreground" use of outside theory. In particular, he spotlights some Jungian ideas in discussing aspects of the therapeutic relationship which are raised in his critique of narrative/conversational modes of therapy. Paul's critique also provides another point for debate when read alongside the paper by Peter Cantwell and Brian Stagoll (Chapter 6), for their discussion is devoted to developing the theory ideas and practices associated with collaborative therapy, and they use this discussion to extend ideas about the therapeutic relationship.

In their paper on supervision, Banu Moloney and Lawrie Moloney (Chapter 10) strike a fine balance in juggling the use of "outside" ideas with a focus on the systemic project, as they place ideas from the wider supervision literature alongside some psychoanalytic ideas and feminist ideas in developing what the ethics of connection and self-disclosure might mean in systemic supervisory practice. Mark Furlong's paper (Chapter 9) on the relationship patterns in public welfare also deserves mention in this discussion of the use of "outside" theory, for he makes a much broader use of a sociological and political analysis in coming to grips with the patterns of blame and volatility in relationships in the field of child welfare.

Another potential point for discussion and debate across papers concerns the theme of the "client's voice", and a commitment to allowing the space for the clients' voices shows itself very clearly in the two papers by Catherine Sanders (Chapter 8) and Amaryll Perlesz, Mark Furlong, and the "D" family (Chapter 7). This idea also crops up in a different form in the supervision discussion of Banu Moloney and Lawrie Moloney (Chapter 10). In her discussion of Part II, Elsa Jones raises the question of who most benefits from eliciting "the client's voice" in forums for systemic therapists, and how the ethics of including marginalized voices needs to take account of this question. Following Elsa's question, it is interesting to go back to the papers to see the different ways in which the different contributors have tackled this issue in the setting-up of their projects.

Of course, there are many other points for debate and discussion which are very well signposted in the two discussion papers by Bebe Speed and Elsa Jones. Again, without wishing to give too much of a preview here, we would like to note the way in which Bebe develops the point that "we cannot not relate" enriches the historical discussion of the way in which systemic therapy has and has not engaged with the therapeutic relationship, and also specifically addresses the importance of the practices of the team in the development of this history. Elsa Jones takes up the themes across the papers in Part II of power and powerlessness, the issue of including clients' voices, the self of the therapist, and the systemic construction of self. In noting some of the very recent European contributions to these discussions, she adds her own reflections on changing the systemic constructions of the therapeutic relationship.

But perhaps that's enough advance information on the content of the papers in this book. We hope that readers will enjoy the collection, both for the ideas held within each paper, as well as for the scope of the combined discussion and the points of commonality and difference. And we would also hope that, like a good symposium, this collection of papers stimulates and promotes further thinking, discussion, and writing about the therapeutic relationship in systemic therapy.

NOTES

1. See, for example, the review in Grunebaum (1988) of clients' perceptions of the importance of qualities of the therapeutic relationship for their experience of therapy.
2. See, for example, the difference in emphases between the use made by Anderson and Goolishian (1988) of social constructionist theory, and Hoffman's (1990) use of it.

REFERENCES

Andersen, T. (1992). Relationship, language and pre-understanding in the reflecting processes. *Australian and New Zealand Journal of Family Therapy, 13* (2), 87–91.

Anderson, H., & Goolishian, H. (1988). Human systems as linguistic systems: preliminary and evolving ideas about the implications for clinical theory. *Family Process, 27* (4), 371–393.

Anderson. H., & Goolishian, H. (1992). The client is the expert: a not-knowing approach to therapy. In S. McNamee & K. J. Gergen (Eds.), *Therapy as Social Construction.* London: Sage.

Andolphi, M., & Angelo, C. (1988). Towards constructing the therapeutic system. *Journal of Marital and Family Therapy, 14* (3), 237–247.

Cecchin, G., Lane, J., & Ray, W. A. (1993). From strategizing to nonintervention: towards irreverence in systemic practice. *Journal of Marital and Family Therapy, 19* (2), 125–136.

Doherty, W. J. (1991). Family therapy goes postmodern. *Family Therapy Networker, 15* (5), 37–42.

Falzer, P. R. (1986). The cybernetic metaphor: a critical examination of ecosystemic epistemology as a foundation of family therapy. *Family Process, 25* (3), 353–363.

Flaskas, C. (1989). Thinking about the emotional interaction of therapist and family. *Australian and New Zealand Journal of Family Therapy, 10* (1): 1–6.

Flaskas, C. (1990). Power and knowledge: the case of the new epistemology. *Australian and New Zealand Journal of Family Therapy*, 11 (3): 207–214.

Flaskas, C. (1994). Exploring the therapeutic relationship: a case study. *Australian and New Zealand Journal of Family Therapy*, 15 (4): 185–190.

Gibney, P. (1991). Articulating the implicate: an invitation to openness. *Australian and New Zealand Journal of Family Therapy*, 12 (3), 133–136.

Grunebaum, H. (1988). What if family therapy were a kind of psychotherapy? *Journal of Marital and Family Therapy*, 14 (2), 195–199.

Hoffman, L. (1990). Constructing realities: an art of lenses. *Family Process* 29 (1), 1–12. Also in *Exchanging Voices: A Collaborative Approach to Family Therapy*. London: Karnac Books, 1993.

Hoffman, L. (1993). *Exchanging Voices: A Collaborative Approach to Family Therapy*. London: Karnac Books.

James, L., & Kirkland, J. (1993). Beyond empathy: seasons of affiliation, intimacy and power in therapy relationships. *Australian and New Zealand Journal of Family Therapy*, 14 (4), 177–180.

Krause, I.-B. (1993). Family therapy and anthropology: the case for emotions. *Journal of Family Therapy*, 15 (1): 35–56.

Luepnitz, D. A. (1988). *The Family Interpreted: Feminist Theory in Clinical Practice*. New York: Basic Books.

MacKinnon, L. K. (1993). Systems in settings: the therapist as power broker. *Australian and New Zealand Journal of Family Therapy*, 14 (3), 117–122.

Perry, R. (1993). Empathy—still at the heart of therapy. *Australian and New Zealand Journal of Family Therapy*, 14 (2), 63–74.

Real, T. (1990). The therapeutic use of self in constructionist/systemic therapy. *Family Process*, 29 (3), 255–272.

Smith, J., Osman, C., & Goding, M. (1990). Reclaiming the emotional aspects of the therapist–family system. *Australian and New Zealand Journal of Family Therapy*, 11 (3), 140–146.

Weingarten, K. (1991). The discourses of intimacy: adding a social constructionist and feminist view. *Family Process*, 30 (3), 285–305.

Weingarten, K. (1992), A consideration of intimate and non-intimate interactions in therapy. *Family Process*, 31 (1), 45–59.

Wilkinson, M. (1992). How do we understand empathy systemically? *Journal of Family Therapy*, 14 (2), 193–206.

PART 1

NEW EXPLORATIONS—
MAINLY THEORY

CHAPTER 1

Leaving well alone: a systemic perspective on the therapeutic relationship

Tom Paterson

INTRODUCTION

In recent years there has been widespread contention that systemic therapists have under-theorized the therapist–family relationship—especially in its emotional aspects. This lack is often attributed to what Smith, Osman, and Goding (1990) call the "dominance of 'male stream' thought in family therapy" (p. 143). This dominance, they argue, has led to a privileging of reason over emotion and objectivity over subjectivity, which has remained unshaken by the emergence of second-order cybernetic theory. Interest has also been shown in the idea of exploring the relevance and possible value of psychoanalytic ideas for filling what is seen as a theoretical vacuum surrounding the therapeutic relationship in family therapy (cf. Flaskas, 1989, 1993, 1994).

I agree that the therapeutic relationship has been ignored for misguided reasons[1], and I also think that psychoanalytic ideas are valuable for some of the things family therapists do. In this chapter, I begin with the simple point, which appears to have been overlooked, that systemic therapists play a more marginal role in the natural groups they join, whereas the one-to-one psychoanalytic therapist–client relationship demands more intense involvement. Thus it is appropriate for the former to focus more on the process in the natural group and for the latter to analyse the therapist–client relationship in depth.

I then make a distinction between the "relational" and "autonomous" aspects of a system or a "self" in order to conceptualize the way problematic patterns range from those that can change relatively easily with a change in relational context, to those that survive contradiction, changes in context, and efforts by therapists to change them. A consideration of the different kinds of therapy that seem appropriate to different kinds of situation suggests that some situations demand an emphasis on theory and technique, whilst others require special attention to feelings and intuitions.

I conclude that an intense personal relationship between therapist and client is not something that should be pursued as a general value. Rather, therapist and client should intrude on each other's lives no more than is necessary to achieve what they will both accept as the therapeutic objective.

THE CONTEXTS OF CHANGE IN SYSTEMIC AND PSYCHOANALYTIC THERAPIES

Perhaps the central idea of family therapy is that healing takes place through the therapist convening what Stierlin et. al. (1980) call a "family-wide encounter", a dialogue between family members, which includes an outsider therapist whose role is to create a context that leads them to change their perspectives on each other. For example, with a couple complaining about their differences, the therapist might help to create a perspective in which each party sees the other as a resource for realizing their aspirations for growth. Systemic therapists' focus on "natural groups" is such that they sometimes forget their presence in the system. Thus Boszormenyi-Nagy and Ulrich (1981) speak of family therapists offering "assistance within the participants' *original* relational context" (p. 162; my italics).

In contrast, the psychoanalytic therapist works in a "substitutive relational context" (Boszormenyi-Nagy & Ulrich, 1981, p. 161). At the outset, the client only knows that he is not happy, and he suspects that the problem lies with him.[2] The ambiguous situation allows the client unconsciously to act out his part in significant relationships transferred from elsewhere in the present or the past. The therapist slowly gains understanding by involving herself in these relationships (Mattinson, 1975, p. 24). Thus therapist and client slowly discover, in Karl Menninger's words:

> that this or that aspect of his feelings and attitudes, this or that technique of behaviour, this or that role in which he casts other people, is of a pattern . . . like the footprint of a bear which has lost certain toes in a trap, [which] originated long ago and stamps itself on every step of his life's journey. [Menninger, 1964, pp. 147–148]

This pattern is present in his everyday relationships, and in the analytic relationship, but originated "for a reason which was valid at the time, and persisted despite changes in some of the circumstances which originally determined it" (Menninger, 1964, p. 148), and it now contains elements that are problematic for both the patient and his cohorts. The work of the analytic therapist is to help the client identify this pattern and free himself from it.

The therapeutic relationship is central to the analytic process and is more marginal to the systemic process. The systemic therapist is always part of the system, but, unlike her analytic counterpart, she may not be as influential as some family members.[3]

THE RELATIONAL SELF AND THE AUTONOMOUS SELF

The psychoanalytic family therapist Jurg Willi (1987) contends that systems therapists tend to believe that different relational frameworks shape different "personalities", whereas psychoanalysts are primarily interested in "personality" structure that remains "stable over time and in different situations" (pp. 430,

431).[4] In this section I build on the "bare bones" ideas of Gregory Bateson and of Humberto Maturana to explore this idea.

According to Mathews (1991), a "self" or a living thing is distinguished not by its boundaries, but by two contrasting elements—autonomy and relatedness. Most obvious is the appearance of autonomy; it is not directly shaped by events, but acts or behaves in accordance with its own organization. On the other hand, it maintains this form or organization by means of its interconnectedness with the environment. The "autonomous" side has been represented in family therapy by the followers of Maturana and Varela (1988), such as Efran and Lukens (1985) and Dell (1982), who emphasize the way clients and their families do not resist change, they just go on being themselves.[5] Bateson (1973) and his followers have emphasized the "relational" side. The autonomous organization of a living thing depends for its existence on its connectedness with information circuits that pass "through" organs such as the brain, and elements in the wider context in which the self is embedded. These circuits generally occupy a much larger space than that bounded by the skin, and they often include other selves.[6]

A brief excursion into Bateson's notorious discussion of a man–axe–tree system will help to clarify the relationship between the autonomous and relational sides of the self. He claims that the total self corrective unit which "'thinks' and 'acts' and 'decides'" (Bateson, 1973, p. 289) is the "tree–eyes–brain–muscles–axe–stroke–tree" system (Bateson, 1973, p. 288). What happens depends on all the elements in the system. The size and shape of the tree will determine what the man does, and the changing shape of the cut in the tree will in turn shape the movements of his arms, which will be different if the axe is blunt or a muscle is sore, and so on. There is a sense in which all the elements in the system determine what happens, but, says Bateson, this is not how "the average Occidental" sees it. "He says, 'I cut down the tree' and he even believes that there is a delimited agent, the 'self', which performed a delimited 'purposive' action upon a delimited object" (Bateson, 1973, p. 288). At this point Bateson forgets the autonomous side. The "average Occidental" is right in the sense that the intention to cut down the tree resides only in him. Being there does not constitute an invitation to him from the tree.

The man's intention is part of the autonomous side of his structure, which has its source, not in the immediate context, but in earlier complementary relationships, in his "learning the contexts of life" (Bateson, 1979, p. 132). The disposition to fell trees has its roots in the man's prior relational learning about what is expected in a social context of trees, axes, timber milling, and so on. He would be unlikely to think of cutting the tree if his life were embedded in a culture in which trees were sacred. This learning is embedded in his structure, but, as Bateson insists, "the relationship comes first; it precedes" (Bateson, 1979, p. 133).

The behaviour of the "relational" self is shaped by all the elements in the system in which it is presently involved. While the relational self is continuously initiating and accommodating, the "autonomous" self may or may not stay the same. The autonomous self carries into the present a dense inscription of prior relational experience in the forms of language, discourse, tradition, and culture. People do not continuously learn, but normally they learn new practices, or develop their autonomous selves, as they meet new circumstances or developmental pressures in the ordinary course of life. The distinction between the relational and the autonomous is much the same as that between "process" and "structure", and "first-" and "second-"order change.[7]

This distinction provides a basis for a discussion of a range of therapeutic domains, ranging from least to most in terms of intrusiveness, time commitment, intensity, therapist's use of self and emotional involvement, and most to least in terms of reliance on theory and technique. The middle of the range demands the greatest investment of authority in the therapist, the most therapist power, and the most prescription for ideological change on the part of the therapist.

ON LEAVING THE AUTONOMOUS SELF WELL ALONE

The sort of therapy I discuss in this section is a matter of "expediting the currents of change already seething in the person and the family" (Erikson, in Watzlawick, Weakland, & Fish, 1974, p. ix). It relies on the fact that people busy themselves with "realization of the imagined" (Kovel, 1991, p. 458). In this process they seek information from friends, radio, television, books, courses, travel, expert advisors, and so on. They visit therapists when they reach an impasse in this process.[8]

Brief systemic therapy is distinctively unintrusive in the way it uses the relational side of the system to suggest positions from which family members can see for themselves the way forward. It thus engages directly with the relational self and only indirectly with the autonomous self—clients are not directly taught what to do. It does not involve pointing out where the clients have gone wrong, but builds on the resources that are there. As an illustration, consider a couple where the more seriously the woman tried to address their sexual problem, the more the man avoided it. The man felt sexy in a context of play, so the therapist suggested that they give up on sex for a while and seek out occasions for play.[9]

This work is a matter of attuning oneself to, and then aligning with, the "language", aspirations, values, and attitudes of family members without depending too much on feedback and correction. Because it does not involve confrontation, it requires a minimal exercise of power by the therapist. Sales persons have minimal authority, yet they get by with these skills. Clients vest far more authority in therapists than the therapists need for this kind of work. Thus the M.R.I. brief therapists (Watzlawick et al., 1974) strategically adopted a "one-down" stance with their clients to minimize the possibility of clients "taking on the expert".

This therapy appears "clever" because it depends greatly on a knowledge of theory and technique and on an ability to think clearly about what to do "on the spot" with the family. Therapy with the sexual problem above depended on a knowledge of deviation-amplifying processes, paradoxical injunctions, and solution-focused techniques. The possibility of contributing "news" to existing structures is greatly enhanced when the therapist carries an awareness of "control hierarchies" (Broderick & Smith, 1979). Individuals and families not only monitor their performances, but they monitor their monitorings and sometimes monitor these monitorings. Clients change when they see what they are doing in the light of overriding or "higher-level" considerations (cf. Paterson, 1985, pp. 444, 445). For example, parents may rethink the need to resolve conflict in their relationship when they see how distressed their children are about it. Here, the changes are "second-order", but in the "lower-order" rules of the system, and once again it is the clients who choose to bring their practices into line with their own values. Sometimes particular experiences of relationships at "lower-order" levels create a "strange loop" (Hofstadter, 1979), which changes general attitudes, values, and principles.[10] This awareness of levels in systems has led to some very detailed work on how to use the therapeutic relationship to provoke "reflexivity" (cf. Pearce & Cronen, 1980; Tomm, 1987, 1988).

It is not possible to cover all the ways in which brief therapists work. Rather, I am concerned to illustrate the unintrusive nature of this sort of work and the way in which it demands theoretical understanding rather than an ability to recognize emotional significance and hidden meanings. The parents of a young boy presented because their fighting over how to bring him up had brought them to the brink of separation. In the course of the first interview the therapist established that each appreciated the other's strength, and neither could contemplate living with a "wimp" she or he could dominate. However, they fought about nearly everything, including how to "come home" from work. He liked to be silent when they got home and to get all the tasks of the evening over before sitting down to talk over a coffee and a port. She liked to "unload" all the worry and frustration of the day from the moment they were together. As a first exercise, the therapist suggested that he should accommodate to her way of coming home from work on even days of the month, and she should accommodate to his way on odd days. They phoned three weeks later to say that they had "got the idea" and did not need to return. The therapist followed the rule that symmetry is reduced by introducing complementarity, but exactly equally, so that it remains within the dominant symmetrical frame of the system (cf. Bateson, 1973, pp. 294–295). The therapist needed a degree of authority for the couple to accept this prescription of a change to a "lower-order" practice, but again she fitted with the way she saw that the system was.

When systemic therapists name what they see, or ask "embedded suggestion questions" (Tomm, 1987, p. 177), or reframe, it would often satisfy the therapist if the clients saw that a situation can be seen through another lens. The method does not depend on re-socialization, but clients do tend to regard the therapist's pronouncements as authoritative. There has been a lot of emphasis in the systemic literature on the importance of "shedding power" and adopting a "collaborative rather than a hierarchical structure" (Anderson & Rambo, 1988; Hoffman, 1985, p. 393, 1991). However, the problem of power, or hierarchy, or authority cannot be solved within the domain of therapy, because the problem belongs to the context of therapy. It arises as soon as a specialist group is formed with "expertise" recognized by audiences to their activity, by means of remuneration and techniques of registration and legitimization. To this extent systemic therapists do participate in re-socializing their clients to accept a mixture of therapist idiosyncrasy and systemic orientation.

Systemic therapists have been overwhelmingly accommodating to the existing organization of selves and systems.[11] This is consistent with the ethical view that therapists ought to allow their clients to determine their own patterns of life, ways of thinking, and values and aspirations, if they do not involve harm to themselves or others. Therapists who respect their clients' values are careful to avoid intimidating or shaming clients into changing their views. This conservative position has been attacked for its insensitivity to political and moral issues. MacKinnon and Miller (1987) argue that family therapists ought to address the autonomous self directly in order to bring about ideological change.

RE-SOCIALIZING THE AUTONOMOUS SELF

I will now consider the direct challenges to culturally embedded patterns of the autonomous self, which systemic therapists mount by enlisting other parts of the client's autonomous self. A starting point for understanding this work is Michel Foucault's idea of "discourses" or tissues of social constraint which determine what can be perceived, thought, and acted upon (Foucault, 1978). He speaks of the individual as "contingent, formed by the weight of moral tradition, not really autonomous" (Miller, 1993, p. 283). Feminists have noted that attitudes, beliefs, and behaviour patterns, embedded over generations, are hard to abandon even though they are untenable in terms of feminist discourse. In practice, family therapists have found ways to help clients free themselves from long-standing habits of thinking and acting by personalizing such habits as modes of domination from which people can "escape". Systemic therapists thus engage with the autonomous self's romantic attraction to battles between good and evil and as a way of helping the person to win against externalized, personalized habits of thought and action (cf. White & Epston, 1989).[12] Once more, this work is so much a matter of capitalizing on readiness that it demands no more than a friendly positive regard between client and therapist. Because it enlists a near-universal human tendency, it does not even demand a great capacity for attunement with idiosyncratic aspirations. However, it does involve a "demolition phase",[13] directed at the old habit, which is absent in the brief systemic approaches described in the previous section.

There are patterns of the autonomous self that appear more resistant to change than these "habits". Because these patterns persist across contexts and because they constrain the usual adaptability of the relational self, they are often experienced in the therapist–client relationship. It usually has little effect to point out that this pattern might have been useful in the past but that it is inappropriate in the present. Influencing the client to change requires an intense and personal relationship and an investment by the client of considerable authority and trust in the therapist.

Bateson (1973, 1979) gives some clues to the persistence of such patterns when he speaks of attitudes and dispositions that persist because of contextual learning that is self-validating.

Case study 1

A man repeatedly bursts out in anger because he feels avoided, left out, and tiptoed around by his family. They do what they are told but leave him out because he is angry and intimidating. He tries controlling his anger, but they do not change because they do not believe it will last, so this confirms his belief, so he gets angry again, confirming their belief. The therapist who "holds" this family in a relationship long enough to change their premises will witness, receive, and express a great deal of emotion. The key family members will be held in the process by an intense involvement with the therapist. In his more reflective moments the man will accept that his behaviour is self-defeating and inappropriate, but this is not sufficient for him to be able to relinquish it. He and the others will stay in therapy to the extent to which each of them feels "understood".

It is not immediately obvious how it is that understanding helps. Yet I am convinced that it is of great importance to clients for therapists to witness and acknowledge experiences that have great significance for them.

BEARING WITNESS

How do we understand? If we leave aside the possibility of access to universal archetypal forms of human experience, we might accept Harré and Secord's (1972) proposal that we use our own life experience and our experience of others' experiences as a formal model for understanding the "enigmatic episodes" in our own and others' lives. The significance of a puzzling episode is slowly brought forth by therapist and client using their imagination and drawing on their own life experience to come up with tentative understandings which might be suggested by the therapist and corrected by the client.

From this view, understanding is a matter of being intimately involved with the client in the sense of sharing or co-creating meaning (Weingarten, 1992). Family therapists sometimes deserve criticism for persisting with therapeutic "moves" in situations that call for understanding. Rushing to a solution could be to negate, once more, the significance of an enigmatic action or emotion that persists just because the feelings connected with it have not been adequately recognized.

Following Harré (1986)[14] and Calhoun and Solomon (1984), emotions may be seen as a means of expressing ethical, moral, and aesthetic judgements about situations. How they are expressed announces the "strength" of our convictions, or the significance of an ordeal, a hurt, or an occasion. From this conception, emotions are an instrument of reason, not opposed to reason.

An expression of emotion is not a reference to an inner state like a sensation. Rather, emotions are constituted by attitudes and accompanying behaviour in a particular situation (Armon-Jones, 1986, p. 47). The psychoanalytic language of "unconscious infection" and of projection and introjection suggests that feelings have a separate existence. Populist therapeutic discourse also speaks of "loss of contact" with feelings, and "getting in touch" with them and "letting feelings out". In contrast, from the social constructionist view, feelings may be expressed more directly in therapy because, unlike many other situations in life, it is an occasion on which such expressions are welcome.

Case study 2

In order to illustrate the model for understanding and the importance of emotional expression in therapy, consider the enigmatic aspect of Martha's problem. She presented with a complaint that she was not coping with her responsibilities. When the therapist inquired about her life she found that Martha was carrying overwhelming responsibilities, far beyond the call of duty, at home, in her workplace, in postgraduate study, and with her friends. The enigma began to dissolve when the therapist heard that from the time that Martha was a small child she had taken sole responsibility for the care of her mentally ill mother and was still doing so. Her father and older brother had completely opted out. The therapist's own life experience of having an aunt who never missed an opportunity to let the family know how difficult it was to care for the therapist's grandparents gave her a clue to making sense of Martha's behaviour. Therapist and client co-constructed the proposition that Martha was carrying a superhuman amount of responsibility whilst feeling overloaded and exhausted as a way of expressing the enormity of her suffering from having to carry an overwhelming degree of responsibility all her life.

Complaining had no effect, so she would not relinquish responsibility until the significance of her lost childhood and her suffering was recognized by the significant audiences to her life. Relinquishing responsibility prematurely would be like lowering the flag which signalled her suffering, and thus relinquishing hope of it being properly recognized. Helping Martha was a long-term process in which the therapist took every opportunity to acknowledge the extent and significance of her suffering and her lost childhood in a dramatic and emotionally intense way, and she invited Martha's husband to do likewise. This went hand-in-hand with the therapist supporting Martha in taking small steps to make her life less burdened and more fun. The therapist drew on her own life experience and her experience of others' suffering in the process of constructing the meaning of Martha's problematic behaviours and in choosing her own emotional response. What happened depended enormously on both the therapist's particular theoretical training and on who the therapist was.

I think that interest in analytic ideas on the part of family therapists stems from the fact that they are searching for ways to be helpful to the increasing number of people who are not seeking out a therapist who might draw attention to something they have overlooked, help unravel a relationship tangle, or point out a pathway through a difficult stage of life. These people do not have value-neutral "disorders" or "dysfunctions". Instead, they present with problematic behaviours charged with emotional significance which express the ways in which their lives have been dominated by loss, hurt, invalidation, and injustice. They include survivors of childhood sexual abuse or violence or neglect, or war or genocide, and, at a less dramatic level, women disadvantaged by patriarchy, ethnic and sexual minorities, and family members who are exploited in their caring for permanently injured or disabled relatives. It is belittling and insulting to suggest that such people "work through" their problems or "come to terms with" their losses or hurts so that they can relinquish the problematic behaviours that signal what has happened to them. If they ever relinquish the sign, they will do so when they are ready.

We have reached an end point in the range of therapeutic domains we have considered. Here, a large part of the work is not concerned with treatment, but with acknowledgement of the clients' survival of events or situations that have great—even overwhelming—ethical and moral significance.

CONCLUSION

I began with the simple point that, if a therapist works with a natural group, her relationship with them will be very different from the one she will have with a single client. By elaborating on the picture of a person as both autonomous and relational and by giving anecdotal accounts of the sorts of approaches that might be appropriate to different sorts of presenting situation, I have put a case for the view that systemic therapists work with a range of situations and that the different "therapies" discussed are not, for the most part, alternatives in competition with each other but complementary approaches appropriate to different domains. Some situations demand, above all, clarity about theory and technique, and others require a very intense and personal relationship. Psychoanalytic ideas, particularly those regarding transference and countertransference, might be useful in elucidating the approaches that depend on an intense personal relationship, since in my view understanding is always a form of transference. Finally, there are situations that require others to bear witness to something that has happened, or an ongoing state of affairs that has great significance for the person.

David Kantor (1985) takes a contrary view when he suggests that therapists have a choice of methods in any given situation. He advises that couple therapists should always begin with clients by using brief systemic methods, avoiding giving too much attention to the roots of these patterns in the families of origin and cultural traditions of each. This is designed to avoid "a politically subtle process of conscription" (p. 26), where clients are induced into an intensely engaging relationship from which they find it difficult to escape, and to which they are unable to give informed consent.

I think that there is something in what Kantor says. Consider the couple with the sexual problem or the symmetrical couple discussed above. Their problems would not disappear with a non-specific change of context, such as going on a holiday. They would persist as long as nothing was done to interrupt the cycles of behaviour that maintained them. These couples could easily have become candidates for long-term, personally demanding therapy.

Where there is a choice, it makes sense for the therapists and clients to adopt a general policy of intruding into each other's lives no more than is necessary to achieve what they will both accept as the therapeutic objective. There are good reasons for thinking that an intense personal relationship between therapist and client is not something that should be pursued as a general value. Firstly, what happens depends enormously on the idiosyncrasies of the therapist. The emotional issues important to both parties inevitably intrude in spite of the relationship being for the client—and the longer and more intense the relationship is, the more therapist issues intrude. Secondly, it is not possible to avoid a significant power imbalance, with its attendant risks of abuse. The most common abuse is financial exploitation. Thirdly, most relationships in which both parties expose their vulnerability are ends in themselves for both parties, whereas therapy is the means to an end for both parties. Fourthly, the therapist–client relationship can intrude into, disrupt, or take the place of other intimate relationships in the client's life. Finally, therapists whose lives are taken up with working in an intense and personal way with the perpetrators and survivors of abuse may be personally hurt by the experience and are at risk of transferring their countertransferences (the feelings they take on from the families) from their client families to their own, and from one client family to another.

Whilst some analytically oriented family therapists could be criticized for developing unnecessarily binding relationships with clients, some brief systemic therapists participate in the invalidation of clients' feelings by persisting with therapeutic "moves" in situations that call for understanding.

This chapter has been about relationships, emotions, and therapy. Concern with emotions and other issues of value takes "therapy" on a "strange loop" out of itself and into the domain of ethics and morals. Once we start working with emotions within the domain of "therapy", we find ourselves without the domain of therapy itself, and back where we started before the advent of therapy, in the realm of practical ethics where it was always thought that how a person lives will have some bearing on his or her well-being and the well-being of others. We are only just beginning to concern ourselves with matters of personal conduct, morals, and politics that may assist with the prevention of such events and circumstances in the future. In some quarters, it is not politically expedient for our work to be seen this way. This could be the most compelling reason for playing down the role of emotions in the domain of systemic therapy.

NOTES

1. The feminist philosopher of science Evelyn Fox Keller (1985) argues that too much "objectivity", seen as distance and uninvolvement, limits our ability to know. She draws on the work of Nobel-prize-winning geneticist Barbara McClintock to show that personal emotional involvement with the subject of study gives access to more, not less, "objective" knowledge. This sort of thinking also stems from the Kantian idea of emotions being opposed to reason. As I argue below, recent work on emotion suggests that emotions are the instrument of reason.

2. For convenience, I use the masculine pronoun when referring to clients and the feminine when referring to therapists.

3. In the middle years of family therapy, this simple systems idea was forgotten, and the belief took hold that all the elements in a system—and, in particular, both parties to a relationship—were equally influential (cf. MacKinnon & Miller 1987, p. 140). It was a commonplace idea in the early history of systems thinking (cf. Buckley 1967, pp. 75, 76).

4. The problem with this is to avoid tautology, because "personality" is the sum of those characteristics that remain relatively stable across different situations and over time.

5. Families, organizations, societies, etc. are not living things or autopoietic systems, to use Maturana and Varela's term. In some respects, however, they operate in analogous ways.

6. It is thus an oversimplification to speak of "intrapsychic and environmental forces" (Slipp, 1984, p. 1). Slipp uses object relations theory as a bridge between individual and family treatment.

7. *First-order change* is a change of behaviour that occurs without change in the organization or structure of the system. *Second-order change* is a change in the system itself (Goding, 1979, p. 10).

8. This leaves out the occasions when people are coerced to seek therapy

because some other person or official audience to their lives wants them to change.

9. A colleague, Irene Gerrard, supplied this example.

10. A "strange loop" occurs when, by moving up or down the levels of a hierarchy, we find ourselves at a level we did not expect (see Hofstadter, 1979, p. 10, for strange loops).

11. An inability to see human systems as open and flexible may stem partly from the fact that the ideas of structural determinism and organizational closure derive from biological metaphors that are inappropriate to the domain of therapy. The organism interacts with its environment in order to maintain a certain body temperature and various fluid levels. These capacities have evolved over hundreds of thousands of years, and the organism dies in an environment that contradicts these values. In contrast, some intentions, attitudes, emotions, perspectives, beliefs, policies, and presuppositions change in a twinkling of an eye, whilst others survive in the face of massive contradiction.

12. The fact that people are exposed to multiple discourses also raises possibilities for selection and creative invention.

13. This is Patrick Pentony's phrase (Pentony, 1981, p. 9).

14. All emotions are about something—"I'm angry at . . .", "afraid of . . .", etc. Some emotions require bodily agitation, and, with the sole exception of fear, they all involve "local systems of rights, obligations, duties and conventions of evaluation" (Harré, 1986, p. 8).

REFERENCES

Anderson, H., & Rambo, A. (1988). An experiment in systemic family therapy training. *Journal of Strategic and Systemic Therapies*, 7 (1), 54–70.

Armon-Jones, C. (1986). The thesis of constructionism. *The Social Construction of Emotions* (chapter 2). Oxford: Blackwell.

Bateson, G. (1973). *Steps To an Ecology of Mind*. Frogmore: Paladin.

Bateson, G. (1979). *Mind and Nature*. New York: E.P. Dutton.

Boszormenyi-Nagy, I., & Ulrich, D. N. (1981). Contextual family therapy. In: A. Gurman & D. Kniskern (Eds.), *Handbook of Family Therapy* (chapter 5). New York: Brunner-Mazel.

Broderick, C., & Smith, J. (1979). A general systems approach to the family. In: W. R. Burr, R. Hill, F. I. Nye, & I. L. Reiss (Eds.), *Contemporary Theories about the Family* (chapter 3). New York: Free Press.

Buckley, W. (1967). *Sociology and Modern Systems Theory*. Englewood Cliffs, NJ: Prentice Hall.

Calhoun, C., & Solomon, R. C. (1984). *What Is an Emotion?* Oxford: Oxford University Press.

Dell, P. (1982). Beyond homeostasis: toward a concept of coherence. *Family Process, 2* (4), 407–414.

Efran, J., & Lukens, M. (1985). The world according to Humberto Maturana. *The Family Therapy Networker, 9* (3), 22–28, 72–75.

Flaskas, C. (1989). Thinking about the emotional interaction of therapist and family. *The Australian and New Zealand Journal of Family Therapy, 10* (1), 1–6.

Flaskas, C. (1993). On the project of using psychoanalytic ideas in systemic therapy. *The Australian and New Zealand Journal of Family Therapy, 14* (1), 9–15.

Flaskas, C. (1994). Exploring the therapeutic relationship: a case study. *The Australian and New Zealand Journal of Family Therapy, 15* (4), 185–190.

Foucault, M. (1978). *Discipline and Punish: The Birth of the Prison.* New York: Pantheon.

Goding, G. (1979). Change and paradox in family therapy. *The Australian Journal of Family Therapy, 1* (1), 9–15.

Harré, R. (1986). An outline of the social constructionist viewpoint. In: R. Harré (Ed.), *The Social Construction of Emotions* (chapter 1). Oxford: Blackwell.

Harré, R., & Secord, P. F. (1972). *The Explanation of Social Behaviour.* Oxford: Blackwell.

Hoffman, L. (1985). Beyond power and control: toward a "second order" family systems therapy. *Family Systems Medicine, 3* (4): 381–396. Also in *Exchanging Voices: A Collaborative Approach to Family Therapy.* London: Karnac Books, 1993.

Hoffman, L. (1991). A reflexive stance for family therapy. *Journal of Strategic and Systemic Therapies, 10* (3/4): 4–17. Also in *Exchanging Voices: A Collaborative Approach to Family Therapy.* London: Karnac Books.

Hofstadter, D. R. (1979). *Godel, Escher, Bach: An Eternal Golden Braid.* London: Penguin.

Kantor, D. (1985). Couples therapy, crisis induction and change. In: A. S. Gurman (Ed.), *A Casebook of Marital Therapy* (chapter 2). New York: Guilford.

Keller, E. F. (1985). *Reflections on Gender and Science.* New Haven, CT: Yale University Press.

Kovel, J. (1991). Speaking truth to power. *Meanjin, 50* (4), 447–462.

MacKinnon, L., & Miller, D. (1987). The new epistemology and the Milan Approach: feminist and sociopolitical considerations. *Journal of Marital and Family Therapy, 13* (2), 139–156.

Mathews, F. (1991). *The Ecological Self.* London: Routledge.

Mattinson, J. (1975). *The Reflection Process in Casework Supervision.* London: Institute of Marital Studies & Tavistock.

Maturana, H., & Varela, F. (1988). *The Tree of Knowledge: The Biological Roots of Human Understanding.* Boston, MA: Shambhala.

Menninger, K. (1964). *Theory of Psychoanalytic Technique.* New York: Harper & Row.

Miller, J. (1993). *The Passion of Michel Foucault.* London: Harper Collins.

Paterson, T. R. J. (1985). Towards an integrated model of marital therapy: a synthesis of systemic, transgenerational and systemic perspectives. *Proceedings of the Sixth Australian Family Therapy Conference.* Melbourne: Victorian Association of Family Therapists.

Pearce, W. B., & Cronen, V. E. (1980). *Communication, Action and Meaning: The Creation of Social Realities.* New York: Praeger.

Pentony, P. (1981). *Models of Influence in Psychotherapy.* New York: Free Press.

Slipp, S. (1984). *Object Relations: A Dynamic Bridge Between Individual and Family Treatment.* Northvale, NJ: Jason Aronson.

Smith, J., Osman, C., & Goding, M. (1990). Reclaiming the emotional aspects of the therapist–family system. *The Australian and New Zealand Journal of Family Therapy, 11* (3), 140–146.

Stierlin, H., Rucker-Embden, I., Wetzel, N., & Wirsching, M. (1980). *The First Interview with the Family.* New York: Brunner/Mazel.

Tomm, K. (1987). Interventive interviewing: Part II. Reflexive questioning as a means to enable self-healing. *Family Process, 26* (2), 167–184.

Tomm, K. (1988). Interventive interviewing: Part III. Intending to ask circular, strategic, or reflexive questions? *Family Process, 27* (1), 1–15.

Watzlawick, P., Weakland, J., & Fisch, R. (1974). *Change: Principles of Problem Formation and Problem Resolution.* New York: W.W. Norton.

Weingarten, K. (1992). The discourses of intimacy: adding a social constructionist and feminist view. *Family Process, 30* (3), 285–305.

White, M., & Epston, D. (1989). *Literate Means to Therapeutic Ends*. Adelaide: Dulwich Publications.
Willi, J. (1987). Some principles of an ecological model of the person as a consequence of the therapeutic experience with systems. *Family* Process, 26 (4), 429–436.

CHAPTER 2

Understanding the therapeutic relationship: using psychoanalytic ideas in the systemic context

Carmel Flaskas

INTRODUCTION

This book has taken as its departure point the impoverishment of the current systemic understandings of the therapeutic relationship. I am not interested so much in developing any further critique of this absence in systemic therapy. Rather, I am looking toward ideas which may extend our understandings of the therapeutic relationship and, specifically, I want to explore some ideas from the psychoanalytic therapies that have this potential.

Systemic therapy has had an ambivalent relationship with the psychoanalytic therapies, and in many ways it has had an oppositional relationship. Though there are probably complex historical and political issues involved in this opposition, nonetheless, at a more straightforward level, it is easy to appreciate why the intra-psychic focus of analytic work has not sat comfortably with the interpersonal and relational focus of the systemic therapies.

This is not to say, of course, that there have been no intersections drawn between analytic ideas and the project of systemic therapy. The earlier collections by Helm Stierlin (1977) and John Pearce and Leonard Friedman (1980) stand out here, as do the integrative projects of Ivan Boszormenyi-Nagy and Geraldine Spark (1973) and Michael Nichols (1987). From quite a different angle, Deborah Luepnitz has juxtaposed object relations therapy as meeting some of the shortcomings of a systemic frame (1988). There has been another body of work (particularly from Britain) that has emphasized the complementarity of these therapy frames (see, e.g., Byng-Hall, 1986, 1988; Campion & Fry, 1985; Crowther, 1988). In the Australian context, a number of recent discussions have raised the renewal of interest in analytic ideas (e.g. Gibney, 1991; Quadrio, 1986a, 1986b; Smith, Osman, & Goding, 1990) and I have also tracked around this area in different ways (Flaskas, 1989, 1992, 1993, 1994).

However, my project with respect to psychoanalytic thinking in this chapter is very specific. I want to explore the usefulness of the analytic ideas of transference, countertransference, and projective identification in understanding issues in the therapeutic relationship in systemic therapy. In applying these ideas in a systemic context, I intend to consider two particular topics—the first is the process of engagement, while the second is an extension of the concept of sequences to the therapeutic relationship.

The plan, then, is this. I begin with some comments about the different therapeutic environments of analytic and systemic therapy, before discussing the concepts of transference, countertransference, and projective identification. The chapter then moves to a consideration of the way in which these analytic ideas may enrich our understandings of engagement and sequences in the therapeutic relationship in systemic work.

ANALYTIC AND SYSTEMIC THERAPIES

If I am to use the analytic ideas of transference, countertransference, and projective identification in the context of systemic therapy, it is important first to draw some distinctions between the therapeutic aims of analytic and systemic work and the different kinds of therapy environments they produce.

In analytic therapy, the focus for change is the client's inner world, and her or his experience of this.[1] The therapeutic aim of analytic therapy is to make a difference to this experience, and changes in clients' experience of their own inner world may then lead to flow-on effects in their current behaviour and relationships. This focus on the intrapsychic world of the clients is quite different from the interpersonal focus of systemic therapy, for in systemic therapy we are primarily interested in facilitating changes in clients' significant relationships, and in their experience of themselves in their relationships with others. The critical shift, then, is attempted at this level of experience. Of course, a change in the experience of current relationships can (and often does) have flow-on effects in the way in which clients come to experience their inner world. However, intrapsychic change is not *the aim* of systemic therapy, even though at times it may be one of its *effects*.

These different aims of analytic and systemic therapy both require and produce different therapy environments and nurture different kinds of therapeutic relationships. In analytic therapy, the main space for therapeutic change lies in the relationship between client and therapist. It is not surprising, then, that there are a number of concepts that have been developed in analytic therapy to understand this relationship. In the analytic relationship, the client may come to know herself or himself differently, and also come to experience core emotional dilemmas differently in the context of the relationship with the therapist. Now, both historically and across the different contemporary analytic therapies, there have been fluctuations in these two emphases of

---

Much of this first section appears in a section entitled "Ideas from analytic therapy: the different environments of analytic and systemic work", pp. 187–188 in C. Flaskas (1994), "Exploring the therapeutic relationship: a case study", *Australian and New Zealand Journal of Family Therapy*, 15 (4): 185–190.

knowing and experiencing in the process of analytic therapy. All analytic therapies privilege both knowing and experiencing in the therapeutic process. However, some analytic therapies balance knowing over experiencing, while others balance the two more evenly.[2]

Although there may be differences in these emphases within the different analytic therapies, the therapeutic environment of systemic therapy contrasts markedly with the processes of knowing and experiencing in analytic therapy. The idea of the client needing to know something differently, let alone needing to come to know it in terms of a specific understanding of the unconscious, the psyche, and human emotions, simply does not feature in the same way in systemic work. The main aim of systemic therapy, particularly the second-order therapies, is to create the space for something different to occur in the client's relationships with others. The act of coming to know something differently may be part of this process, but particular ways of knowing are not privileged, and knowing, itself, is not privileged over other routes to change.

Moreover, in analytic therapy, the different experience that counts comes to lie in the experience of the client with the therapist, and this leads to a centring of the therapeutic relationship in analytic therapy. However, in systemic therapy, the different experience that counts lies in the clients' experience with their significant others. *Thus in systemic therapy the therapeutic relationship is "de-centred" in favour of the clients' current relationships with their significant others.*

It may be that the very practice of de-centring the therapeutic relationship in systemic therapy has contributed to the failure of systemic therapy to theorize this area. Leaving this issue aside, though, it is nonetheless clear that in systemic therapy, the relationship between therapist and clients still significantly aids or hinders the work with the client's significant relationships. This is so regardless of whether the work is with individuals, with couples, or with families. Moreover, engagement issues can be very complex, and sometimes it is not at all easy to form and maintain a positive therapeutic connection with clients. As well, in some situations in systemic therapy it is easy to enter into a problematic therapy sequence with clients.

All these factors in the therapeutic relationship in systemic therapy make it attractive to turn to the understandings offered by the analytic therapies, despite the differences in the therapeutic aims and environments of the two frameworks. However, a recognition of these differences means that we should be looking for *intersections* with analytic ideas, rather than attempting simply to "import" analytic ideas into the systemic context.

TRANSFERENCE, COUNTERTRANSFERENCE, AND PROJECTIVE IDENTIFICATION

I would like to move directly to the analytic ideas of transference, countertransference, and projective identification, three related concepts that are integral to an understanding of the therapy process in analytic therapy. I hope to avoid any major detour into the historical developments and changes in the analytic therapies, not least because of the complexity of the history of analytic theory—at the same time, though, it is important to locate these three ideas as accurately as possible here before mapping their potential value in systemic work.[3]

There has been a tendency in systemic therapy to regard the intrapsychic focus of analytic therapy as *necessarily* a lineal and non-systemic arena (e.g. see Hoffman, 1981). While this assumption may match a stereotype of analytic therapy based on its earlier versions, I do not think it is fair comment with respect to contemporary analytic theory. Analytic theory in the past four decades, particularly in the English-speaking environments, has shifted more and more towards a relational understanding of intra-psychic development and a relational understanding of the therapy process itself. This same trend may be seen in the development of the two quite different contemporary analytic therapies of self-psychology and object relations theory. It may also be seen in the current analytic thinking around the concepts of transference, countertransference, and projective identification.

Understandings of transference and countertransference have a long history within the analytic tradition, these two processes having first been identified by Freud. Projective identification is a relatively more recent concept, having emerged in the early 1950s during the period of Melanie Klein's foundational development of object relations theory. Throughout the history of these concepts, the understandings of them have been worked and re-worked, so that by now, within contemporary analytic thinking, they have become much richer theory and practice concepts as compared to their first appearances.[4]

Within contemporary thinking, transference describes the process of a person re-creating her or his patterns of experience in the context of a present relationship. Transference, then, is about an individual's patterns of relating; as such, it occurs only in the context of a relationship, and it occurs in any significant relationship, not just the therapy relationship. As "the living history of ways of relating" (Scharff & Scharff, 1991, p. 203), transference patterns are able to show core emotional dilemmas and struggles, and it is for this reason that the transference of the client in the analytic relationship is seen as centrally valuable in showing the way for the analytic work. Analytic therapy, then, attempts to structure a therapeutic relationship in which maximum use may be made of the client's experience of transference with the therapist. As Ruth Riesenberg Malcolm writes of the analytic therapy transference:

... transference is an emotional relationship of the patient with the analyst which is experienced in the present, in what is generally called "the-here-and-now" of the analytic situation. It is the expression of the patient's past in its multiple transformations. [Riesenberg Malcolm, 1986, p. 433]

If transference refers to the patterns of experience that the client brings and enacts in the therapy, countertransference refers to the involvement of the therapist in the relationship and the emotions, attitudes, and patterns of relating that the therapist may begin to feel and enact in the context of the therapeutic relationship. The "circular" nature of transference and countertransference is explicitly acknowledged in some of the current analytic discussions. For example, Neville Symington notes that "at one level the analyst and patient together make a single system" (Symington, 1986a, p. 262), and Gregorio Kohon writes:

The analyst is never an "outsider"; he is part and parcel of the transference situation. In fact, one could argue that the transference is as much a function of the countertransference as the countertransference is a result of the transference. [Kohon, 1986, p. 53]

Within this understanding of the relational context of countertransference, there have been two ways in which the therapist's own involvements and responses to the specific analytic therapy situation have been understood. The first understanding has been focused on the countertransferences that primarily come from the therapist's own experiences and emotional dilemmas, which become triggered in the process of her or his relationship with the client. This kind of understanding of countertransference began with Freud, though he shifted across time from seeing the process of countertransference as being always a hindrance to the analytic work to seeing its potential helpfulness in giving more information to the therapist about the client's situation.

However, there is a second understanding of countertransference which moves much further in linking the therapist's experience in the therapy to the client's experience. This is the concept of projective identification. The idea here is that sometimes in therapy the client communicates at an unconscious level very powerful information about her or his emotional position. The therapist comes to know this, not through a direct verbal or non-verbal communication, but rather by finding herself or himself feeling or enacting the client's dilemma. This kind of unconscious communication happens when the feeling or dilemma the client is experiencing is too difficult to bear—in this sense, projective identification on the part of the client is both a protective defence and a communication in the context of a particular relationship.

Projective identification, then, is very much a recursive process. It describes not just the projection of the client, but the willingness and ability of the therapist to both receive and respond to (or identify with) this kind of communication. The question of the ability of the therapist to respond depends partly on the extent to which the communication of the client is able to resonate with the therapist's own emotional possibilities. In analytic therapy, the process of projective identification has come to be understood as central to the therapy process, for it is through projective identification that the therapist, and the therapist and client, may come to know something about the client's unbearable emotions and dilemmas and experience them in a more tolerable way.

Of course, there is a significant difficulty in the clinical application of projective identification. In projective identification, the therapist experiences the client's feelings for a time as if they were her or his own experience, and during this period it is impossible for the therapist to distinguish whether her or his feelings are primarily a response to her or his own dilemmas (as in the first understanding of countertransference), or the client's unconscious communication (as in projective identification). Analytic thinking suggests that it is only by the therapist holding on to this uncertainty, and maintaining the ability to reflect on it, that there may be a tentative unravelling of the experience of projective identification in the therapy relationship.

Analytic training is meant, of course, to teach therapists to be able to do just this. However, the clinical (mis-)use of projective identification allows the space for abuse in analytic therapy, for the client may well become the recipient of the therapist's unconscious projections in the guise of the therapist coming to know the client's projections. Within contemporary analytic discussions, there is an ongoing struggle with precisely this concern (see e.g. Kohon, 1986, p. 72).

THE PROCESS OF ENGAGEMENT IN SYSTEMIC THERAPY

But let us leave the understanding of these concepts within analytic therapy. I am more interested, in this chapter, in exploring their potential value in systemic therapy, and I particularly want to explore the way in which these ideas may be intersected in our thinking about engagement issues and in the application of the idea of sequences to the therapy relationship.

The question of engagement in systemic therapy is usually discussed in quite a stunted way. In the textbooks, engagement is often written about as something that happens at the beginning of the first session, and the idea of "engagement skills" in systemic training has become almost synonymous with the therapist's role in the initial joining process with clients. In one of the few wider discussions of the place of engagement in family therapy, Sue Jackson and Daniel Chable write:

> Engagement is a complex, reciprocal process concerning the relationship between the therapist and family. It refers to the specific adjustments the therapist makes to him/herself over time to accommodate to the particular family. [Jackson & Chable, 1985, p. 65]

I agree with this view wholeheartedly and would like to reinforce that engagement is a process in therapy, not an event. Although sometimes engagement with a family may be quite straightforward, very often it has to be negotiated and renegotiated throughout the course of therapy. If I were to hazard an alternative definition of engagement in systemic therapy, I would say that it is a process of forming and holding a good-enough personal relationship between therapist and clients so that the work of that particular therapy can occur. Different families and different clients need different styles of engagement with their therapist. Also, a "good-enough" engagement in the beginning of therapy may not be good enough to hold the work of the therapy when the family or client begins to hit some rockier patches in the process of change.

I would be inclined to add to the definition the idea that systemic therapy requires that the therapist finds and holds respectful and compassionate connections with the client/family members, and that the clients/family members are able to experience this. I am aware that this kind of language has not been so popular in systemic therapy, although it is heartening to see two quite recent discussions from Australia and the United Kingdom exploring the translation of the idea of empathy in a systemic context (Perry, 1993; Wilkinson, 1992).

Of course, I am not meaning to suggest that the practices of systemic therapy pay no attention to the need for the therapist to have compassionate connections with clients. This is certainly not the case, and different systemic therapies have developed techniques that attempt to ensure a positive therapeutic orientation, and positive connections between therapist and clients. In Milan therapy, for example, the techniques of circular questioning and positive connotation both allow for and create a stronger therapeutic bond between the therapist and the family's experience of their dilemmas (see MacKinnon & James, 1987). In a very different way, the technique of externalization used by Michael White achieves similar benefits in therapeutic engagement (see White, 1989). However, my point here is that the engagement function of these techniques is scarcely acknowledged. The danger, then, is that when systemic techniques *fail* to ensure a positive therapeutic engagement, it becomes difficult to understand the territory of a problematic therapeutic engagement.

It is in understanding this territory of impasse and failure in the therapeutic relationship that the potential use of analytic ideas comes to the fore. Transference, countertransference, and projective identification are concepts that provide ways of thinking about problematic interactions in therapy around engagement. Thinking in terms of transference can generate some ideas for the therapist about the relationship patterns that clients may be bringing to bear on the therapeutic relationship. Moreover, the capacity to think about this helps the therapist stay "meta" to recurrent difficulties and so hopefully to avoid re-enacting an unhelpful sequence for the clients. Thinking in terms of countertransference also helps the therapist recognize (and take responsibility for) the way in which her or his own responses or involvements may be contributing to, or even sometimes triggering, the difficulties in engagement.

The concept of projective identification also offers the therapist the opportunity actively to use the problems in engagement to think about the clients' dilemmas, and to maintain a space for thinking about their dilemmas even when quite difficult things may be happening in the therapeutic relationship. Perhaps of more value, though, is the potential that using the idea of projective identification has in generating and allowing compassionate connections between the therapist and family in situations in which the ability of the therapist to do this has been compromised. Being on the receiving end of feelings that someone else cannot bear is generally not much fun, and an unreflective stance on the part of the therapist in this situation very often means that her or his capacity for empathy is diminished, which in turn compounds the engagement difficulties.

I could become a Milan therapist for a moment in describing this benefit of using the idea of projective identification. We can imagine an opinion being given to a therapist struggling with a difficulty in finding herself wanting to denigrate a particular client, and finding herself beginning to enact this by an off-handedness and a "pleasant" cut-and-dried professionalism. We could say to her:

> "Although you feel bad about finding yourself on the edge of attacking your client, and it's true that what you are doing in the therapy is not helping the engagement, we were wondering whether at least some of what you are experiencing relates more to your client's dilemma. It may be that things have happened for her that have led her often to feel like attacking people she is close to, but it is hard for her to know about this given the image she has of herself. This would certainly compound things for her in her relationships with others, and may help to make some sense of the difficulties she is presenting to you. Your response shows your ability to be sensitive to this, and your ability to know something about her dilemma. Though you are experiencing your desire to attack her as a therapeutic negative, we think that in the long term it may turn out to be very useful in your ability to engage with this client in her current situation."[5]

Of course, I am phrasing these ideas in the form of a Milan opinion partly in a light-hearted way; at another level, though, I am quite serious. Difficulties in the therapeutic relationship are in some ways no different from the difficulties people experience in their "ordinary" relationships, and the systemic ways of using ideas to re-cast difficulties and forge compassionate and positive connections are equally useful in examining the therapeutic relationship. The analytic ideas of transference, countertransference, and projective identification may be very helpful in this project, precisely because they address processes that describe complex emotional interactions, and because the implications of these ideas have been developed in the specific context of understanding the (analytic) therapeutic relationship.

In summary, then, if engagement is understood as a process in therapy, not as an event, the analytic ideas of transference, countertransference, and projective identification may be helpful in a number of ways. They offer recursive understandings of interactions in the engagement process; they offer a different kind of information about the relationship dilemmas of the client/family, which can be put alongside other information from the therapy; they allow a more challenging examination of the therapist's personal involvement in the engagement process; they allow potentially negative sequences in the therapy relationship to be understood in constructive and positive ways; they allow a greater space for compassionate connections on the part of the therapist in the engagement process, and this is especially valuable in situations in which there is some interference in the therapist's ability to be respectful and compassionate.

These are, if you like, some of the intersection points in using analytic ideas in systemic therapy. It would be misleading, though, to fail to note some of the points at which these ideas do not translate so well into a systemic context. The central analytic concern in using these ideas to guide an exploration of the client's/family's inner world simply does not fit into the systemic therapy project—in systemic therapy, we are more interested in using these ideas alongside other ideas in our work with clients. In a similar way, the analytic priority given to unconscious material translates into a more conditional and strategic use in systemic therapy. In systemic practice, it is likely that analytic ideas become especially attractive in situations in which the engagement process is difficult, and when there is the potential for a negative therapy sequence—in analytic work, these ideas are always primary in understanding the therapeutic relationship.

I am inclined to add that, especially in the systemic context, ideas generated by the analytic concepts of transference, countertransference, and projective identification need always to be treated as strictly tentative. However, in theory the same comment applies equally to contemporary analytic work, although the legacy of the historical position of the analytic therapist as the "explorer" of the territory of the client's unconscious may still compound this issue in analytic practice.

SOME THOUGHTS ON SEQUENCES

The second and related systemic concept that may be enriched by analytic thinking is the idea of sequences, and its application to the therapeutic relationship. In exploring engagement as a process rather than an event, the application of the concept of sequences to understanding the therapy relationship makes easy sense. We could re-cast much of what I have written on engagement using the term "engagement sequence", and this would be useful in the same way that thinking of patterns within families as sequences is useful in systemic therapy. The idea of sequences is generally helpful in therapy because it draws the broader relational patterns that "hold" the difficulties being experienced by the client/family; it is also a very useful idea because it links particular events with patterns of relating.

As with the concept of engagement, though, the concept of sequences has remained quite narrow in systemic therapy. The usual definition of a sequence is the pattern of behaviour across time, and in therapy we are usually interested in the repeating sequences of behaviour in which the presenting problem is embedded. Douglas Breunlin and Richard Schwartz argue that the "idea of recursive patterned behaviour connected to problems" is indeed generic to many models in systemic therapy (Breunlin & Schwartz, 1986, p. 68).

However, in the common understanding of sequences, the behavioural dimension of relationship patterns has been privileged, and this privileging has restricted the concept in both its theory and its practice dimensions. The development of the idea of sequences owes much to the strategic therapies, and this context partly explains the behavioural emphasis. But to reduce patterns of relating simply to patterns of behaviour negates one of the central ideas of contemporary systemic therapy—that systems of meanings often underpin and hold behaviour in relationships. I would add to this the idea that emotions are inextricably linked to meaning and behaviour in people's experience of themselves in relationships. If we were to broaden the behavioural orientation of the idea of sequences, then we could consider sequences as descriptions of patterns of relating across time, recursively linking the levels of behaviour, meaning, and emotions in people's experience of these patterns.

Moreover, the idea of sequences has been restricted by a tendency to use it to plot just the immediate interactions around the presenting problem. In their excellent discussion, Breunlin and Schwartz (1986; Breunlin, Schwartz, & MacKune-Karrer, 1992) consider the different time-contexts of patterns of behaviour. If you like, they consider the sequencing of sequences, and look at the relationship of patterns of behaviour across minutes to hours, then hours to days, then days to years, then across at least two generations. They refer to these respectively as S1, S2, S3, and S4 sequences and develop the hypotheses that presenting problems are most likely to involve at least S1 and S2 sequences, that they are very often embedded in S3 sequences, and that perhaps the most "chronic" and difficult problems are likely to be embedded in S4 sequences.

I am giving this description of the ideas of Breunlin and Schwartz, because I think that their work significantly extends the potential of sequences as a theory and practice concept. In combination with the extension of the idea of sequences to include meanings and emotions as well as the behavioural aspects of relationship patterns, it becomes possible for us to consider some further intersections with analytic ideas.

Transference, countertransference, and projective identification are all interactional descriptions, and transference and countertransference in particular describe special sequences in the therapeutic relationship. That they are primarily used in analytic work to understand emotional experience does not mean that they do not also describe behavioural and meaning sequences, and it is this broader description of these analytic concepts as specific sequences in emotions, meanings, and behaviour which makes them potentially very valuable ideas to be used in the systemic context.

In addition, though, transference, countertransference, and projective identification are ideas that describe the immediacy of people's experience across time in their current interactions, and so they offer one very particular way of connecting relationship sequences across time. In terms of the work of Breunlin and Schwartz, the analytic ideas describe S1 sequences that are embedded in S4 sequences, and they also link the way in which therapists may be involved in complex S4 issues of their own in their experience in working with clients.

In many ways, the potential of the idea of sequences in generating very specific understandings of the therapeutic relationship is untapped in systemic therapy. Sequences would help us to understand our own relationships with clients in much the same way as we might understand the family's pattern of relationships. Analytic ideas may give particular ways of considering the sequences in the therapeutic relationship; they may yield understandings that connect immediate sequences in the therapy with sequences across time; and they may also be used to consider sequences in emotions and meanings, as well as behaviour. As in the consideration of the use of analytic ideas in engagement, though, we would need to be clear about the different kinds of ways in which we would be using these ideas in a systemic context, and in the boundaries of the therapeutic aims and environment of systemic therapy.

CONCLUSION

In this chapter, I have considered the potential use of some psychoanalytic ideas in understanding the therapeutic relationship in systemic therapy, with a particular focus on issues surrounding the process of engagement, and the idea of sequences in the therapeutic relationship. My argument is not that we "import" analytic ideas into systemic therapy, or that we try to use them in the way in which they are used in the psychoanalytic context. Rather, I would argue that we appreciate the differences in the aims and therapeutic environments of analytic and systemic therapy, and that this appreciation can guide us in choosing the ways in which we intersect these ideas in the systemic project.

Psychoanalytic ideas become attractive because systemic therapy has failed to theorize the therapeutic relationship, and examples of this include the failure to offer understandings of the complexities of the process of engagement and therapy sequences. However, in terms of the project of systemic therapy, I would hope that we might use the ideas of transference, countertransference, and projective identification in a conditional, strategic, and tentative way—conditional, in the sense of allowing these ideas to sit side-by-side with other ideas; strategic, in the sense of using them especially when they are directly helpful in supporting the therapeutic environment of systemic therapy; and tentative, in the sense of always allowing ourselves and our clients the space for other possibilities, while maintaining the benefit of a serious exploration of the situation at hand.

NOTES

1. Throughout this chapter, I refer to analytic theory and practice in its broader contemporary individual usage, rather than singling out the particular project of object relations family therapy. Both the American and British versions of object relations family therapy are directly derivative of current analytic theory and practice with respect to individual analysis—see, for example, the American work of Slipp (1984) and Scharff and Scharff (1991), and the British collections of Box et al. (1981) and Szur and Miller (1991). The only analytic family therapy framework that uses group analytic theory versus individual analytic theory is Robin Skynner's work (Skynner, 1987).

2. For example, it could be argued that both traditional Freudian therapy and contemporary Lacanian therapy privilege the process of coming to know the unconscious over the process of re-experiencing core emotional dilemmas differently, and that contemporary object relations therapy and self-psychology balance these two emphases more evenly.

3. It is not possible to do justice to the complexities of these concepts in analytic theory in the brief space here, as my overriding concern is with their potential usefulness in the systemic context. I would refer readers interested in the psychoanalytic discussions of these concepts to Kohon (1986), Ogden (1982), Orr (1988), Sandler (1989), Symington (1986b), Tansey and Burke (1989), and Wolstein (1988).

4. An interesting account of the historical development of the concepts of transference and countertransference is given by Douglass Orr (1988).

5. For an extended discussion of a case example of a specific therapeutic relationship, see Flaskas (1994).

REFERENCES

Boszormenyi-Nagy, I., & Spark, G. M. (1973). *Invisible Loyalties: Reciprocity in Intergenerational Family Therapy.* Hagerstown, MD: Harper & Row.

Box, S., Copley, B., Magagna, J., & Moustaki, E. (Eds.) (1981). *Psychotherapy with Families: An Analytic Approach.* London: Routledge & Kegan Paul.

Breunlin, D. C., & Schwartz, R. C. (1986). Sequences: toward a common denominator in family therapy. *Family Process, 25* (1): 67–87.

Breunlin, D. C, Schwartz, R. C., & MacKune-Karrer, B (1992). *Metaframeworks: Transcending the Models of Family Therapy.* San Francisco, CA: Jossey-Bass.

Byng-Hall, J. (1986). Family scripts: a concept which can bridge child psychotherapy and family therapy thinking. *Journal of Child Psychotherapy, 12* (1), 3–13.

Byng-Hall, J. (1988). Scripts and legends in families and family therapy. *Family Process, 27* (2): 167–179.

Campion, J., & Fry, E. (1985). The contribution of Kleinian psychotherapy to the treatment of a disturbed five-year-old girl and her family. *Journal of Family Therapy, 7* (4), 341–356.

Crowther, C. (1988). A psychoanalytic perspective on family therapy. In G. Pearson, J. Treseder, & M. Yelloly (Eds.), *Social Work and the Legacy of Freud.* London: MacMillan Education.

Flaskas, C. (1989). Thinking about the emotional interaction of therapist and family. *Australian and New Zealand Journal of Family Therapy, 10* (1), 1–6.

Flaskas, C. (1992). A reframe by any other name: on the process of reframing in strategic, Milan, and analytic therapy. *Journal of Family Therapy, 14* (2), 145–162.

Flaskas, C. (1993). On the project of using psychoanalytic ideas in systemic therapy: a discussion paper. *Australian and New Zealand Journal of Family Therapy, 14* (1), 9–15.

Flaskas, C. (1994). Exploring the therapeutic relationship: a case study. *Australian and New Zealand Journal of Family Therapy, 15* (4), 185–190.

Gibney, P. (1991). Articulating the implicate: an invitation to openness. *Australian and New Zealand Journal of Family Therapy, 12* (3), 133–136.

Hoffman, L. (1981). *Foundations of Family Therapy.* New York: Basic Books.

Jackson, S., & Chable, D. G. (1985). Engagement: a critical aspect of family therapy practice. *Australian and New Zealand Journal of Family Therapy, 6* (2), 65–69.

Kohon, G. (1986). Countertransference: an independent view. In G. Kohon (Ed.), *The British School of Psychoanalysis: The Independent Tradition*. London: Free Association Books.

Luepnitz, D. (1988). *The Family Interpreted*. New York: Basic Books.

MacKinnon, L. K., & James, K. (1987). The Milan systemic approach: theory and practice. *Australian and New Zealand Journal of Family Therapy, 8* (2), 89–98.

Nichols, M. P. (1987). *The Self in the System: Expanding the Limits of Family Therapy*. New York: Brunner/Mazel.

Ogden, T. H. (1982). *Projective Identification and Psychotherapeutic Technique*. Northvale, NJ: Jason Aronson.

Orr, D. W. (1988). Transference and countertransference: a historical survey. In B. Wolstein (Ed.), *Essential Papers on Countertransference*. New York: New York University Press.

Pearce, J. K., & Friedman, L. J. (Eds.) (1980). *Family Therapy: Combining Psychodynamic and Family Systems Approaches*. New York: Grune & Stratton.

Perry, R. (1993). Empathy—still at the heart of therapy. *Australian and New Zealand Journal of Family Therapy, 14* (2), 63–74.

Quadrio, C. (1986a). Analysis and system: a marriage. *Australian and New Zealand Journal of Psychiatry, 18,* 184–170.

Quadrio, C. (1986b). Individuation as a life process—the interface of intrapsychic and systems theories. *Australian and New Zealand Journal of Family Therapy, 7* (4), 189–193.

Riesenberg Malcolm R. (1986). Interpretation: the past in the present. *International Review of Psycho-Analysis, 13,* 433–443.

Sandler, J. (Ed.) (1989). *Projection, Identification, Projective Identification*. London: Karnac Books.

Scharff, D. E., & Scharff, J. S. (1991). *Object Relations Family Therapy*. Northvale, NJ: Jason Aronson.

Skynner, R. (1987). *Explorations with Families: Group Analysis and Family Therapy*. London: Tavistock/Routledge.

Slipp, S. (1984). *Object Relations: A Dynamic Bridge between Individual and Family Treartment*. Northvale, NJ: Jason Aronson.

Smith, J., Osman, C., & Goding, M. (1990). Reclaiming the emotional aspects of the therapist–family system. *Australian and New Zealand Journal of Family Therapy, 11* (3), 140–146.

Stierlin, H. (Ed.) (1977). *Psychoanalysis and Family Therapy: Selected Papers*. New York: Jason Aronson.

Symington, N. (1986a). The analyst's act of freedom as agent of therapeutic change. In: G. Kohon (Ed.), *The British School of Psychoanalysis: The Independent Tradition*. London: Free Association Books.

Symington, N. (1986b). *The Analytic Experience*. New York: St Martin's Press.

Szur, R., & Miller, S. (Eds.) (1991). *Extending Horizons: Psychoanalytic Psychotherapy with Children, Adolescents and Families*. London: Karnac Books.

Tansey, M. J., & Burke, W. F. (1989). *Understanding Countertransference: From Projective Identification to Empathy*. Hillsdale, NJ: The Analytic Press.

White, M. (1989). The externalizing of the problem and the re-authoring of lives and relationships. In: M. White, *Selected Papers*. Adelaide: Dulwich Centre Publications.

Wilkinson, M. (1992). How do we understand empathy systemically? *Journal of Family Therapy*, 14 (2), 193–206.

Wolstein, B. (Ed.) (1988). *Essential Papers on Countertransference*. New York: New York University Press.

CHAPTER 3

Empathy and the therapeutic relationship in systemic-oriented therapies: a historical and clinical overview

Edwin Harari

INTRODUCTION

"there are between heaven and earth things . . . which demand not to be developed or explained but understood"

J. G. Droysen—*Outline of the Principles of History*
[cited in Burger, 1978, p. 8]

From Antigone to Princess Diana, from Cain and Abel to the Kennedys of Massachusetts, family relationships have been an inexhaustible source of fascination for people. That family relationships could be a force for happiness or misfortune in a person's life, whose effects could be transmitted across the generations, was widely appreciated, and variously attributed to the workings of Divine Will, Fate, History, Blood, Race, and Nation. Implicit in the account of such influences was the idea that they were beyond people's capacity to change.

The Enlightenment of the eighteenth century challenged this view. Inspired by the success of science to explain, control and change the natural world, the thinkers of the Enlightenment (and the social and political revolutions they encouraged) sought to explain Human Nature and the social order in human terms. This quest could not begin until two fundamental questions were answered:

1. Was Human Nature made of a different (i.e. "higher") "stuff" than the natural world? That it appeared to be so seemed obvious, given the existence of Culture, Morality, Social Progress, and Reason, though Darwin's theory of evolution was to undermine some of the confidence in this view.

2. Could Human Nature, social life, and organization be studied through the methods of natural science, or were specific methods required? The French scholar Auguste Comte articulated the doctrine of positivism, which situated the fledgling disci-pline of sociology as the apotheosis of scientific practice, claiming that the methods of natural science could be applied to the study of human beings and their social organization. The English philosopher John Stuart Mill argued that the principles of inductive reasoning upon which the natural sciences were based could also be applied to the complexities of human psychology and social life.

However, dissenting views were expressed by German scholars (Dilthey, Droysen, Rickert, and to a degree Max Weber), who argued for a unique method appropriate to the study of the subject matter of human history and human social formations. These scholars turned to the discipline of hermeneutics, which had originated in the exposition and interpretation of biblical texts. They argued that human activities could be studied through the same method, central to which was the concept of *"verstehen"*, or "understanding derived from empathy". In the *verstehen* method the researcher is empathically connected with the phenomena of study, whereas in the natural sciences the researcher seeks an objective, detached position. While the *verstehen* method provides a meaning of the phenomena, the method of natural science seeks a cause for the phenomena.

The project of the Enlightenment applied to the study of the characteristics of individuals. Their formation through biology and family relationships and their transmission across the generations were described in the models of the mind proposed by Sigmund Freud. Freud's model of developmental psychology and psychopathology, as well as the associated therapeutic method of psychoanalysis, straddled both of the approaches to science summarized above. Furthermore, in his account of unconscious mental functioning, Freud (along with Friedrich Nietzsche and Karl Marx) challenged the confidence of the Enlightenment in the apparent rationality of conscious thought and the veracity of immediate experience.

The tensions and contradictions between an objective position in search of a causal explanation, and an empathic understanding in search of the meaning of an experience, runs like a faultline through the history of psychotherapy, as does the question of the participants' awareness of their motives and intentions that influence their actions.

This chapter summarizes the therapeutic principles of several widely practised models of family therapy, paying particular attention to the role (if any) that they accord to empathy in their formulations of the therapist's stance and of the therapeutic relationship. The overview suggests that these systemic models of therapy rely on empathy and attend to emotional states and to the therapeutic relationship to a greater degree than has hitherto been recognized by critics of family therapy (e.g. Smith, Osman, & Goding, 1990). This discrepancy may reflect a failure to distinguish between the *practice* of empathy and its attendant concerns about the therapeutic relationship, and *theorizing about* empathy and the therapeutic relationship. The latter has indeed been neglected by family therapists, whereas in clinical practice empathy and attention to the therapeutic relationship are important aspects of most, if not all, systemic therapies. These aspects of clinical practice are the focus of this overview.

EMPATHY

The concept of empathy has its origins in aesthetics, the branch of philosophy concerned with the appreciation of art and the reflection of life in art. Empathy is generally used as the English translation of the German word *"Einfühlung"* (literally, "feeling into"). Although not the first to use the term, Theodore Lipps in 1885 described *Einfühlung* in his study of optical illusions, and he argued that every visual art object (i.e. sculpture and painting rather than literature) represents a living being. Using psychologically sophisticated concepts, Lipps argued that people who project themselves into such an art object and identify with it experience a particular psychic state (Sharma, 1992).

Freud's personal library contained several of Lipps' books, in which he made marginal annotations. His essay on Michaelangelo's statue of Moses shows that Freud appreciated the imaginative act of placing one's self in the emotional state of another so as to understand the other. In his study of Leonardo da Vinci, Freud described how this capacity could be a source of both creativity and psychopathology, a reflection of the phenomenon of narcissism. In a later paper on the technique of psychoanalysis, he states:

> . . . it is certainly possible to forfeit this first success (i.e. establishing the transference) if from the start one takes up any standpoint other than one of empathic understanding, such as a moralising one. [Freud, 1913, p. 140]

However, despite endorsing the importance of the therapist's empathy, Freud wrote very little on this subject. This may have been because he took it for granted that empathy was a self-evident, non-mysterious activity by the analyst; or it may have been that he lost sight of the importance of empathy in his determination to give psychoanalysis the status of a science, according to the norms of natural science (Wolf, 1983). Yet Freud had to struggle with the inescapable evidence that even if psychoanalysis was a science, its practice, theorizing, and research were based on the conversations and the evolving relationship between two sentient, sapient human beings.

THE FAMILY PERSPECTIVE IN PSYCHOANALYSIS

While references to family life abound in Freud's writings (Sander, 1978), and while he made many astute observations on the influence of family relationships on the individual, Freud's clinical models of psychopathology and therapy remained focused on the individual, whose early childhood experiences in the family of origin were replayed in the context of the transference relationship with the analyst. While the deepening exploration of the transference was gradually recognized as the central activity of the psychoanalyst, American analysts—particularly those of the school of ego-psychology—adopted the stance of the objective, emotionally detached, "blank-screen" observer. There were some notable exceptions. Of particular relevance to the future development of family therapy was Harry Stack Sullivan (1953), whose method of participant observation in the clinical setting and close attention to the client's social context (including the family), and whose descriptions of how the developing child appraises its mother's feelings through empathy, were ideas that influenced the pioneers of family therapy such as Don Jackson, Murray Bowen, and Salvador Minuchin.

In the United Kingdom, Melanie Klein and her students (Klein, Heimann, & Money-Kyrle, 1955) emphasized the diagnostic and therapeutic value of the therapist attending to his or her countertransference, the functions of the therapist as a container for disowned, projected parts of the analysand's personality, and the process of projective identification which, in its benign, reversible form, constitutes the basis of empathy.

British Object-Relations therapists such as John Bowlby (1979) and Donald Winnicott (1965) emphasized the facilitation of attachment and provision of an adequate "holding" environment as vital experiences that the mother provided for her young child, and they modelled therapy in an analogous way to the "good-enough", emotionally-attuned mother. Empathy as the key epistemic and therapeutic principle of psychoanalysis was promoted by the Chicago psychoanalyst Heinz Kohut in his model of Self-Psychology, which has many similarities with Object Relations theory (Bacal & Newman, 1990). Object Relations theory enabled a shift from the intra-psychic to the inter-subjective field. The principles of Object Relations theory were readily translated into marital therapy, group therapy, and the child-guidance model of child therapy, but, rather curiously, not into a model of therapy with the whole family. This had to await developments in the United States.

However, interest in psychodynamic models of family therapy based on Object-Relations principles has grown in recent years (Box et al., 1981; Brighton-Cleghorn, 1987; Scharff & Scharff, 1991; Skynner, 1976; Slipp, 1991). This renewed interest has been stimulated by feminist psychotherapy (Luepnitz, 1988) and by the Milan model of family therapy (see below), which may be viewed as a bridge between psychodynamic and systemic therapies.

FAMILY THERAPY

Family therapy developed simultaneously in several centres in the United States (Gurman & Kniskern, 1981). It is possible to discern two broad streams of thought and clinical practice.

Communication models

In California, Gregory Bateson and others developed the "communication" model of psychopathology, which emphasized violation of tacit rules of family communication, contradiction between levels, and dissonant feedback between "the organism" and its environment (Bateson et al., 1956). The Mental Research Institute (MRI) School is the prototype (Watzlawick, Weakland, & Fisch, 1974). Don Jackson was a founding member of this group, and as a psychoanalyst he was interested in the symbolic meanings of problematic behaviours and their homeostatic function in the family. However, his untimely death limited the contribution he made to the description of the therapist's position. Virginia Satir, another early member of this group, brought the humanistic psychotherapy perspective which paid great attention to the therapist's empathic understanding of the anxieties and predicaments of each individual in a family; however, Satir's stay with MRI was brief.

The emphasis of MRI and subsequent therapies that it influenced, including solution-focused and problem-solving approaches, is to look for repetitive patterns of behaviour that have a communicative import relevant to the presenting problem.

Drawing on cybernetic theory, the therapist's task appears to be that of a detached observer who monitors the patterns of meaningful signals (information) that family members exchange with one another, the form of such communication (analogical or digital), and the behavioural consequences of such signals. The principal activity of the therapist seems to be pattern-recognition. The concept of homeostasis is not relevant to MRI, for it is assumed that the family is trying to change and adapt but has become trapped in failed solutions which inadvertently amplify the presenting problem (positive feedback). The family is seen as having its own self-healing capacities, which are not utilized currently because of inappropriate or confusing patterns of communication and problem solving.

Accordingly, the therapist's task is to perturb the pattern of communication in terms of its sequences, logical level, form, and behavioural consequences. It is assumed that comparatively minor input from the therapist may lead to significant changes in the family, at least for those members who are most interested in changing. The MRI therapist appears to pay little attention to empathy or to the therapeutic relationship.

In contrast, the development of family therapy in the metropolitan centres of the East of the United States reflects the influence of psychoanalysis. Although often determined to highlight how systems-oriented therapies differ in theory and practice from psychoanalysis, many of the tensions and debates that were summarized above in the work of Freud and his successors are also to be found in these models of family therapy.

Nathan Ackerman

As a young psychiatrist in the great Depression of the 1930s, Ackerman was struck by the massive and wide-ranging effects of unemployment on the family life and family relationships of coal-miners in Pennsylvania. Twenty-five years later, in his seminal work *The Psychodynamics of Family Life*, he noted that to label clients as uncooperative or untreatable may reveal a serious deficiency in the therapist's understanding of the client, for:

... one cannot administer psychotherapy to a starving person or one who is in danger of freezing to death. In these socially and economically maimed families the human situation is critical and demands emergency measures. There is real danger, not merely neurotically imagined danger; and the danger is a shared one. It is only natural that members of such families should resist individual psychotherapy. [Ackerman, 1958, p. 101]

In mobilizing practical help and then in the exploration of interpersonal conflicts, their intra-psychic consequences. and the reciprocal influences between the individual and the family, the therapist's role, according to Ackerman, is one of empathic understanding of each individual in the context of the family. This is the foundation upon which the therapist helps the client to understand himself or herself better and to feel understood by the therapist.

Contextual therapy

Ivan Boszormenyi-Nagy (1987; Boszormenyi-Nagy & Spark, 1973) has described family organization in terms of a "ledger" of justice, made up of debts and entitlements that each individual accumulates in childhood and seeks to redress through marriage, parenthood, and other social relationships. Implicit in these descriptions of interpersonal and transpersonal influence are many of the concepts of Object Relations theory. Nagy's relational ethics emerged from the therapist's empathic understanding of the three levels of relationship that human beings experience: purely intrapsychic, the internal aspects of interpersonal relationships, and the existential aspects of the interpersonal.

These are formulated by the therapist after carefully listening to the client's history and detailed description of relationships with significant others in his current life and childhood. The therapist formulates (reframes) the presenting problems in terms of the expressions of these relational ethical imperatives, in a way that shows the therapist's understanding of the "ledger" in the life of each family member (multi-lateral partiality).

Bowen's systems therapy

As a psychoanalyst, Murray Bowen treated children suffering from psychoses in which the pathology appeared to be a symbiotic tie between the child and its mother. Bowen gradually realized that this symbiotic relationship was but one thread in a network of family relationships, often extending across several generations, which could be conceptualized as many overlapping triangular relationships among family members. The intensity of these relationships, based on projection, introjection, and physical distance, had powerful effects on the developmental processes of individual differentiation among family members. Bowen, like Nagy, emphasized the importance of the extended family and of obtaining a detailed history of such influences, but, unlike Nagy, Bowen conducted most of his therapy with the marital couple in a troubled family. Sometimes one couple was observed behind the one-way mirror by other troubled couples.

The therapist's main formal activity was to explore the history and consequences of emotional closeness and differentiation of the individual and the pressures within the family that led to states of fusion with, or excessive detachment from, the family. The therapist also had to monitor his or her own position in the family so as to stay out of the triangulated emotional pressures that all families inevitably bring to bear on their therapist. To the extent that the therapist has not differentiated appropriately from his or her own family of origin, so he or she will get caught up in the fusing and triangulating processes of the family (Bowen, 1978).

While the Bowen-style therapist uses a high degree of empathy for individual family members and monitors the transference, this is primarily to avoid the transference and to remain sufficiently detached so as to be able to ask relevant questions. Accordingly, doing one's own family-of-origin work is an integral part of the training and practice of therapists in this model.

Structural family therapy

Perhaps the most influential of the early models of family therapy was Salvador Minuchin's model of Structural Therapy (Minuchin, 1974). The model appears deceptively simple. It explains psychopathology in terms of particular family structures, often imposed by adverse environmental circumstances, which result in a variety of problem-inducing patterns of family structure: for example, inverse hierarchies, extremes of enmeshment and disengagement, inappropriate boundaries between the various functional subsystems of the family, and so forth.

The structural therapist is very active, aiming to "join" the family and then to intervene in order to change the family structure. The therapist is the instrument of change—unbalancing, siding, tracking, physically moving around the room to get closer to or further away from some family members, asking them to do likewise—all in accordance with the family map. The therapist talks a great deal, cajoles, encourages, cautions, plays, and jokes in an attempt to lead the family into new patterns of relationship.

Clearly, the family must accept the therapist, and joining the family is the most important initial task. Minuchin describes how the therapist alternates between the "outsider-looking-in" stance, which he calls the transferential position, and the "working-inside-the-family" stance, which he calls the existential position. The high degree of therapist activity requires that he or she be attuned to how the family is responding, individually and in their relationships with one another, otherwise there is the risk that the therapist will be perceived to be authoritarian or destructive. Unlike many other approaches in individual or family therapy, the structural therapist accepts the need to form temporary alliances with one family member, which may be resented by others in the family. However, this alliance is not a coalition against another family member and does not seek to devalue or undermine them. Nevertheless, it is important for the structural therapist to remain alert to the possibility of becoming inducted by the family into its power struggles.

A further safeguard, as well as a source of useful interventions for the therapist, is to have colleagues observing behind the one-way mirror. Unlike Milan (systemic) therapy, the relationship between the therapist and the observing team is not usually the subject of discussion and intervention, a position consistent with the notions of first-order cybernetics, which situated the therapist as an observer of the family system.

Strategic therapy

Jay Haley's original strategic therapy, with its emphasis on family homeostasis, and his later version of problem-solving therapy, reflects a passionate mistrust, indeed a contempt, for ideas that do not lead to practical, change-oriented, hope-enhancing manoeuvres by the therapist (Haley, 1976). The therapist's stance, though not as active as in structural therapy, is that of the principal agent of change in the family. The strategic therapist places emphasis on the power hierarchy of the family, whose problems are seen to reflect the inappropriate inversion or blurring of power relationships between the generations. Influenced by Milton Erikson's methods of tacit communication, the strategic therapist may redefine the presenting problem in such a way that it can be more easily solved. As well as direct suggestions and specific homework tasks, the therapist may use symptom prescription, rituals, and ordeals that challenge the function that the symptom is purported to serve by maintaining family homeostasis; the therapist thereby gives the family rapid experiences of success in altering the problem.

While Haley exhorts the therapist to try any intervention that might work regardless of its lack of theoretical elegance, he also emphasizes the importance of the therapist's willingness to "go to the mat" with the family and to struggle with them until a solution is found. Particularly when prescribing the symptom as an intervention, or the setting of tasks that may be difficult and onerous for the family, the therapist must be attuned to the responses of family members. However, this aspect of strategic therapy is often overshadowed by the impression of a therapist who wishes to obtain change at any price, even if this ignores the real inequalities suffered by women and minority groups in society which are reflected in the family's structure (Luepnitz, 1988).

More recently, in her strategic therapy with survivors of incest and child abuse, Cloë Madanes has emphasized the need for the perpetrator to atone and make reparation so that the survivor and the family can gradually leave the traumatic past behind them. Such activity requires a high degree of therapist empathy with all the participants if the intervention is not to become persecutory or destructive (Madanes, 1990).

Symbolic–experiential family therapy

Carl Whitaker has been called the Zarathustra of family therapy. His model of therapy advocates and encourages the therapist's use of self in order to understand the family members' experiences which are symbolized in their problems—in particular, their unspoken (and often unconscious) fears and desires (Napier & Whitaker, 1978; Neill & Kniskern, 1982). While refreshingly free of theory and jargon, Whitaker respects the unconscious of the therapist as a source of information about the family. The therapist's stance is to enter fully the experiential world of the family, while at the same time remaining aware of his or her own individuality.

In the early phase of therapy, and again at various critical points during the course of therapy, the therapist engages the family in two battles: the "battle for structure" is the therapist's efforts to learn about the family, not merely about their problems and history, but about their relationships with one another, their fears and fantasies which may be symbolically represented in the symptoms; the "battle for initiative" is the family's attempts to put the therapist into particular roles (e.g. giving advice, pursuing a particular line of inquiry while neglecting another line).

The therapist's use of empathy and countertransference is crucial in order to maintain a therapeutic stance without becoming absorbed by the family or rejecting them. The therapist's own fantasy life can be a source of humour, play, exaggeration of problems, provocative suggestions, and story-telling, all of which are expressed in the context of the therapist's empathic understanding of the anxiety and fears of family members. Co-therapy is a feature of this model, and the therapists' empathic attunement to one another enables them to support each other, to model disagreement and conflict resolution, and to adopt particular standpoints that may mirror those of various family members. A guiding principle of Whitaker's method is that the therapist will be affected and changed and will grow emotionally in the encounter with the family.

Milan (systemic) therapy

The repetitive three-stage sequence of Milan therapy—hypothesis, circularity, and neutrality (Selvini Palazzoli et al., 1980)—may give the appearance that the therapist adopts a detached, intellectualized, and objective position with regard to the family. This may reflect the influence of the MRI model on the early years of the Milan group, the group's transition from psychoanalytic to cybernetic language, and their advocacy of counter-paradoxical techniques, all of which implied a chess-game quality to therapy. After the split in the original Milan team, Mara Selvini Palazzoli's proposal of the "invariant prescription" added to this impression of therapy as a technical activity (Selvini Palazzoli, 1986).

In practice, hypothesizing by the therapist and the team about the family, which occurs before, during, and after a session, requires a high degree of empathy with the family. Similarly, the circular questions that the therapist asks, while they may appear mechanical and little more than an endless list of differences and rank-ordering of responses among family members, are meant to highlight differences that may be of significance to the family members in their attempts to define and understand their problem. While the emphasis in the earlier Milan model was on the impact of the end-of-session message delivered by the team to the family, attention more recently has been on the family's experiences in the session itself, including the experience of the family-plus-therapist system that is transiently formed.

The Milan group highlights the therapist's curiosity about the family; this is not an inquisitive intrusiveness, but the therapist's respectful interest in the family, their lives, and the issues that the family finds relevant to itself (Cecchin, 1987). The neutrality of the therapist does not mean an indifference to the family's distress or the dangers that they may face individually and collectively. Indeed, the therapist's empathy with such feelings is often a source of fruitful hypotheses and questions, which may lead the family to construct a different view of their problems and of possible solutions.

If the therapist's empathic resonance with the plight of family members suggests that they are at risk of illness, suicide, violence, or abuse, the therapist's role may change to one of advocate, social controller, or doctor. This requires the therapist to attend constantly to his or her ever-changing relationship with the family and with the wider professional, social, and political context in which therapy takes place. The observing team monitors such issues, which may, in turn, become the subject of further hypotheses.

Narrative therapy

Narrative approaches in family therapy have reminded clinicians of the importance of listening carefully to clients and allowing them to tell their story in their own time and their own way. The psychoanalyst Theodore Reik's celebrated phrase "listening with the third ear" implies that listening is not merely polite attention, but is an active process. While psychoanalysis uses this listening to discern and articulate transference issues, the family therapist uses the narrative as an opportunity for the client to express experiences that are important for the experience of self. Empathic understanding in the narrative view is not merely a preliminary activity before setting tasks or enacting interventions, but is part of the essence of therapy (Anderson & Goolishian, 1988). From such understanding the therapist can encourage the client to recount other stories that family members may have been reluctant to tell or might have assumed were well-known or irrelevant. Such stories may also guide the therapist to encourage the family to consider alternative outcomes to their stories and the consequences if such outcomes had occurred in the past or were to occur in the future (White & Epston, 1990).

Similarly, the Reflecting Team discussion entails a high degree of empathy with the family, individually and collectively, their view of the world, family rules, and life-cycle anxieties. The team discussion, conducted with the family observing and listening, positively connotes and reframes the behaviour of family members. The team advances possible solutions, their risks and advantages—all of which are proposed with respect and empathy for the current concerns, limits, and competencies of the family (Andersen, 1987).

Behavioural family therapy

The genealogy of behavioural therapies is based on learning theory, which emphasized the observable, objective, testable, replicable nature of its concepts and methods. The therapist serves as an educator, as a model (explicit or implicit) for particular behaviours, as a teacher of skills, and as an advocate of new methods of problem solving or of more effective use of competencies that the family has. The therapist views the family members as rational agents whose problem-solving skills have been depleted or wrongly learned.

While the behavioural therapist is respectful of each family member's experiences, empathy is not commonly described as a therapist's requirement; yet to explore, often in great detail, behavioural sequences and their associated cognitions requires patience and empathy by the therapist. The growing emphasis on the cognitive dimension that accompanies most human actions has led behavioural therapists to pay closer attention to historical, transgenerational, and current contextual experiences that influence patterns of cognition. As a result, the intersubjective experiences of the therapist and family members during the therapy session are increasingly acknowledged to be relevant and not merely "confounding variables" in therapy (Patterson & Forgatch, 1985).

CONCLUSION

The therapist's empathy appears to be a necessary, though by no means sufficient, ingredient in all models of systemic therapies. This is explicitly encouraged and highly prized in Whitaker's symbolic-experiential model of therapy and to varying degrees in psychodynamically influenced models, including transgenerational, Milan (systemic), and narrative therapies. While MRI, problem-solving, solution-focused, and behavioural models give little explicit attention to the therapist's empathy and to the therapist–family relationship, these are still important features of the clinical application of these models.

Empathy has been rediscovered by family therapists (Perry, 1993; Wilkinson, 1992). Where psychoanalytic and humanistic therapies addressed the individual and the original models of family therapy addressed contextual and systemic issues, empathy may provide the link that facilitates the study and the therapy of individuals-in-context in their roles as therapists and family members. The therapist may be thought of as a temporary attachment figure for the family (Byng-Hall, 1988).

The ability of the therapist both to experience the family "from the inside" and yet still to be able to step "outside" the family in order to observe and plan intervention is a skill all models of therapy require. How this activity by the therapist can be studied, taught, and researched in order to provide more effective forms of therapy is part of a debate that began in the eighteenth century with the Enlightenment and continues to this day.

REFERENCES

Ackerman, N. (1958). *The Psychodynamics of Family Life*. New York: Basic Books.

Andersen, T. (1987). The reflecting team: dialogues and meta-dialogue in clinical work. *Family Process*, 26, 415–428.

Anderson, H., & Goolishian, H. A. (1988). Human systems as linguistic systems. *Family Process*, 27, 371–393.

Bacal, H. A., & Newman, K. M. (1990). *Theories of object relations: bridges to self psychology*. New York: Columbia University Press.

Bateson, G., Jackson, D. D., Haley, J., & Weakland, J. H. (1956). Towards a theory of schizophrenia. *Behavioural Science*, 1 (4), 251–264.

Boszormenyi-Nagy, I. (1987). *Foundations of Contextual Therapy* (collected papers). New York: Brunner/Mazel.

Boszormenyi-Nagy, I., & Spark, G. (1973). *Invisible Loyalties: Reciprocity in Intergenerational Family Therapy*. New York: Harper & Row. (Second edition, New York: Brunner/Mazel, 1984.)

Bowen, M. (1978). *Family Therapy in Clinical Practice.* New York: Jason Aronson.
Bowlby, J. (1979). *The Making and Breaking of Affectional Bonds.* London: Tavistock.
Box, S., Copley, B., Magagna, J., & Moustaki, E. (1981). *Psychotherapy with Families: An Analytic Approach.* London: Routledge & Kegan Paul.
Brighton-Cleghorn, J. (1987). Formulations of self and family systems. *Family Process,* 26 (2), 185–201.
Burger, T. (1978). Droysen and the idea of Verstehen. *The Journal of the History of the Behavioural Sciences,* 1, 6–19.
Byng-Hall, J. (1988). Scripts and legends in families and family therapy. *Family Process,* 27, 167–179
Cecchin, G. (1987). Hypothesizing, circularity and neutrality revisited: an invitation to curiosity. *Family Process,* 26 (4), 405–413.
Freud, S. (1913). On beginning the treatment. Further recommendations on the technique of psychoanalysis. *Standard Edition of the Complete Psychological Works of Sigmund Freud,* edited by J. Strachey. London: Hogarth Press, 1955, Vol. 12, pp. 121–144.
Gurman, A. S., & Kniskern, D. P. (Eds.) (1981). *Handbook of Family Therapy.* New York: Brunner/Mazel.
Haley, J. (1976). *Problem Solving Therapy.* San Francisco, CA: Jossey Bass.
Klein, M., Heimann, P., & Money-Kyrle, R. (Eds.) (1955). *New Directions in Psychoanalysis.* London: Tavistock.
Luepnitz, D. (1988). *The Family Interpreted. Feminist Theory in Clinical Practice.* New York: Basic Books.
Madanes, C. (1990). *Sex, Love and Violence.* New York: W.W. Norton.
Minuchin, S. (1974). *Families and Family Therapy.* London: Tavistock.
Napier, A. Y., & Whitaker, C. (1978). *The Family Crucible.* New York: Harper & Row.
Neill, J., & Kniskern, D. (Eds) (1982). *From Psyche to System: The Evolving Therapy of Carl Whitaker.* New York: Guilford Press.
Patterson, G. R., & Forgatch, M. S. (1985). Therapist behaviour as a determinant for client non-compliance: a paradox for the behaviour modifier. *Journal of Consulting and Clinical Psychology,* 53, 846–851.
Perry, R. (1993). Empathy—still at the heart of therapy. *Australian and New Zealand Journal of Family Therapy,* 14 (2), 63–74.
Sander, F. (1978). Marriage and the family in Freud's writings. *Journal of the American Academy of Psychoanalysis,* 6 (2), 157–174.

Scharff, D., & Scharff, J. (1991). *Object Relations Family Therapy.* Northvale, NJ: Jason Aronson.
Selvini Palazzoli, M. (1986). Towards a general model of psychotic family games. *Journal of Marital and Family Therapy, 12,* 339–344.
Selvini Palazzoli, M., Boscolo, L., Cecchin, G., & Prata, G. (1980). Hypothesizing—circularity—neutrality: three guidelines for the conduct of the sessions. *Family Process, 19,* 3–12.
Sharma, R. M. (1992). Empathy—a retrospective on its development in psychotherapy. *Australian and New Zealand Journal of Psychiatry, 26* (3), 377–390.
Skynner, A. C. R. (1976). *One Flesh, Separate Persons: Principles of Family and Marital Psychotherapy.* London: Constable.
Slipp, S. (1991). *Object Relations. A Dynamic Bridge between Individual and Family Treatment.* Northvale, NJ: Jason Aronson.
Smith, J., Osman, C., & Goding, M. (1990). Reclaiming the emotional aspects of the therapist–family system. *Australian and New Zealand Journal of Family Therapy, 11* (3), 140–146.
Sullivan, H. S. (1953). *The Interpersonal Theory of Psychiatry.* New York: W. W. Norton.
Watzlawick, P., Weakland, J., & Fisch, R. (1974). *Change: Principles of Problem Formation and Problem Resolution.* New York: W. W. Norton.
White, M., & Epston, D. (1990). *Narrative Means to Therapeutic Ends.* New York: W. W. Norton.
Wilkinson, M. (1992). How do we understand empathy systemically? *Journal of Family Therapy, 14* (2), 193–205.
Winnicott, D. (1965). *The Maturational Processes and the Facilitating Environment.* London: Hogarth. [Reprinted London: Karnac Books, 1990.]
Wolf, E. S. (1983). Empathy and countertransference. *The Future of Psychoanalysis* (pp. 309–326), edited by A. Goldberg. New York: International Universities Press.

CHAPTER 4

Embedded and embodied in the therapeutic relationship: understanding the therapist's use of self systemically

Vivien Hardham

INTRODUCTION

Our "use of self is . . . the only tool available to (us)" (Real, 1990, p. 255). Every beginning therapist is painfully and humbly aware of the meaning in practice of this statement. Our selves are what we use to do therapy. The beginning systemic therapist may also note that to help us in our practice we have literature that describes techniques or styles of therapy, theory that implies certain approaches, or vague statements about the existential or intuitive aspects of therapy. Yet somehow, none of this directly helps us understand how we use *ourselves* as feeling and thinking people within dynamic action-packed therapeutic relationships.

This chapter presents a stage in the development of my thinking about the use of self of the therapist. It is addressed to therapists who identify their theory of practice as systemic, and it was inspired by a personally felt need arising from my wish not to have to "step outside" my theory of practice in order to understand how I do therapy. The essay is strongly shaped by two allegiances that I should own from the outset. Firstly, I wished to be consistent with systemic (ecological/second-order cybernetic) understandings of therapy, and so I am trying to focus on the therapist and the therapist's use of self, while still seeing the therapist as inextricably and recursively a part of a dynamic relationship/system. Secondly, I wished to do this in a way that meant that I did not compromise a commitment to the broader issues of power, and to the ethics that are consistent with feminist and culturally sensitive practice.

Systemic theory brought us the valuable notion that nothing makes sense except in context, and later the idea that this can be seen through many different lenses—for example, systems' organization, epistemologies, language (Boscolo, 1993). Understanding the patterns that connect added "outsight" to our therapeutic project and enhanced our capacity to work within, and influence, broader systems of meaning. The ideas of multipartiality, multiple engagement, circularity, and curiosity were thus made possible, and we were able to understand what we do from "out-of-there" perspectives (Boscolo et al., 1988; Campbell & Draper, 1985).

However, this "big picture" approach of systemic theory does not give a language for talking about an individual's felt experience and activity, except in relation to the specific context in which it occurs. There is an apparent contradiction involved when one tries to look at individual therapists "systemically". How can we focus upon individual (therapists') selves and experience, and yet stay within systemic theory, when this theory primarily maps the big picture?

Some feminist critiques have taken issue with the way in which systemic notions of power and neutrality have seemed to place a focus on values and subjective experience impossible (see Hoffman, 1990; Luepnitz, 1988; MacKinnon & Miller, 1987; McIntyre, 1991). In response to the acknowledgement of this problem, some writers have moved away from systemic theory and investigated the possibility of adding in ideas from other approaches. Both psychoanalytic theory and social constructionism have been used to do this (see e.g Flaskas, 1993; Hoffman, 1990; Luepnitz, 1988). While turning to outside theories may be very valuable, I am choosing in this chapter to stay more strictly within a systemic framework. Flaskas (1989) notes that systemic or second-order cybernetic theory leaves the space for further development of systemic theory in relation to the therapeutic relationship, and it is this space that I would like to explore in investigating the therapist's use of self in the therapeutic relationship.

I was first intrigued by "systemic" language linking individuals and contexts. I then became intrigued by any language that seemed to require this kind of dual focus. Stierlin (1987) writes about "coevolving" and coins the complementary term "coindividuation". He quotes Hegel—"The doing of the one is the doing of the other" (in Stierlin, 1987, p. 100)—and points out how the process of definition of one term implies a definition by difference of the other, complementary, term. For example, if we define an "in" we also define an "out". As Stierlin elegantly notes, all evolution involves individuals changing, and all individuation is in relation to others. Throughout this chapter, I use this kind of dual focus/"other side of the coin" approach.

The chapter is shaped as a cumulative layering of ideas and is structured in three parts. The first part explores the idea of the self in the big picture and sets the stage for a "systemic" understanding of an active intentional self in relationship. Systemic/ecological ideas are used in developing a simple language, which provides a framework for further elaboration.

The second part considers the qualities of the self as embodied and embedded within therapeutic relationships and begins to map a systemic way of understanding the therapist's use of self. The third part explores embeddedness and positioning in the therapeutic context and takes the ideas developed in the earlier sections into the broader context of socio-political concerns, personal ethics, and therapeutic responsibility.

THE SELF IN THE BIG PICTURE

Introducing the ideas of "embedded" and "embodied"

We can begin this exploration of the self in the big picture by considering the systemic/ecological idea that we as individual selves are *embedded* within our contexts. We are a *part* of complex, evolving webs of meaning, interactions, and patterns of connection. As embedded individuals we are not outside our contexts, and we could be likened to pieces of cellular genetic material inextricably embedded within complex and shifting cellular and organismic environments.

And, to follow Stierlin's use of Hegel's idea, if we define ourselves as embedded, by implication we also define ourselves as *embodied*, discrete individuals. Thinking of ourselves as embedded also means thinking of ourselves as boundaried, biological individuals. We are inextricably "in-there" as finite, embodied people. This is a shift from the "big picture" focus to a "close-up" focus. We shift focus to ourselves as individuals embodied and situated within the big picture or webs of meaning.

As Benhabib (1992) notes: "the illusion of a disembedded and disembodied subject, . . . situated beyond historical and cultural contingency . . . (has) long ceased to exist" (p. 4), and further, that we "(as) the subjects of reason are finite, embodied fragile creatures, and not disembodied cogitos . . ." (p. 5).

The "big picture" and our embeddedness— the idea of outsight

If we focus upon the embedded nature of our existence, we will see ourselves as determined by our contexts. We will notice the sociocultural meanings and patterns of interaction within which we exist. We will notice things like co-evolution, interdependence, connections, reciprocal influence, and (therapeutic) responsibility for others. Understanding our embeddedness involves looking for such things as the patterns that connect, and the social constructions that shape our experience. This is the closest we can get to an "out-of-there" appreciation of the webs of interaction and/or meaning in which we act as therapists.

"Outsight" is a term coined by Stagoll (1987) to describe the way of seeing things in the "out-of-there" part of the "there and out-of-there" circular dynamic of the therapist as described by Boscolo (in discussion with D. Campbell, R. Draper, and G. Cecchin: Campbell & Draper, 1985, p. 282). An outsight could be seen as the use of a contextual, big-picture understanding to make sense of individual experience. We are going *from* the outer social/cultural meaning *to* the inner experience. For example, I could say:

> Many of my clients have the impression that I am a kind of child protection worker, even though I work in a counselling service independent of child protection. No wonder I often feel as though I am being rejected as some kind of alien.

This "outsight" helps me to recognize and make visible the context within which I work and so from there understand my felt experience. Outsights, then, assist us in making sense of our embeddedness.

Embodied individuals within the big picture— the idea of insight

Many writers argue that it is unhelpful, if not inaccurate, to view individuals as separate social atoms (e.g. Bateson, 1972; Mathews, 1991). I would agree, and so I have chosen to use the word *"embodied"* rather than "bodied". "Embodiment" is not a quality that exists independently of relationships and connections. It is an active rather than descriptive term. In this chapter "embodiment" refers to the defining of self (biological individuality) and to the defining of others as discrete individuals. These are the active constructions of individuals or subjects. As individuals we experience ourselves as biologically discrete, as contained within our skins. Thus, we experience ourselves as embodied and largely define our selves and our boundaries by our bodied experience. But also importantly, despite the ecological reality of our inextricable embeddedness, we are boundaried, defined, and located by others—and, so, we are also embodied by others.

"Insight" could be understood as the idea that is complementary to "outsight". In this way an "insight" could be seen as the view from "in-there" rather than "out-of-there", as going *from* the inner subjective experience *to* the outer, contextual or relational, meaning. For example, consider these "insightful" statements:

I always feel rotten and withdraw from interaction when my clients reject or criticize me. I guess this is because it reminds me of my early experiences of criticism as attack and elicits my habitual defensive response.

These "insights" move from a description of an inner feeling, to a description that contextualizes, or gives relational meaning to, my subjective experience.

Insights place our embodied experience in the context of a relationship or narrative, and so we come to know ourselves as feeling and acting people a little more completely. As we reflect upon our experience in relationships, we develop more and more insight. We gradually define our personal boundaries, and come to see ourselves as self-creating people with agency in our choices and actions. We come to see our selves as the embodied authors of our own life stories. We are no longer un-self-consciously embedded in webs of narratives.

This process of self-definition or self-embodiment is an ongoing process of evolution (or co-individuation). We have an evolving self-consciousness and experience of ourselves as feeling, acting selves. If we focus upon the embodied nature of our existence, we will notice things like autonomy, independence, personal ethics, self-responsibility, and feelings.

Insights are vital for therapists. Yet, however important, they are not the whole story. Insights alone cannot make the big picture visible. We need outsights, the other focus, as well.[1]

Both embedded and embodied

However, it seems that systemic literature has neglected to address what it means to be embodied as well as what it means to be embedded. Systemic theory has helped us analyse our selves in context, in relation to others. We can see how we are interconnected, constrained, reciprocally influential, and defined by our context. It has not helped us paint ourselves into the picture as embodied, actively, and intentionally relating people.[2]

It has become axiomatic within systemic theory of practice to recognize that the therapist cannot be an observer from nowhere. The therapist is within the therapeutic relationship and broader system and culture. It seems that with the acceptance of postmodern and constructivist ideas, which posit that there are as many valid realities as there are individuals, the therapist has been encouraged to become an observer from everywhere. We are encouraged to be sensitive to multiple realities, and to put aside our own. The very real contradiction here is that embedded/embodied individuals cannot be everywhere. We cannot slide around, unattached, in the big picture. Embodiment brings with it limitations to our ability to be multipartial, curious, or neutral.

This first part of the chapter has introduced a number of related dualities which may be helpful in conceptualizing the self of the therapist in the context of therapy. In particular, I have introduced the ideas of the therapist as both embedded and embodied in the therapeutic relationship, and the recursiveness of the ideas of "outsight" and "insight" as ways of thinking about the therapist's position. The next section develops the ideas of embeddedness and embodiment as relational concepts and begins to draw out some of the implications of these ideas for how we think about ourselves within therapeutic relationships.

EMBODIED/EMBEDDED WITHIN THERAPEUTIC RELATIONSHIPS

The gap—language and expressive action

I begin this second part of the chapter by noting the gap between language and expressive action, and the way in which this gap has not been sufficiently acknowledged or theorized in systemic theory. This gap was highlighted for me as I watched the (live) work of gifted therapist/theorists. The systemic literature had not given me a language to make sense of the way in which (for example) Luigi Boscolo gently rocked towards different family members, or the significance to the therapeutic relationship of the tear in his eye. I knew that these activities, or uses of self, were consistent with the systemic theory of practice, but there was little to help me link theories and the ways in which we as therapists use ourselves in practice. I found myself needing to step outside the systemic theory of practice as it is currently developed in order to provide myself with a simple framework to address this gap. I was looking for a way to expand my (systemic) theory usefully, and wanted to bring the use of ourselves as embodied people into systemic/family therapy language.

In exploring the gap, I turned to the current approaches in systemic therapy. When I considered the way in which constructivist and narrative ideas have become influential in systemic thinking, it seemed to me that these ideas are being used in ways that imply that all the action of therapy is in words. The therapist is a "co-author" (White & Epston, 1988) or "in conversation" (Goolishian & Anderson, 1989) in the process of therapy. In one of the few papers that directly address the therapist's use of self, Real (1990) restricts himself to a discussion of only the verbal activity or questioning styles of the proponents of different "schools" of systemic/constructionist therapy.

Yet when I am doing therapy, I am doing a lot more than just talking or reflecting. I am also reacting and feeling in ways that are pre-reflective (perhaps physiologically based), not in words or thoughts. I experience my feelings and emotions as being within me—within my personal boundaries. This is my embodied experience of my self in the relationship. To address the part played by our pre-reflective, feeling reactions in shaping our felt experience, we need to bring ourselves as embodied, biological individuals into the picture. We need to bridge the gap between language and expressive action.

The step—
feelings, reflections (theory), and felt reality

My step outside systemic theory involved a simple construction based upon this intuitive idea. The activity of any therapist necessarily involves dynamic and recursively-shaping interactions between both feeling reactions and cognitive reflections. This dynamic process creates the evolving, individual, felt reality of the therapist. Both the pre-reflective feelings and the language-based reflections create my felt reality. Both influence what I do, how I use myself. A "both/and", both feeling and reflective, dual-focus approach seems useful in linking our theory (reflections) and our practice (use of self).

Different models of therapy will provide different frameworks or shaping principles which will play a part in the construction of our reflections. A systemic therapist will be aware of the importance of widening the context, of using as many lenses as we have at our disposal, as we reflect. To address the part played by our pre-reflective and feeling reactions in shaping our felt reality, we need to bring ourselves as embodied people into the picture.

Krause (1993) traces the development of ideas within both family therapy and anthropology as they moved from implicit understandings of emotions as being of the body and residing within the individual (and so being unaddressable when understanding systems and cultures) towards understanding emotions as culturally and socially constructed appraisals and communications. She begins to open discussion of the implications for the practice of family therapy. Here, following Krause (1993) and Solomon (1993), I use the term "feeling" to denote our pre-reflective sensations or responses. Krause and Solomon use the term "emotion" to denote the more complex constructions of individuals as they respond and give meaning to or reflect upon those feelings. In this chapter I generally use the alternative term, "felt reality", as this seems to encompass both the pre-reflective and reflective.[3]

Emotions or felt realities are cultural or social constructions in that the meanings, values, or reflections that participate in their creation are constructed and shaped in the social/cultural domain. For therapists, these reflections will be constructed in part by our theories of practice. Understanding our felt realities as socially constructed gives us a way of understanding how our embeddedness shapes our experience.

However, meanings or reflections alone do not constitute our felt realities. We are not "disembodied cogitos" (Benhabib, 1992, p. 5). We have feelings or bodied responses that also participate dynamically or recursively in the evolving construction of our felt realities. Understanding our felt reality is understanding the link between our embeddedness and our embodiedness.

Felt reality—embedded and embodied

Our emotions or felt realities can only be understood in relation. That is, I can only make sense of my felt reality in the context of this particular therapeutic relationship. My feelings are inextricably embedded in relation. If my felt reality is not related to the context in which it is expressed, experts with the power to name will describe me as having "inappropriate affect". My felt reality is the most immediate way in which I am embedded within the relationship.

Our felt realities (or emotions) may also be the most significant way in which we are embodied. When I suffer, desire, or fear, I experience myself as a separate unique being. My felt reality defines me (at least to myself) as alive and unique. I may feel overwhelmed, but at least I know that I am real. When my reality or self-definition is at stake, I will not appreciate having my feelings externalized.

To summarize, then, understanding our felt reality is understanding the link between our embeddedness and our embodiedness. To make a systemic sense of our felt reality in relationships we need to address the way in which relational, cultural, and theoretical constructions shape our individual experience, and the ways in which our felt reality shapes our relationships and our practice. Our felt reality, as shaped by our pre-reflective reactions and our rational (even if "forgotten") theoretical reflections, is what is enacted in the process of therapy. The expression of our felt reality is use of self in relationship. I will turn now to look at what this may mean within the therapeutic relationship.

Felt reality and action and therapeutic positioning

Empathy could be understood as the expression or enactment of our felt reality as it evolves dynamically within the therapeutic relationship. This expression/enactment is in the realm of analogic communication. As Boscolo (dialogue at workshop, Sydney, in 1993) and Gibney (1994) remind us, analogic communication cannot be negated. If my face "drops" when I see a child apparently rejected, it stays "dropped" in the memory of the family members who saw it. No words, no reframing, no change of mind after more considered reflection can undo that communication. I am visible within the therapeutic relationship as an embodied person. Family members will create their own image of me. They will have "embodied" me, located me in the webs of meaning and interaction that constitute and construct this therapeutic relationship.

Every use of self, whether intended or unintended, is an expression of our felt reality. Each action, or inaction, effectively embodies and positions us within the therapeutic relationship. Though not expressed in these terms, Andolphi and Angelo (1988), Haber (1990), and Real (1990) describe how we can choose to enact our felt reality (i.e. use ourselves), and all refer to the therapist as "positioning" in relation.

Andolphi and Angelo (1988) write:

> the therapist is continually positioning himself at one pole of various triangles. [p. 241]

Haber (1990) says:

> Awareness of the therapist's position/role and internal experience provides information that can help the therapist act in a more congruent, flexible, and creative fashion. [p. 377]

Real (1990) describes "systemic positioning, *multiple engagement*" as the act of "positioning" oneself:

> vis-à-vis the many contrasting currents in this system, its multiple realities and agendas, in such a way as to promote a healing conversation. [p. 260]

I have come to see every thing we do as positioning. "Positioning" is an active relational term. As therapists we are "positioned" or "have a position" in relation to moral issues or political "isms". "One-up(or down)ness" refers to a strategic positioning. Our emotional closeness (or distance) is reflected in our physical orientation. All of these may be relatively fixed positions or may be in a process of dynamic flux. We may choose our positions, or we may find we are positioned by others.

In the dropped-face example above, I have probably described an unintended expression of my felt reality, an unintended use of self. Yet this effectively positioned me in the therapeutic relationship. It limited my capacity to vary my style and still relate congruently. In many ways it limited my manoeuvrability. My felt reality (a value- and meaning-full reality) had been shaped by my previous experience and my meaning and value construction in many contexts. The expression of my felt reality in turn shaped the therapeutic relationship.

So, what choices do I have when my face drops? Can I position myself in ways that allow me to be curious and respectful and still be congruent with my values and felt reality as expressed? The answer is yes, but my curiosity is no longer *unlimited*.

For us all, this is to some extent unavoidable. Some circumstances evoke such a strength of feeling that the much-needed opportunity to reflect is not accessible to us. The expression/enaction of our felt reality will be without any consideration of the bigger picture and the meaning of that response. If we are stuck in a reactive mode, our therapy will be human and responsive, but we risk acting inappropriately or irresponsibly. We may be "flung by the tail of the tiger", or in a "black hole of empathy".[4] If, in an attempt to avoid unhelpful, judgemental positioning, I tried to detach from my values and felt reality (some see this as neutrality), I would be trying to ignore my feelings, my embodiedness. The therapy could well become technocratic and impersonal. In systemic therapy this lack of responsiveness is "circularity in the head". In a workshop in Sydney in 1989, Boscolo used this term (with circular hand motions beside his head) and contrasted this with a circularity joining therapist and family. Interestingly, he indicated this by circular hand motions moving between his stomach (gut level?) and the imagined family. Without this recursive process I would be simply testing static hypotheses, nothing would be co-evolving, I would not be engaging in therapy. Family members will make their own sense of this lack of human engagement. Again, they will position me in ways beyond my control.

To avoid either of these untherapeutic possibilities, I can express my felt reality strategically or with awareness of the meanings within this relationship of my reactions and actions. If I have an insightful and outsightful understanding of my sense of self and felt reality as it is evolving in this relationship, I will have an enhanced capacity to use myself intentionally.

This second part of the chapter has identified the gap between language and expressed action in the current systemic understandings. The idea of "felt reality" has been used to describe the way in which therapists come to experience themselves as a result of being both embedded and embodied in the therapeutic relationship, and the notion of the therapist's "position" has been used to incorporate these ideas. It is now possible to move to a consideration of the therapist's position as embedded and emodied in the broader context.

EMBEDDED/EMBODIED IN THE BROADER CONTEXT

The context defines and positions

I turn now to the broader system or culture that embeds the therapeutic relationship and shapes and locates it. For example, I may think that I am saying to my clients: "This is just a conversation, and you are the expert here." But this statement may well be made a confusing nonsense by the context created by my gender, my professional status, my middle-classness, my culture, my office, my employers' expectations, the respect with which others treat me, etc. . . . Family members will of course make their own sense of such a statement.

I can have little or no control over some factors creating the context. There are also some factors I would not choose to change. For example, an expert status can be influential, and perhaps, without some form of socially constructed status as a helpful change agent, "not knowing" is merely ignorance. However, as MacKinnon (1993) eloquently points out, there is a potentially less-than-rosy side to this. All these "context" factors also define my clients as my "other" (non-professional, non-white/middle class, non-competent, unemployed . . .). I too may become the "other" to my clients, and "in this position of 'other' . . . I cannot be 'just a person'" to my clients (MacKinnon, 1993,

p. 120). When my face drops, then the meaning to the family will depend partly upon how strongly the context (including the philosophy of my workplace and the referral and intake process) has defined me as an expert in "correct parenting".

This focus on our embeddedness in a position by the broader context can lead us to see ourselves as determined or defined by our contexts. It is useful (and refreshing!) to shift the focus to ourselves as embodied people. Through this lens we can see our creativity, our flexibility, and our ability to influence the ways in which we are seen or positioned as proactive choices.

Self-embodiment as positioning

Self-embodiment is in contrast to both unintentional expression of our felt reality and un-self-conscious embeddedness. Intentionally expressing our felt reality, positioning ourselves, with the awareness of the relational meanings this creates, is self-embodiment of ourselves in the therapeutic relationship/context. Awareness of the relational context will help us see precisely what kind of freedom we have to be creative and curious.

In some situations our personal values and/or our legal and social/cultural responsibilities are strongly challenged (e.g. child abuse or domestic violence). Our context and our individual felt realities seem to require us to define our position clearly and explicitly—to say, "here I stand", and limit our curiosity. This limits the space in which we can be therapeutic. Some situations or work contexts (e.g. statutory child-protection work with severe abuse) may limit the therapeutic space so markedly that only social control is possible.

Saying or enacting "here I stand" is expressing our personal ethics. This is the statement or action of a concrete embodied person who can actively locate or position herself in relation to the broader context in which she is embedded. We cannot have a personal ethic without addressing both our embodiedness and our embeddedness. Every use of self is an ethical, positioning act. Even my "dropped face" is an act that positions me in the broader context within which this therapeutic relationship is embedded.

Ethical (self- and context-aware) positioning prevents us sliding around ambiguously, being positioned despite ourselves. We each need to be careful that this does not rigidly define ourselves as right/well/good and everyone else as wrong/ill/bad. The attempt to stay in touch with the bigger picture and the meanings attributed to our self-positioning helps prevent the creation of a no-change dichotomy. We can only be therapeutic where we have flexibility and mobility in positioning. Somewhere between rigid self-definition (fixing our position in concrete) and ambiguous slipperiness (refusal to acknowledge our embeddedness) we find therapeutic leverage and therapeutic responsibility.

Creating therapeutic contexts

As Flaskas (1989) succinctly outlines, the therapeutic relationship is understood in systemic therapy as the unit of change or evolution. The systemic theory of Boscolo and Cecchin acknowledges the defining power of context, and, in the "systemically optimistic" tradition (Stierlin, 1988), they redefine therapy as the influencing of context. Cecchin (in Campbell & Draper, 1985) writes:

> Whether therapy is good or not depends on the context you create around it . . . In therapy, you work to create a context in which *whatever* you do becomes effective. [p. 280]

Thus, the therapeutic relationship is not only the unit of change, it is the context of change. To rephrase Cecchin, we work to create a relationship that enables whatever we do to be effective. In working to create a therapeutic relationship, we are working to create a context within which we have maximum flexibility and can relate or position ourselves in many ways.

Therapeutic responsibility and positioning

Cecchin (1987) also writes: "Therapeutic responsibility begins with seeing your own position in the system. Many times this simply means recognizing what little power you have and, at the same time, maintaining respect for the system." (p. 410). Recognizing what little power I may have means recognizing what little capacity I have for mobility in positioning. Cecchin understands that this is a limited capacity. It is limited by the way in which the context defines my position as well as by the way in which my own felt reality limits my creativity or flexibility and fixes my position.

We continue, optimistically, to try to be therapeutically influential (or powerful). Being therapeutically influential means being good at influencing context. To do this we need to create contexts within which we have maximum manoeuvrability. For this we need good understandings of ourselves as embedded in the broader context and therapeutic relationship. We need to engage curiously and respectfully with people and their meanings, and to recognize ourselves, our actions and felt realities, as visible and influential (embodied) within the therapeutic relationship. To be effective for each client, couple, or family we work with, we require imagination, playfulness, even "irreverence" (Cecchin, Lane, & Ray, 1993). Therapeutic responsibility requires an awareness of how the context we create by our actions, our positioning in relation, fits within the broader context.

CONCLUSION: BACK TO THE BEGINNING— UNDERSTANDING MY USE OF SELF SYSTEMICALLY

This chapter has moved through a number of different ideas. Beginning with the dualities of embedded and embodied, outsight and insight, it moved to a consideration of the idea of the therapist's felt reality and the way in which the therapist comes to be positioned both by her or his own felt reality and the broader context of the therapy. It has also looked at the way in which the positioning of the therapist in the therapeutic relationship is a recursive process—the therapist both positions and is positioned by her or his felt reality, and the broader context shapes both the embodied and embedded aspects of the therapist's position.

All these ideas are, I believe, consistent with the systemic theory of practice. The feminist critique of systemic theory has at least partly been based upon an understanding of neutrality as a strategy or approach that creates a therapy of no values, no individual felt reality. In terms of the ideas developed in this chapter, it seems that perhaps an assumption has been made that a therapy that highlights the embedded nature of being (our place in the patterns that connect) is necessarily out of touch with the embodied experience of being. I have wanted to argue that a dual focus is possible. Perhaps this both/and, embedded and embodied, approach can help us find the language that can enrich our capacity to see the therapist's self in the process of therapy.

Seeing myself as embedded/embodied within the therapeutic relationship means that I have a way to address my feeling reactions, my cognitive (theoretical) reflections, and my intentional and unintentional positioning in relationships/contexts. This acknowledgement of myself as an individual in connection with others also means that I acknowledge my responsibility for the effects of my use of self. I am more able to paint myself into the picture. I begin to fill the gap between systemic theory and the practice of systemic therapy. And I begin to make sense of what Boscolo perhaps means when he says that a good therapist is one "who has many ways of getting in relation" (dialogue at a workshop in Sydney in 1993).

NOTES

1. It is tempting to theorize that this is why we came to need systemic theory in the project of theorizing networks of relationships.

2. Krause (1993) gives a historical account of the conceptualization of emotions in systemic and anthropological theory which indicates how this neglect occurred.

3. This also avoids possible confusion due to the interchangeability in current English usage of "emotions" and "feelings".

4. I am indebted to past supervisors, Bill Buchanan and Jenny Smith, for these gems.

REFERENCES

Andolphi, M., & Angelo, C. (1988). Towards constructing the therapeutic system. *Journal of Marital and Family Therapy, 14* (3), 237–247.

Bateson, G. (1972). *Steps to an Ecology of Mind.* New York: Ballantine.

Benhabib, S. (1992). *Situating the Self: Gender, Community and Postmodernism in Contempary Ethics.* New York: Routledge.

Boscolo, L. (1993). Time and Therapy. Plenary address, Australian Family Therapy Conference, Canberra, Australia.

Boscolo, L., Cecchin, G., Hoffman, L., & Penn, P. (1988). *Milan Systemic Family Therapy.* New York: Basic Books.

Campbell, D., & Draper, R. (Eds.) (1985). *Applications of Systemic Family Therapy—The Milan Approach.* London: Grune & Stratton.

Cecchin, G. (1987). Hypothesizing, circularity, and neutrality revisited: an invitation to curiosity. *Family Process, 26* (4), 405–413.

Cecchin, G., Lane, J., & Ray, W. A. (1993). From strategizing to nonintervention: towards irreverence in systemic practice. *Journal of Marital and Family Therapy, 19* (2), 125–136.

Flaskas, C. (1989). Thinking about the emotional interaction of therapist and family. *Australian and New Zealand Journal of Family Therapy, 10* (1): 1–6.

Flaskas, C. (1993). On the project of using psychoanalytic ideas in systemic therapy: a discussion paper. *Australian and New Zealand Journal of Family Therapy, 14* (2), 9–15.

Gibney, P. (1994). Time in the therapeutic domain. *Australian and New Zealand Journal of Family Therapy, 15* (2), 61–72.

Goolishian, H. A., & Anderson, H. (1987). Language, systems, and therapy: an evolving idea. *Psychotherapy, 24,* 529–538.

Haber, R. (1990). From handicapped to handicapable: training systemic therapists in the use of self. *Family Process, 29* (4), 375–384.

Hoffman, L. (1990). Constructing realities: an art of lenses. *Family Process, 29* (1), 1–12. Also in: *Exchanging Voices: A Collaborative Approach to Family Therapy.* London: Karnac Books, 1993.

Krause, I.-B. (1993). Family therapy and anthropology: the case for emotions. *Journal of Family Therapy, 15* (1), 35–56.

Luepnitz, D. (1988). *The Family Interpreted.* New York: Basic Books.

MacKinnon, L. K. (1993). Systems in settings: the therapist as power broker. *Australian and New Zealand Journal of Family Therapy, 14* (3), 117–122.

MacKinnon, L. K., & Miller, D. (1987). The new epistemology and the Milan approach: feminist and sociopolitical considerations. *Journal of Marital and Family Therapy, 13* (2), 139–155.

Mathews, F. (1991). *The Ecological Self.* London: Routledge.

McIntyre, D. (1991). Social justice. *Australian and New Zealand Journal of Family Therapy, 12* (2), 79–84.

Real, T. (1990). The therapeutic use of self in constructionist/systemic therapy. *Family Process, 29* (3), 255–272.

Solomon, R. (1993). *The Passions: Emotions and the Meaning of Life.* Indianapolis/Cambridge: Hackett.

Stagoll, B. (1987). Insight and outsight. *Australian and New Zealand Journal of Family Therapy, 8* (4), 212–217.

Stierlin, H. (1987). Co-evolution and co-individuation. In: *Familiar Realities: The Heidelberg Conference.* New York: Brunner/Mazel.

Stierlin, H. (1988). Systemic optimism—systemic pessimism: two perspectives on change. *Family Process, 27* (2), 121–127.

White, M., & Epston, D. (1989). *Literate Means to Therapeutic Ends: Selected Papers.* Adelaide: Dulwich Centre Publications.

CHAPTER 5

To embrace paradox (once more, with feeling): a commentary on narrative/ conversational therapies and the therapeutic relationship

Paul Gibney

THE GROUNDWORK

Family therapy has undergone a major shift in theoretical emphasis in the last twenty years. In the 1970s, family therapists spread themselves between the technical and theoretical certitudes of the strategic and structural schools of family therapy. In the late 1970s to mid-1980s, therapists embraced systemic therapy with its stylized practice format, its rigorous questioning, and its complex theorizing. The late 1980s to the mid-1990s have been increasingly characterized by a move towards narrative/conversational models of therapy. These latest models de-emphasize the power of the therapist and speak of the co-construction of meaning, a collaborative approach, the shedding of power, and the challenging of dominant paradigms. There is an accompanying sense of having attempted to address the arrogant certainties of yesteryear with a more tentative, more politically correct stance of today.

The epistemology debates of the early 1980s invited therapists to reconsider how they thought, knew, and decided about families; once they did that, with any amount of earnestness, the possibility of constructivism became available and the promise of certainty seemed to recede forever.

In those epistemology debates, writers such as Keeney, Dell, and Auerswald often referred to Richard Rabkin (1978), who had said that the disagreement between Gregory Bateson and Jay Haley over the issue of power lay at the heart of the epistemology of family therapy. Bateson (1972) had said that power did not exist and that the thought of power corrupted those who believed in it. Haley (1969) said that power existed, and that the therapist had best use power and control to meet his or her therapeutic goals.

The new narrative/conversational models of therapy seemed to have "overcome" the problems of power. Lynn Hoffman and Harlene Anderson encourage therapists to "shed" power, to seek a more equitable relationship with their clients. Michael White invites clients to critique institutions of power, so that he and the client family might re-author another version of their lives that contains more options.

It is the purpose of this chapter to argue that nothing much has changed, in the last twenty years, in the world of family therapy theorizing, and that the theoretical mistakes of the 1970s have now been balanced by the theoretical mistakes of the 1990s. In essence, both generations of theorists have avoided construing the paradoxical nature of the combination of power and love that characterizes a therapeutic relationship.

Carl Jung's student and collaborator, Marie Louise von Franz, has noted: "Where love is absent, power occupies the vacancy" (von Franz, 1993, p. 243).

It will be suggested here that in therapy, power and love play a balancing role with each other and that both must be kept alive in the therapeutic equation. By power, I suggest that the therapist has more say in the therapy by his or her expertise, context, and societal sanction, and that this power must be used in a loving way—that is, it must be used in a way that increases the family's options. Furthermore, psychotherapeutic love distinguishes itself from romantic love, in that the therapist does not ask for his or her own emotional needs to be met, nor indeed attempts to meet all the emotional needs of the family, but rather helps to attend to, and to articulate, the emotional processes that occur in therapy both between family members and between family members and himself or herself. This difficult dual process—maintaining an expert monitoring of an emotional process whilst articulating one's own involvement in it—is the therapeutic paradox, the healing paradox par excellence, that family therapy theorists of many persuasions over the past twenty years have steadfastly refused to discuss.

This chapter examines the recent changes in family therapy theorizing and the nature of change in the theorizing. An argument is then presented in three parts: that the new models of therapy are not particularly new but often proceed through a theoretical and historical myopia; that the emotional interaction between therapist and family is consistently neglected; and that the power issues in the therapeutic relationship are not resolved by the new models. The conclusion emphasizes the role of paradox in theorizing and practising the art and discipline of family therapy.

TALK AND ONLY TALK: THERAPY AS A CO-CONSTRUCTION OF MEANING

Family therapy theory and practice in the 1990s has emerged in the new form of the conversational/narrative models—forms that emphasize therapy as a process in which meaning is constantly co-constructed between client and therapist. Though it is beyond the scope and purpose of this chapter to address the causes of this shift in any depth, a number of possible elements that contributed to this change are clearly evident. The epistemology debates, which included the work of Bradford Keeney and Paul Dell, raised to consciousness the notions that therapists could not *control* systems, that such pragmatism was only one side of the pragmatic/aesthetic possibility, and that we, as therapists, must be included in the therapeutic equation. Concurrently, a rich feminist literature (e.g. the works of Betty Carter, Rachel Hare Mustin, Virginia Goldner, to name but a few of the influential authors) began to challenge many family therapy tenets as artefacts of the dominant patriarchal systems of thought, and gave voice to the possibilities of practice based on shared expertise, less emphasis on hierarchy, valuing connection over independence, and with a bold willingness to address the difficult issues of violence, rape, and abuse (issues that were not adequately conceptualized by systemic thinking).

As feminism and more learned debate questioned the previous theoretical arrogance of family therapy, a new technical innovation further eroded any arrogance on this practice front. Andersen's (1987) model of the reflecting team, in which client families saw directly the debate between team members about the interview and thus received direct feedback, dispensed with much of the *faceless*, omniscient expert status of the observing team. With these theoretical expansions, and with a new practical openness, family therapy found itself talking less about cures, and talking more about talking.

Goolishian and Anderson (1987) were amongst the first theorists to describe therapy from a linguistic/social constructivist position. They wrote:

> The role of the therapist is to create a space in which the opportunity for dialogical communication between self and self, and between self and others is maximised. That is, therapy should be thought of as an emerging context that promotes the infinite revision and elaboration of meaning. [p. 535]

In a paper, published shortly after Goolishian's untimely death, they referred to their model of therapy as a *social constructionist model*:

> Therapy is transformed in this social constructionist model into a co-participant conversational action. The emphasis is on doing something *with* and talking *with* as opposed to doing something *to*. Change is not defined in terms of social structure. Change is defined as changing narrative, story and meaning. [Goolishian & Anderson, 1992, p. 12]

Similarly, de Shazer has in recent years evolved his brief solution-oriented therapy into a system that includes an explanatory framework from poststructural thought (de Shazer, 1991, 1994). Using Wittgenstein's phrase, de Shazer suggests that therapy is about a *language game*. Poststructuralism, de Shazer informs, rejects the notion of a captured truth but stresses the interaction of people as an activity through which meaning is constructed. From this point of view:

> the therapy unit can be seen as a self-contained linguistic system that creates meaning through negotiation between therapist and client. [de Shazer & Berg, 1992, p. 80]

The work of Michael White and David Epston is now referred to in the Australian and New Zealand context as Narrative Therapy. White sees his work as being based on questioning his clients in such a way that:

> these questions serve to deconstruct the dominant and impoverished stories that persons are living by. [White, in Wood, 1991, p. 209]

O'Hanlon (1994), describing the Narrative Therapy as a Third Wave in family therapy, writes of their method:

> The more time I have spent reading and watching the work of Third Wave therapists, the more I see similar patterns—a willingness to acknowledge the tremendous power of the past history and the present culture that shape our lives, integrated with a powerful, optimistic vision of our capacity to free ourselves from them once they are made conscious. Third Wave approaches talk to the Adult Within. [p. 23]

This translates into everyday therapy as a process in which the therapist asks highly structured questions that enable the clients to glimpse how their lives have been *storied* by the dominant narrative, and then to construct a new narrative by highlighting and concentrating on those times when the client family acted outside the impoverishing dominant paradigm (White & Epston, 1990).

While de Shazer uses poststructural ideas to describe his search for *solutions* and while White and Epston use deconstructionist ideas to describe their deliberate re-authoring with clients of the clients' narratives, Harlene Anderson takes up the *narrative/constructivist* argument from an *ethics-first* position. Her position, following on from her work with Goolishian, seems not to be about structuring a conversation that leads to a certain end (e.g. a solution or a new sense of freedom). But, rather, she starts from an *ethical stance* that if the client family is allowed enough space to tell their story, if that story is respected, if the therapist openly and genuinely responds to that story, then new options will become available via that very process. The therapist needs to structure little, apart from being available to help create the space, to witness, and to respond. Anderson describes this ethical position:

> Genuinely respecting people, allowing people to experience dignity in their relationship with you and in their lives—that is an ethical base. To be open and public rather than closed and private in my thoughts as a therapist, to allow my views, my ethics to be questioned by the other, to reflect continuously on my own values and morals. [Anderson, in Holmes, 1994, p. 156]

Anderson further responds to the issue of "being an expert" by saying that the therapist is an expert in creating a dialogical space and process and, in doing so, recognizes the expertise that clients have about their own lives, desires, and uniqueness. Therefore, therapy becomes a combination of client and therapist expertise (Anderson, in Holmes, 1994, p. 156).

Lynn Hoffman, that venerable commentator of the family therapy field, has arrived from her own reflections at a similar position to Anderson's—a position that Hoffman calls a *reflexive stance* (Hoffman, 1991). Hoffman, similarly, does not use *postmodernism, deconstructionism,* or *poststructuralism* to arrive at another definite form of therapy. Rather, she uses these intellectual tools to critique family therapy's previous certainties and to outline, tentatively, a stance, an ethical position, from which one might begin to practise a less hierarchical, more inclusive therapy.

Hoffman, in reviewing her own changing attitudes to therapy, sets out to reconsider some of the implicit and explicit tenets upon which a good deal of traditional therapeutic theory and practice are based. In deconstructionist style, she challenges what she sees as "five sacred cows": she debunks the possibility of any *objective* social research; she suggests that the *self* might be a concept that suits Western thinking; she questions whether individual development occurs in an orderly predictable pathway; she contextualizes *emotions* as a newly discovered concept; and she ponders whether we even need a notion of *levels* to consider interpersonal phenomena (Hoffman, 1993, pp. 118–122). Hoffman goes on to argue that the certainty with which some of these concepts were held as "true" led to a state of "the colonialism of mental health", in which experts told clients the "truth" about their lives, with little to no regard for the client's experience, thus leaving the client mystified, dependent, and impotent.

As a response to this critique, Hoffman suggests a much more open-ended style of interviewing, a style in which the ethos developed for her where "listening came to seem more important than talking" (Hoffman, 1993, p. 114). From her descriptions, Hoffman's interviewing has become less structured and aims at making the expert "disappear" (1993, p. 127). Hoffman speaks of an ethic of participation, where the power differentials in therapeutic relationships are acknowledged and thus given less emphasis and less capacity for misuse and abuse.

THE NATURE OF THE CHANGE

From the preceding descriptions of the major thrusts of family therapy theory in the 1990s, it can be seen that the emphases in theory and practice have clearly changed. Family therapy developed almost as a movement against the individually pathologizing models of psychiatry and sought to locate dysfunction within interpersonal interactions instead of within the individual. When, with positive connotation, family therapy no longer dwelt on pathology, the field's hubris shifted from an arrogance of diagnosis (that is: we know what is wrong), to an arrogance of technique (that is: we know how to go about correcting whatever might be wrong). Family therapy now seems keen to be unsure that anything is wrong and just wishes to have conversations about stories, narratives, solutions, and discourses.

Ethically, the move away from pathologizing and towards an optimistic belief in families' and individuals' capacities to actively contribute to the resolution of their own difficulties is a welcome one. A clear difference, however, can be seen between the works of de Shazer, Epston, White, O'Hanlon, and so on and the works of Anderson, Hoffman, and so forth. The solution-focused therapists, such as O'Hanlon (1987; O'Hanlon & Weiner-Davis, 1989) and de Shazer (1991, 1994), may utilize constructivist theories and deconstructionist critiques to question whether there is such a thing as "reality" beyond the language used to describe it, but then, with a fervour, they go about creating with the client a new reality that contains solutions. White and Epston (1990) similarly use deconstructionist notions to question cultural and political prescriptions, and then with a singular determination actively seek to construct a new story by their own tenacity. They clearly believe that some stories are better than others, and, unwilling to leave issues in a deconstructed state, they direct the client in the construction of what they believe to be a more edifying tale.

Harlene Anderson mentions that Tom Andersen has questioned her as to why she speaks of her approach as a "philosophical stance" as opposed to a "theory". She states that she is hoping to get away from the usual connotations of "theories" (presumably pathologizing) and to emphasize that she "is talking about a way of being and a way of viewing the world and experience" (Anderson, in Holmes, 1994, p. 156). Both Anderson and Hoffman seem to take this position, this *philosophical stance*. The belief seems to be that an open, respectful practice that demonstrates a deep interest in the client's beliefs and experiences will lead to a new set of options and possibilities for the client. Hoffman (1993) acknowledges that when she does share her own stories, they do tend to have something of an agenda attached to them:

> I, myself, encourage people to play with stories, and will offer some of my own to push the idea along. I admit that my stories tend to be positive and transformative, meaning that I try to turn what is experienced as a difficulty into something that contains some hope. [p. 134]

Though clearly on the side of hope and optimism, Hoffman and Anderson seem more trusting of an open process and feel less need to be as actively seeking different story lines than do White, Epston, de Shazer, O'Hanlon, and other writers within the narrative/solution genre.

FAMILY THERAPY THEORIZING: TOO MUCH IMAGINATION AND NOT ENOUGH RIGOUR?

One of the most pleasing aspects of family therapy has always been its willingness to consider new theories, new vantage points, new ways of conceptualizing theory and practice. This willingness has freed family therapy from the empirical dilemmas of behavioural psychology, which seems to be forever limited to discussing what can be construed by a positivist framework and from the constrictures of some therapeutic modalities that never wander far from the dogmatic truths of their founders. However, one of the disadvantages of family therapy's willingness to venture abroad has been its failure at times to build theory upon existing theory, to relate new theory to old theory, to borrow respectfully from existing therapeutic theory, and to articulate the links between the new and old, and the possible advantages of the new schemata.

An argument in three parts

1. *The new narrative therapy as good strategic therapy and the new philosophical stance as good manners*

It can be seen that family therapy has two major theoretical problems. First, it suffers from a theoretical myopia in which the often wonderful insights of other schools of therapy (psychoanalytic, Jungian, etc.) are generally ignored while our own theorists tediously reconstruct the wheel. Second, family therapy theorists often fail to build new theory on old theory or to seek to articulate the connections between the two. For example, I remain unconvinced that the new narrative/conversational models are not in fact strategic therapy. And if indeed this is so, do they warrant new names?

White and de Shazer's penchant for quoting poststructural philosophers (in particular, Foucault and Derrida) obscures the recognition that technically what they both practise is good, in fact excellent, strategic therapy. White reframes the problem, choosing frames from a cultural and political critique, the choice of which distances the client from ownership of the perceived pathology. Small changes are then aimed at, and each small achievement is cast as a major achievement in a struggle against oppression. The techniques are strategic reframing and the highlighting of exceptions and small changes. This is in no way different pragmatically to the template that White eloquently expressed in his 1986 paper (White, 1986). The current emphasis on political themes and the language of oppression/emancipation may be more appealing to White and his advocates, but the failure to link the model with the fine tradition of strategic therapy robs family therapy of an embeddedness and cohesiveness of development of its major themes.

Similarly, though de Shazer (1994) has taken to quoting Lacan's complicated theories of language, at the end of the therapy day de Shazer still looks for solutions. Unlike White, he often bypasses the reframing and heads straight for the exceptions and small changes. Clearly, both these practitioners have valuable practice methods to offer, but is the family therapy community best served by their attempts to locate themselves in French poststructuralist philosophy, as opposed to their more obvious connections with American pragmatic therapy?

Likewise, the new "philosophical stance" of Anderson (in Holmes, 1994) and Hoffman (1993) could be considered either good manners, old practice, pragmatic common sense, or a higher form of professional development, depending on your vantage point.

In describing her encounter with Tom Andersen's Norwegian teams' format of doing therapy, using a specific style of questioning and a reflecting team approach, Hoffman (1993) was struck by a difference in their style of talking. She writes:

> Their questions or comments are marked by tentativeness, by hesitancy, and by long periods of silence. Often, the voice of the interviewer sinks so low that it is difficult to hear. They tend to begin their sentences with "Could it be that?" or "What if?". At first I thought this strange way of talking was due either to their difficulties with our language or else a cultural difference that came from the well-known modesty of the Norwegian personality. This turns out to be untrue. The interview-

ing method embodies in a most graphic way the deliberate immolation of the professional self, and the effect on clients is to encourage both participation and invention. [p. 128]

One is tempted to ask here: are these attitudes actually the operationalization of a new philosophical stance of family therapy and/or the deliberate immolation of the professional self, or are they just what is commonly known as *plain good manners*? Since when was it useful, decent, appropriate, polite—or, for that matter, professional—to lord it over people, to be absolutely certain of your own opinions and to dismiss others in the process? Not only might this be a reinstatement of manners, it might also be an honouring of old, time-honoured practice principles, as outlined by social work academics some forty-plus years ago. I seem to remember Felix Biestek's principles of a casework relationship including such elements as empathy and respect for the client's self-determination (Biestek, 1957).

In another sense, the stances or positions of Hoffman, Anderson, and Andersen also reflect common good sense: since when did anyone, in their right mind or otherwise, enjoy cooperating with, consulting with, or even talking to people who treated them disrespectfully? Furthermore, one might add, is this new "philosophical position" nothing more than the final stance of most mature therapists towards their clients? I am sure we are all familiar with T.S. Eliot's famous quote regarding how we finally arrive at the place from whence we started and know it for the first time. Is this not what happens to most practitioners? We start out innocent and trusting. Our anxiety and desire for mastery invite us to learn models, tricks, strategies, and techniques that keep us safe and clever. But, over the years, the failures, the anomalies, the *bad* cases that went well, the *good* cases that went bad, the cases that contradicted the theories but still went well—all of these reduce hubris, instil humility, and invite us to be as open and as honest as we can be. Should we elevate this to be the correct "philosophical stance", or should we respect this as the end point of a practitioner's initiation into the vocation of therapist? Either way, I am unconvinced that this should be seen as new, or as a discontinuous jump unconnected to the therapeutic tradition.

2. *Both new positions do little to address the emotional interaction between therapist and family*

In the past ten years, family therapy has adopted a number of new metaphors to invite its practitioners to re-evaluate their frameworks. We have been invited to re-language, to re-vision, to give voice, to question our epistemology, and to challenge dominant paradigms. It has been a very long time since we have been asked *to feel, to have emotions*.

Virginia Satir was quite clear that families had feelings and that therapists should attend to them. Strategic therapists at times had suggestions as to how to make feelings come and go, how to practise them at certain times, and so forth, so as to have more control over their feelings. I have seen narrative therapists question children as to how they might become the *boss* of *their feelings*. But what about the therapist? How does she or he feel? What about the family? How do they feel when they are with the therapist? Should any of this be elicited? Should any of it be articulated? Is there therapeutic benefit in discussing feelings, including those evoked by the therapeutic process, in the sessions?

As Paterson (1994) noted, one of family therapy's recent failings has been its inability/unwillingness to consider feelings, and to consider those occasions when the narrative changes but the feelings do not:

> the current preoccupation with narrative and discourse invites us to suppose that a person's feelings will change when the narrative changes. This is often the case, but it is perhaps part of the human condition that some feelings only change painfully and slowly. [p. 38]

Mercifully, there are traditions of therapy, and even family therapy, that deal with emotions—both the family's feelings and those in the therapist/family field. These models come from psychoanalytic theories, such as the work of Skynner (1987), based on group analytic concepts, and Scharff and Scharff (1987) and Luepnitz (1988), based on object relations theory. Psychoanalytic models make two important contributions to working with families' and clients' emotions. First, it is one of the therapist's tasks to *contain* the family and the therapeutic situation, or to develop a context in which feelings can be safely expressed. Second, feelings that are experienced by the therapist during the sessions are considered as possible countertransference feelings, or feelings that contain information about the family. Skynner (1987), for example, considers this the essence of therapy: for the therapist to be able to feel and articulate emotions with which the family cannot deal.

Perhaps, as well as taking a new philosophical stance of openness and a willingness to pursue victories over oppressions, the therapist should also be able to be open emotionally, to feel and to discuss feelings with the family. Paterson's point, I suspect, is correct: that some feelings change only slowly and painfully, and often not concurrently with shifts in vision and thinking. However, it could be argued that feelings would be more likely to change if they were experienced in sessions and included in the therapeutic dialogue. This inclusion not only honours the second-order cybernetic principle that "the observer is connected to the observed" in a profound way, it also offers the opportunity of demonstrating to the family the therapist's connection to them, and ways of dealing with painful emotions constructively and honestly.

Family therapy's lack of attention to psychoanalytic thinking these past thirty years is another example of its theoretical myopia. Recently, considerable work has been done to reintegrate systemic thinking with psychoanalytic thought by such writers as Luepnitz (1988), Flaskas (1993), and Smith, Osman, and Goding (1990). It is no coincidence that these authors also embrace a feminist framework. It would seem that once a search has begun for a model that reduces hierarchy, honours connection, and aims at including the experiences of the therapist, then feelings and emotions have to be included in the equation. To date, psychoanalysis—with the work of its pioneering mothers (e.g. Horney, Deutsch, Klein, and Anna Freud: see Sayers, 1991)—has best provided a map for the deep, emotional intersubjectivity that often characterizes a therapeutic relationship.

3. *Family therapy needs to acknowledge power in the presence of nurturance, responsibility, and accountability*

Family therapy has never lost its fascination with power. Haley believed that power is inevitable in all interpersonal situations and hence should be actively used by the therapist in therapy. Bateson believed the concept of power was based on an epistemological error and that the very idea of power corrupted. Feminist family therapists critique the power differentials that lead to discrimination along gender lines. Narrative therapists critique the power of institutions, while seemingly seeking *non-expert* status for themselves.

Perhaps the time has come for therapists to consider that, while we may do our best to be respectful, to practise up, to recognize the clients' expertise, and to eschew unnecessary professional pretensions, we have power—personally, professionally, archetypally, and contextually. Whether we wish to see this or not, when we accept payment for therapeutic practice, when we are employed by agencies that are socially sanctioned to provide therapy, and when others seek out our expertise, we are imbued with the cultural role of "healer" (von Franz, 1993, p. 238). Despite our philosophical protestations or aesthetic preferences to the contrary, once we accept the role, we are manifested with the power of expectations of others and of society in general.

My contention here is that family therapy has had problems with power, not because it is inherently a wicked thing, but rather because we have ignored emotional issues, and we have failed to balance power with the responsibilities that go with it. If we accept therapeutic power, it stands to reason that we must accept the responsibility to be nurturant to those for whom we conduct therapy, and to be accountable to clients, colleagues, and society in general.

As foreshadowed in the introduction of this chapter, I would suggest, as Jungian practitioners have done before me, that power and love are part of the same complex, having some type of ongoing relationship with each other. In the past, family therapists were keen to be powerful experts tricking clients out of the perverse games/patterns in which the family was caught. Now, practitioners seem to wish to be non-powerful equals who share concepts. Both of these images of practice avoid the recognition that many clients for some period of their lives wish to be looked after, cared for, supported, and emotionally helped through difficult periods of change. Clearly, therapy involves all of these aspects: helping to change patterns, sharing concepts, and emotionally supporting the clients. As mentioned, this emotional supporting—this psychotherapeutic love—is accomplished through attending to, as well as articulating, the clients' emotional processes including those in therapy of which the therapist is a part. This is a powerful experience that is tempered by the humility of being a part of it. Here, love and power are balanced in a demanding, illuminating experience.

We cannot avoid power. What we can do is to challenge ourselves to manage power within an ethical framework, to constantly question ourselves and others about the juxtaposition of power and accountability within a nurturant framework in therapy.

CONCLUSION: RESTORING PARADOX TO ITS APPROPRIATE PLACE

Paradox in family therapy, once celebrated as the pinnacle of therapeutic efficacy, has in recent years fallen into disrepute, as a memory of a time when therapists outwitted the client family. In short, paradox in family therapy has got a bad name for itself.

Paradox, however is also mentioned in the Jungian literature. There, paradox—an unsolvable riddle—is precisely from where psychological and spiritual growth emanates. As von Franz (1970) writes:

> Jung has said that to be in a situation where there is no way out, or to be in conflict where there is no solution, is the classical beginning of the process of individuation. [p. 4]

Johnson (1991) says:

> When the unstoppable bullet hits the unpenetrable wall ... It is precisely here that one will grow. [p. 9]

What I would like to suggest here is that family therapy as a field and each family therapist as a practitioner must, in maturity, embrace a number of unsolvable paradoxes. We must accept our power, but aim at giving it away. We must aim at being non-expert and yet accept responsibility for the process of therapy. We must attend to feelings, while aiming to alter cognition. We must attend to and support new beginnings, while attending to and honouring the past. We must nurture a new sense of self, while not dismissing the experience of suffering. We must be open to feel something of what our clients feel, while aiming to take them to a different emotional position.

Paradox, I would argue, is at the heart of the therapeutic experience. It demands an emotional maturity of a practitioner who is capable of sitting with uncertainty, resisting the premature solution, and helping the family to bear the tensions involved. This is more an emotional process than a question of method or technique.

Family therapy, it has been suggested in this article, has undergone a profound theoretical shift in the past twenty years: from a certainty regarding therapeutic assessment and practice, to an embracing of uncertainty and an active challenging of our expert status. However, a middle ground exists where the emotional interaction between the therapist and client family is valued and articulated. In that process, hubris melts away and the therapist finds herself or himself sitting in the middle of unresolvable paradoxes that often give space to healing. This chapter concludes with the hope that the family therapy field might theoretically spend less time pursuing newness, and more time considering the paradoxes that underlie our theorizing and our practice.

REFERENCES

Andersen, T. (1987). The reflecting team: dialogue and meta dialogue in clinical work. *Family Process*, 26, 415–428.

Bateson, G. (1972). *Steps to an Ecology of Mind.* New York: Ballantine Books.

Biestek, F. (1957). *The Case Work Relationship.* Chicago, IL: Loyola University Press.

de Shazer, S. (1991). *Putting Difference to Work.* New York: W. W. Norton.
de Shazer, S. (1994). *Words Were Originally Magic.* New York: W. W. Norton.
de Shazer, S., & Berg I. K. (1992). Doing therapy: a post-structural revision. *Journal of Marital and Family Therapy, 18,* 71–81.
Flaskas, C. (1993). On the project of using psychoanalytic ideas in systemic therapy. *Australian and New Zealand Journal of Family Therapy, 14* (1), 9–15.
Goolishian, H. A., & Anderson, H. (1987). Language, systems and therapy: an evolving idea. *Psychotherapy, 24,* 529–538.
Goolishian, H. A., & Anderson, H. (1992). Strategy and intervention versus non-intervention: a matter of theory? *Journal of Marital and Family Therapy, 18* (1), 5–14.
Haley, J. (1969). *The Power Tactics of Jesus Christ: And Other Essays.* New York: Avon Books.
Hoffman, L. (1991). A reflexive stance for family therapy. *Journal of Strategic and Systemic Therapies, 10,* 4–17. Also in: *Exchanging Voices: A Collaborative Approach to Family Therapy.* London: Karnac Books, 1993.
Hoffman, L. (1993). *Exchanging Voices. A Collaborative Approach to Family Therapy.* London: Karnac Books.
Holmes, S. (1994). A philosophical stance, ethics and therapy: an interview with Harlene Anderson. *The Australian and New Zealand Journal of Family Therapy, 15* (3), 155–161.
Johnson, R. A. (1991). *Owning Your Own Shadow: Understanding the Dark Side of the Psyche.* San Francisco, CA: Harper Collins.
Luepnitz, D. A. (1988). *The Family Interpreted: Feminist Theory in Clinical Practice.* New York: Basic Books.
O'Hanlon, W. (1994). The third wave. *Family Therapy Networker* (November–December), 19–29.
O'Hanlon, W. H. (1987). *Taproots. Underlying Principles of Milton Erickson's Therapy and Hypnosis.* New York: W. W. Norton.
O'Hanlon, W. H., & Weiner-Davis, M. (1989). *In Search of Solutions: A New Direction in Psychotherapy.* New York: The Guilford Press.
Paterson, T. (1994). Family therapy in the age of isms. *Australian and New Zealand Journal of Family Therapy, 15* (1), 33–38.
Rabkin, R. (1978). Who plays the pipes? *Family Process, 17,* 485–488.

Sayers, J. (1991). *Mothering Psychoanalysis: Helene Deutsch, Karen Horney, Anna Freud, and Melanie Klein*. London: Hamish Hamilton.

Scharff, D., & Scharff, J. (1987). *Object Relations Family Therapy*. Northvale, NJ: Jason Aronson.

Skynner, A. C. R. (1987). *Explorations with Families, Group Analysis and Family Therapy*, edited by J. R. Schlapobersky. London: Methuen.

Smith, J., Osman, C., & Goding, M. (1990). Reclaiming the emotional aspects of the therapist–family system. *Australian and New Zealand Journal of Family Therapy, 11* (3), 140–146.

von Franz, M. L. (1970). *Interpretation of Fairy Tales*. New York: Spring Publications.

von Franz, M. L. (1993). *Psychotherapy*. Boston, MA, & London: Shambhala.

White, M. (1986). Negative explanation, restraint and double description: a template for family therapy. *Family Process, 25* (2), 169–184.

White, M., & Epston, D. (1990). *Narrative Means to Therapeutic Ends*. New York: W. W. Norton.

Wood, A. (1991). Outside expert knowledge: an interview with Michael White. *The Australian and New Zealand Journal of Family Therapy, 12*, 206–214.

DISCUSSION PAPER I

You cannot not relate

Bebe Speed

INTRODUCTION

As the Editors of this volume indicate, the therapeutic relationship within systemic approaches has been little theorized about or discussed, at least in the public domain. But because it hasn't been much written about doesn't mean it hasn't existed. By definition, every time a therapist sees a client, a relationship comes into being—"you cannot not relate". But somehow this medium in which our practice is embedded has been taken for granted, and little commented upon, and its potential significance as a crucial part of our encounter with clients has therefore been underplayed. This volume makes a substantial and innovative contribution to placing the topic of the therapeutic relationship within the formal discourse of the systemic therapies.

THE RELATIONSHIP IN THERAPY
OR THE THERAPEUTIC RELATIONSHIP?

The Editors have chosen a nicely ambiguous phrase in their title for the book. "The therapeutic relationship" can be taken to mean the relationship which comes into being between clients and therapist as the vehicle carrying the content of therapy, or it can imply that the relationship between clients and therapist may in itself be therapeutic—that the quality of the relationship itself may be change-enhancing or, at the very least, may affect the content of the work for better or worse.

This is like asking: how does the style of relationship between a doctor and patient affect the medical task? Generally, that relationship would tend to be seen as the taken-for-granted backdrop to the more central business of diagnosis and treatment. Certainly, we have a relationship with our doctor, but this is secondary to the content of the medicine on offer. The way in which the doctor relates to us, whether in a detached, gruff, hierarchical way, or in a more connected, warm, concerned way, will be less an issue than obtaining the specific, technical, medical help we need, for example, with the diagnosis of ear infection and the prescription for antibiotics. At other times, when what we want to discuss is less straightforward or when our emotions are more engaged (when the issue is, for example, cancer or failure to become pregnant), the way in which we and our doctor relate becomes more central. Then, a detached and hurried stance on the part of the doctor may seem unsympathetic and rejecting, and this relationship process itself may adversely come to affect the course of the content of treatment.

Whilst we cannot separate the content of the medical consultation from the relationship within which it occurs, we can talk about one aspect or the other being more or less significant at different times. Similarly, within relationships between clients and therapists using systemic approaches, different sorts of relationships and different balances between the content of therapy and the relationship process can be discerned and seen to evolve over time as the practice of these therapies has developed.

RELATIONSHIPS BETWEEN THERAPIST AND FAMILY IN SYSTEMIC WRITINGS

Systemic therapists have traditionally been concerned, in written accounts at least, primarily with doing something active in as short a time as possible to facilitate change for clients. This focus developed partly as a response to the perception of existing therapeutic approaches such as psychoanalysis and social casework concentrating primarily on a minute examination of the psyche of the client via the relationship between client and therapist as it developed, often over many years. Such approaches were seen by many family therapists to be doing very little, as well as taking a long time to do it.

As an aspect of differentiating themselves in the process of professionalization from these approaches, it was not then surprising that many family therapists paid relatively little explicit attention to the relationship between themselves and clients. Some attention was given to how the relationship should be established, with Haley and Minuchin amongst others writing about the importance of engagement and joining techniques, and Cade (1982) discussing the use of humour. Beyond that, however, how the therapist maintained engagement—a therapeutic alliance—and related to the family throughout the course of therapy was often implicit. Various systemic practices such as positive connotation or circular questioning or other interventions which the family might perceive as addressing their core issues probably often had the effect of maintaining a positive engagement with clients. But as Flaskas here points out, the function of these techniques in supporting the continuing relationship between clients and therapist has scarcely been acknowledged—that was not what these techniques were overtly for.

In first-order days, the systemic therapist was construed as a detached and objective observer and evaluator of the wider family process, or the narrower more-of-the-same sequence revealed in front of them, whether by the circular questioning of the Milan approach, or enactment techniques used within the structural approach, or the problem-solving questions of the Mental Research Institute's strategic approach. Family therapy's focus was on behaviour between individuals rather than feelings inside them, and, congruently, the focus was also on the behaviour between the therapist and family members. When attention was paid to how the therapist was relating to the family and how rapport could be built, the focus was (e.g. within the Milan approach) on the therapist's behaviour, such as even-handedness, neutrality, and positive connotation, and what that communicated.

The therapist was an expert, a sleuth uncovering what exists and conjuring up ideas to provoke change. The relationship between family and therapist came across in the literature as one of observer/observed, charismatic leader/led, teacher/taught, doer/done-to. Sometimes there was more of a flavour of a personal, emotional involvement, particularly in the writings of the more proximal therapists such as Minuchin, Satir, and Whitaker. Even within the more detached Milan approach, some emotion could, at times, be detected—for example, when therapy turned into a bit of a battle, as Hoffman describes it, "a benevolent contest" with the family that is "too richly crossjoined" (Hoffman, 1981, p. 328) trying to outwit the therapist and vice versa. But, on the whole, as evidenced by their writing at least, many family therapists at this time were not relating to clients, as Flaskas and Perlesz in their Introduction indicate, on a basis of intimacy and engagement of feelings. There was often an avoidance of emotion, and "feelings" for many became a dirty word. This, however, is not the same as saying that clients and therapists were not relating at all.

WRITING IS NOT DOING

I agree with Harari's point here that written descriptions probably often fell far short of the powerful emotional connectedness and immediacy of what happened between therapists and families in the room. In the Introduction, Flaskas and Perlesz comment that "clients . . . are stubborn in their consistency in experiencing therapy as a very human endeavour". Therapists, too, were very much human and engaged when you saw them at work. I remember in Cardiff in 1979 when Minuchin visited the Family Institute and saw a family I brought for consultation. It was clear to see how he established an intense, powerfully empathic, emotionally highly connected relationship with the family. He encountered them in a very personal way and established an intense relationship with them, at the same time as maintaining a meta-perspective, or an ability to think and talk about them in a more detached, evaluative way. He talked about the family more colloquially than he did in his writings. For example, he labelled his particular style of working with the family as one of "stroke and kick", describing how he joined with each family member by respecting them and their values, confirming and complimenting them, empathizing with them, and then from that basis powerfully and expertly using his leadership of the therapeutic system to challenge them to change.

Similarly, being in the room with a Milan therapist gave a rather different impression from that gained from a reading of their papers, of the relationship on offer. Both in a consultation by Boscolo and Cecchin to my work team at the Family Institute, Cardiff, in the mid-1980s, and through an experience of being interviewed in a role-play family by Cecchin at one of the Oxford team conferences, I experienced their warmth, humour, understanding, strength, optimism, and empathy interwoven with their particular techniques. Boscolo's and Cecchin's attentive gaze, the series of highly appropriate questions they asked, and the perceptive, challenging, long-reverberating intervention at the end left me in no doubt of their empathic understanding. I felt entirely engaged. Neutrality and curiosity are generally written about as techniques but are also, more implicitly, aspects of the relationship offered to the client and, used with sensitivity, may be received by the client as evidence of the therapist's empathy, non-judgemental interest, and concern.

Seeing therapists of this calibre at work was very different from our own, often tortured, attempts to learn these techniques. Inexperienced therapists attempting to learn a technique new to them, such as circular questioning, focus on this rather rigidly, and therapy becomes mechanistic and wooden. In our efforts to get the technique "right" we would inevitably be less engaged with the family, less attentive, more fearful of being diverted by them into waters we did not know how to navigate. As we became more experienced, we were freer to develop richer, more complex relationships with our clients, to have room again for relaxed relating as well as for reflecting about hypotheses and technique. In this, family therapists share common ground with other approaches: the careful, technique-following practice of an analyst in training will be quite different from the breaking of "rules" and idiosyncratic, freer use of self by an experienced analyst.

THERAPEUTIC RELATIONSHIPS AND THE TEAM

One significant influence on the sort of relationship offered to clients by systemic therapists has been the existence of the team behind the screen. The team itself had a relationship of sorts with the family. It offered messages of support and encouragement, challenges, expert opinion, dire warnings, either in strategic agreement or disagreement with the therapist. The therapist and the team were, of course, also relating, often in a complex, long-term, intense sort of way, almost at times like a family themselves. In my view, this is where much of the therapist's and team members' emotions were earthed, feelings about the family as well as their more personal feelings and associations triggered by the family and each other. Behind the screen was perceived to be the place where despondency, amusement, sadness, and irritation with the family or each other belonged. Therapists' emotional engagement was thus largely with their team, not with the family—just as family members' emotional involvement was with each other, not with the therapist. Some teams varied this practice; for example, Selvini and Selvini Palazzoli (1991) describe the way in which, in their team, over time, the therapist in the room began to engage more with the family, became necessarily, in their view, more involved. Nevertheless, the detachment of the team behind the screen, gathering and processing information, was still seen to be important.

This sort of balance and separation tended at the time to be seen as helpful (see, e.g., Speed et al., 1982), though judged from a different vantage point, such working arrangements can also be seen to have their disadvantages (see Cade, Speed, & Seligman, 1986; Speed, 1992). They may, for example, have predisposed family therapy to the development of an "us and them" view, thus contributing in themselves to the development of a contest with families; they may sometimes also have led to a lack of appropriate empathy with family members and to an overvaluing of the expertise of the therapist and team in hypothesizing and devising clever strategies.

As Hoffman (1993) describes, the introduction of the idea of the reflecting team in the late 1980s changed this situation substantially. With the team in the room, the therapist and team's relationship to clients became more affiliative, tentative, and positive, and clinical, pathologizing language was dropped. Working alone without a team has for me had some similar effects of decreasing distance between myself and clients. I now tend to become closer to clients and more emotionally connected with them. A greater degree of intimacy develops than might with a team either in the room or behind the screen. I am more tentative partly because I no longer have colleagues with whom I can carefully hone a series of questions or an intervention. I use myself—my personal experience, resonances to the clients' experiences, and my feelings—as a resource much more (see Hildebrand & Speed, 1995). I use myself as my "internal supervisor" (Casement, 1990) or "internal consultant" (Haber, 1994).

THERAPY RELATIONSHIPS IN RECENT TIMES

Other aspects of second-order approaches, besides the use of the reflecting team, have affected the style of relationship between some therapists and their clients. As therapists have moved from the objective to a more co-constructed position (Speed, 1994), relating with clients has shifted from the expert to the more collaborative, conversational, participatory, and "user-friendly" style (Treacher & Carpenter, 1993). There has been something of a shift from offering clients what Inger (1993), using Buber, has called an I–It relationship to an I–Thou relationship. In such a relationship, the personal, genuine dialogue and the connection between therapist and client is itself seen by some therapists (e.g. Hoffman, 1993) to be therapeutic.

As the content of our approach changes, so too will the relationship we build with clients' change and vice versa. But change, as Gibney here observes, doesn't necessarily mean something new. Some of the ideas of Hoffman (1993) and Anderson and Goolishian (1992) seem to overlap with what many of us learnt years ago in our social work courses. The relationship once again is central, feelings are fashionable, and old teachers—Biestek (1961), Hollis (1964), and Rogers (1959)—can be disinterred. Empathy once again becomes respectable, along with positive regard, respect, a non-judgmental stance, silence, tentativeness on the therapist's part (including once-abandoned phrases such as "I wonder if . . ."), and client self-determination—otherwise known as "helping clients develop their own stories". And here again, we do not have to look far to find some psychoanalytically minded therapists who have also addressed these matters. Hobson (1985), who also refers to Buber, is one, whilst another, Lomas (1977), has this to say:

> Moreover, if the personal factor in the encounter is crucial then it will seem less one between expert and novice than between two equals both of whom bring their experience of living to the set-up. [p. 12]

But hang on—wasn't one of the reasons I left social work in 1979 that it didn't seem to offer any solid ideas for how to help people other than this sanctified casework relationship . . . ?

WHAT SORT OF RELATIONSHIP BEST ACCOMPLISHES THE TASK?

It may be that there are some core qualities and conditions of relating that all therapists explicitly or implicitly must offer clients in order to form an essential matrix to the work. These probably include careful, empathic listening, a non-judgmental attitude, respect, a sense of safety both of time and space, and something that can trigger the beginning of trust in the therapist's ability to understand and help. Byng-Hall (1995) describes this process as providing a secure base from which the family can face up to what needs to be done. How these necessary qualities will be conveyed and how involved the therapist becomes will vary greatly from approach to approach. Empathy, for example, as Harari indicates here, and as Perry has shown elsewhere (1993), may be conveyed in many ways, and may imply more or less involvement on the therapist's part—astute questioning throughout the session or an insightful remark/interpretation at the end of the session, the offer of a behavioural task that for the clients fits like a glove, or even an ordeal that is felt by the family to challenge them appropriately, perhaps with humour, may all convey the therapist's empathy and involvement.

Systemic therapists, because of their focus on the content of therapy, on what to do, may not have been explicit about their everyday, taken-for-granted, though highly skilled use of such core qualities. Before taking up family therapy, many of us had had prior training in social work, psychotherapy, clinical psychology—approaches that gave us a grounding in skills that we by now use automatically but are nevertheless of great significance. We have also had the experience our personal relationships have given us, including as Gibney says the learning of "plain good manners". But perhaps we generally underestimate the relevance of the development of our personal self in our personal lives to our work with clients. As Lomas (1977) puts it:

> the greatest part of his (the therapist's) capacity to help is learned in the "school of life"; or, to put it another way, his capacity to help depends more on being able to apply a realistic experience of ordinary living to the special situation of psychotherapy than on any other factor. If he comes to believe that the efficacy of his specialised experience (or, worse, that the rigour of his scientific theory or technique) can supplant or transcend the application of his ordinary experience of people, then the whole endeavour is threatened. [p. 11]

But are these core qualities and experiences enough? Exactly what sort of relationship should we attempt to establish, and what is the appropriate balance between relating and drawing on the content of the particular approaches we have learnt? How important is technique (whether systemic, behavioural, or analytic) and how important is the person of the therapist and the sort of relationship the therapist offers? What is an appropriate balance between involvement and detachment, between working-inside-the family and being the outsider-looking-in?

WHAT CLIENTS OFFER

I agree with many of the points Paterson makes in Chapter 1, that any particular therapy encounter will be shaped by a number of interrelated factors. First of all, it depends on the clients themselves. There is a tendency when discussing therapeutic relationships to focus much more on what the therapist offers than on what the client offers, initially and in an ongoing way, to the relationship and what difference that may make to what is established. We often talk about therapist power but rarely about the balance of power that exists between therapist and client and the way clients influence the interaction or relationship. A client coming alone might, for example, be more likely to wish to relate intimately, emotionally, and dependently and propose more of an I–Thou relationship than might a family who have each other to be intimate and emotional with and dependent upon. Or again, a family, more than an individual, might be more inclined to talk about problematic behaviour than explore contentious or shameful feelings in front of each other, which will also influence the basis for engagement with the therapist.

What difference, too, does it make what issues individuals or families bring in influencing how they relate to the therapist? Different clients with different sorts of problems, whether a story of childhood sexual abuse or a 10-year-old child who still wets the bed, will need and want different things and show that in the way they attempt to relate. Some problems and relational patterns will be relatively autonomous (Elias, 1971) of the wider system, some not, and, as Paterson here says, some will be more or less amenable to change. How, too, do wider social changes affect clients and their expectations of therapy? How are clients influenced by culture—in the United States, for example, by what Hoffman (1993, p. 79) calls "American pragmatism and the can-do spirit"—in what they expect of therapy and in what they themselves offer as clients?

WHAT THERAPISTS OFFER

The therapeutic approach that we have trained in (which we are, partly because of the investment of time and money, deeply committed to) will determine in part the sort of relationship we offer to our clients and expect from them. As Flaskas and Paterson here both indicate, psychoanalysis, for example, depends upon clients showing the analyst what their patterns of relating are within the analytic relationship. In family therapy, such patterns appear in front of the therapist enacted between the family members, and the relationship between family and therapist is consequently quite different. Pinsof (1994) makes a useful distinction between aspects of the therapeutic alliance—agreement on tasks and goals and the development of emotional bonds—the relevance of which will vary according to the job in hand. As Paterson says here in Chapter 1, an "intense personal relationship between therapist and client is not something that should be pursued as a general value"; rather, it should be pursued because it fits the requirements of the task. As touched on earlier, the presence or absence of a team will also influence the development of the work, both the style of relationship between clients and therapist and the definition of the task in the clients' and therapist's eyes.

Therapists vary in their personal qualities and how these develop over time. This will also partly determine what the therapist feels able to offer any client and, indeed, what approach the therapist has chosen to learn in the first place and how that approach is then made use of. One key influence in my continuing development as a therapist was having, in the early 1980s, personal, individual, analytically informed psychotherapy. There, I came to value the experience of being understood and listened to carefully and non-intrusively and also to realize how long it might take for sufficient trust to develop in a therapeutic relationship for a client to reveal what matters the most. Some of this experience, so different from the systemic approaches I had been absorbing in my professional life, inevitably began to creep into my work with clients.

FAMILY THERAPY'S MISSING LINK

Because we have concentrated so much on the "between", family therapists have tended to overlook what is "within"—both within clients and within ourselves. As Hardham here puts it, systemic therapy has not addressed how the self fits within relationships, how we are embedded in contexts but also embodied, separate selves within them, how the self is both interdependent with and relatively autonomous from (Elias, 1971) the relationships of which it is a part. This missing link has recently come more to the fore with writers in this collection and elsewhere (e.g. Breunlin, Schwartz, & MacKune-Karrer, 1992; Gorell Barnes & Henessy, 1995; Pocock, 1995), arguing that what is inside individuals is a relevant part of the whole. What from inside ourselves—emotions, thoughts, motivations, memories, hopes—fuels how we behave towards others and how does that behaviour out there fuel what is within? How is the family represented in each person's mind? How does what people have in their minds influence their interactions? How are "within" and "between" connected? Byng-Hall (1995) offers some new directions in his application of attachment theory to family therapy, but we can also make use of the work of therapists like Skynner (1979) and Pinsof (1994 and earlier), which has been rather neglected by the mainstream.

Such explorations will inevitably, as they have done already, influence the type of relationship we as therapists establish with clients. As we become more interested in the selves of our clients, we also focus more on our own selves, and vice versa. If we are to think more about the self, how are we to do that? Flaskas suggests the potential helpfulness of some analytic concepts as they intersect with systemic ideas. Even though our aim is to enable change in the client's relationships with others rather than in the clients' relationship with the therapist, the quality of the client/therapist relationship will help or hinder the work. Therefore, she suggests, analytic concepts may be useful if there are impasses either at engagement or at later stages. Of course, the systemic approaches have already developed many ways to reflect on and respond to stuckness within the client–therapist relationship. A debate between therapists who are attempting to integrate analytically derived ideas with their systemic practice and those without such a background who nevertheless want to explore the individual-self–system interface should generate many further creative ideas.

CONCLUSION

Family therapists have written at length about approach, method, and technique (Burnham, 1992), but we have tended to overlook ourselves, and the quality of the relationship we establish, as one of the critical ingredients in the therapeutic encounter. I like Gibney's idea about love and power in psychotherapy. We are perceived to have power by others and by ourselves, but we must use power in a responsible, ethical, loving, enabling, and sponsoring way. And to do that, we need, in my view, to be both involved and detached, to be able to relate in a range of ways and intensities, as well as to retain and use our personal and professional knowledge, according to the particular needs of the specific client or family.

REFERENCES

Anderson, H., & Goolishian, H. (1992). The client is the expert: a not-knowing approach to therapy. In: S. McNamee & K. Gergen (Eds.), *Therapy as Social Construction*. London: Sage.

Biestek, F. P. (1961). *The Casework Relationship*. London: Allen and Unwin.

Breunlin, D., Schwartz, R., & MacKune-Karrer, B. (1992). *Metaframeworks: Transcending the Models of Family Therapy*. CA: Jossey-Bass.

Burnham, J. (1992). Approach–method–technique: making distinctions and creating connections. *Human Systems*, 3 (1), 3–27.

Byng-Hall, J. (1995). *Family Scripts: From Secure Attachment to Systems Change*. London: Guilford Press.

Cade, B. (1982). Humour and creativity. *Journal of Family Therapy*, 4 (1), 35–34.

Cade, B., Speed, B., & Seligman, P. (1986). Working in teams: the pros and cons. In: F. Kaslow (Ed.), *Supervision and Training: Models, Dilemmas and Challenges*. New York: Haworth Press.

Casement, P. (1990). *Further Learning from the Patient: The Analytic Space and Process*. London: Tavistock/Routledge.

Elias, N. (1971). Sociology of knowledge: new perspectives (Part Two). *Sociology*, 355–370.

Gorell Barnes, G., & Henessy, S. (1995). Reclaiming a female mind from the experience of child sexual abuse: a developing conversation between writers and editors. In: C. Burck & B. Speed (Eds.), *Gender, Power and Relationships*. London: Routledge.

Haber, R. (1994). Response-ability: the therapist's "I" and role. *Journal of Family Therapy*, 16 (3), 269–285.

Hildebrand, J., & Speed, B. (1995). The influence of therapists' personal experience on their work with couples. In: J. van Lawick & M. Sanders (Eds.), *Family, Gender and Beyond*. Heemstede, Netherlands: LS Books.

Hobson, R. (1985). *Forms of Feeling: The Heart of Psychotherapy*. London: Tavistock.

Hoffman, L. (1981). *Foundations of Family Therapy: A Conceptual Framework for Systems Change*. New York: Basic Books.

Hoffman, L. (1993). *Exchanging Voices: A Collaborative Approach to Family Therapy*. London: Karnac Books.

Hollis, F. (1964). *Casework: A Psychosocial Therapy* (2nd edition, 1972). New York: Random House.

Inger, I. (1993). A dialogic perspective for family therapy: the contributions of Martin Buber and Gregory Bateson. *Journal of Family Therapy*, 15 (3), 293–315.

Lomas, P. (1977). The nature of psychotherapy. *Tract*, 23, 3–19.

Perry, R. (1993). Empathy—still at the heart of therapy. *The Australian and New Zealand Journal of Family Therapy*, 14 (2), 63–74.

Pinsof, W. (1994). An overview of integrative problem-centered therapy: a synthesis of family and individual psychotherapies. *Journal of Family Therapy*, 16 (1), 103–121.

Pocock, D. (1995). Searching for a better story: harnessing modern and post-modern positions in family therapy. *Journal of Family Therapy*, 17 (2), 149–175.

Rogers, C. R. (1959). A theory of therapy, personality and interpersonal relationships as developed in the client-centred framework. In S. Koch (Ed.), *Psychology: A Study of a Science, Vol. 3*. New York: McGraw-Hill.

Selvini, M., & Selvini Palazzoli, M. (1991). Team consultation: an indispensable tool for the progress of knowledge. *Journal of Family Therapy, 13* (1), 31–53.

Skynner, R. (1979). Reflections on the family therapist as family scapegoat. *Journal of Family Therapy, 1* (1), 7–23.

Speed, B., Seligman, P., Kingston, P., & Cade, B. (1982). A team approach to therapy. *Journal of Family Therapy, 4,* 271–284.

Speed, B. (1992). One head is better than two (or more): the advantages of the lone therapist. In: J. Schweitzer, A. Retzer, & H. R. Fischer (Eds.), *Systemische Praxis und Postmoderne.* Frankfurt: Suhrkamp.

Speed, B. (1994). Reality exists o.k.? An argument against constructivism and social constructionism. *Journal of Family Therapy, 13* (4), 395–411.

Treacher, A., & Carpenter J. (1993). User-friendly family therapy. In: J. Carpenter & A. Treacher (Eds.), *Using Family Therapy in the 90s.* Oxford: Blackwell.

PART II

NEW EXPLORATIONS—
MAINLY PRACTICE

CHAPTER 6

The therapeutic moment: a double-sided drama

Peter Cantwell and Brian Stagoll

> It was inevitable that in the consulting room there would be two dramas played out, and one of them was going to occur in the unconscious of the therapist.
>
> (Kahn, 1991, p. 118)

A new voice being heard more frequently in the systemic world stresses the therapeutic relationship. Emphasis on the therapeutic relationship is not new in systemic thinking (a fact sometimes overlooked by writers in the systemic tradition—Skynner, 1987), but it is now receiving more attention. This is a reflection of the rising influence of feminist-informed therapy and the elaboration of social constructionist thinking (Cantwell & Holmes, 1994). Earlier family/systemic therapies originating from work with highly dysfunctional and stuck systems needed to be preoccupied with strategies for shifting rigid structures and behaviour patterns. In its time, this pioneering work was a significant addition to psychotherapeutic thinking. Now, with systemic approaches more fully established, systemic therapists can turn to paying more attention to the therapeutic relationship itself.

This chapter explores the therapeutic relationship in three parts. In the first part, after outlining contemporary theory on the nature of a collaborative therapeutic relationship, we extend the notion of collaboration to a more profound challenge to therapist self-awareness and self-complacency. In the second part, we offer some simple vignettes from our clinical work to illustrate these principles. Finally, and in the light of our earlier discussion, we muse on our own personal journeys as therapists as a way of inviting the readers to reflect on their own development and unspoken assumptions about therapy.

THE THERAPEUTIC RELATIONSHIP: SYSTEMIC THINKING LISTENS TO NEW VOICES

There are many ways of understanding the therapeutic relationship

Traditionally, different therapeutic schools have understood the therapeutic relationship in different ways. We do not believe it necessary to coalesce these different ideas into a single way of thinking and working. Indeed, this is to be avoided. There are many ways to be therapeutically effective. Many tributaries enrich psychotherapy. One stream of thinking that is dwindling in importance is the "blank-screen" therapist, detached from and inaccessible to the client. Even within traditional analysis, whence this model arose, there is considerable questioning of the value of the remote, untouchable therapist whose views and interpretations are not subject to client negotiation. Bader and Chernin (1993) propose that:

> the analyst's alleged privileged capacity to interpret what is "inside the patient" is actually a pathological fantasy shared by patients and analysts alike. [p. 36]

They further point out that contemporary currents of psychoanalytic thought are:

in favour of a more democratic, less tilted view of the analytic relationship in which the analyst is a co-equal participant. [p. 37]

Kohut's self-psychology approach is described by Kahn (1991) as:

softening of the diamond-hard discipline of psychoanalytic practice by introducing into it the warm softness of humanism. [pp. 81–82).

Rogers (1967), representing the humanistic tradition which emphasizes the concrete presence of the therapist, states that:

if the therapy were optimal, . . . then it would mean that the therapist has been able to enter into an intensely personal and subjective relationship with the client . . . as a person to a person. It would mean that the therapist is genuine, hiding behind no defensive facade, but meeting the client with the feelings which organically he is experiencing. . . . It means that the therapist has been comfortable in entering this relationship fully. [pp. 184–185]

*Social construction theory:
an invitation to a different order with clients*

Recent social construction theory invites systemic therapists to reflect more profoundly on the place and nature of the therapeutic relationship. Such a move is an extension of the logic of second-order cybernetics, with its emphasis on the involvement of the person of the therapist *within* the therapeutic system. This is in contrast to a pre-supposed observer sitting outside the feedback loops, in the detached world of first-order cybernetics. But systemic thinkers have been rather hesitant to operationalize the clinical implications of this line of thought. The Galveston school of Goolishian and Anderson (1992) has been in the forefront of clinical experiments in this area, teasing out and developing the notions of the non-expertise and the not-knowing of the therapist and the need for the therapist to be open to "always changing". The therapist is in a continuous state of being informed and never comes to know fully. The therapist is challenged to assimilate his or her own biases—whether cultural, professional, gender, or racial—and to be aware that there is no privileged standpoint for understanding any client.

Lynn Hoffman (1993) has proposed an "ethic of participation" for therapy, emphasizing the collaborative nature of the therapeutic endeavour. She teases out the qualities of collaboration in an earlier article:

> We express our ideas about therapy, tell relevant stories from our lives, share concern about mistakes we may have made. ... We can be extremely open about our rationales, our practices and our more personal thoughts. Instead of keeping up a pretence of "neutrality", we can acknowledge and share the subjective nature of our understandings. For instance, we might tell the family about some personal experience that we think might interfere with our effectiveness, or we might share with the family the all too frequent feeling of being stuck. [Hoffman, 1991, p. 5]

Tom Andersen's (1992; personal communication 1994) ideas on the reflecting team arose from his reflections on the appropriate ethical stance within any therapeutic relationship. Andersen has come up with novel ways to operationalize second-order cybernetics. His suggestion that therapists make available to clients their own internal thoughts and feelings, rather than share them with colleagues behind the protection of a one-way mirror, proposes a different dynamic for the client–therapist relationship. The reflecting team prompts systemic therapists to search for the inherent resources of clients and their ability to define and realize their own choices. There is promising research that indicates that clients find the reflecting method a richer, more collaborative and participatory format for therapy (Smith, Yoshioka, & Winton, 1993).

Cecchin, Lane, and Ray's (1992) notion of irreverence moves the therapeutic relationship away from the manoeuvrings and strategies of earlier Milan to a respectful irreverence. We have dubbed the new Milan method as "hypothesizing, circularity, and jocularity"! Madanes' (1993) description of strategic humanism emphasizes a similar collaboration. Once we take on board the *mutuality* of the therapeutic relationship, the *human reality and presence of the therapist*, and the necessary readiness of the *therapist to be open to change*, we have a new constellation for guiding clinical work. Kahn (1991) reminds us that it is the relationship that *is* the key to client change: "the therapist–client relationship itself holds enormous therapeutic potential" (p. 2).

Collaborative therapeutic relationships: the interactive moment

A collaborative therapeutic relationship, such as is being proposed here, can offer potential for client *and therapist* growth and change. Shotter (1994) argues that the knowledge that is most formative of our sense of ourselves and our identity formation is not abstract theoretical knowledge or skill-based practical knowledge. It is rather that knowledge/experience that emerges from "the interactive moment". Such interactive moments are not the product of any casual presence of one person to another, but moments where we experience ourselves as deeply involved with and deeply connected to another. In this "interplay of voices" new meanings that profoundly influence our sense of ourselves emerge most clearly. This is expressed by Carl Rogers, in a paper written towards the end of his life, where he mused that when he was at his best, his inner spirit seemed to reach out and touch the other person in a profoundly healing way (Thorne, 1992). Baur (1991) quotes Judith Horgan's telling point: "To be understood deeply and intelligently and to be treasured is a combination that deflects the course of any life. The rest is stuff" (p. 87).

Therapy as two interlocking dramas

The style of therapeutic relationship that we are offering touches deeper currents than those sometimes depicted as collaborative. We are not talking about a superficial matter of "caring and sharing". The relationship of therapist and client comes out of the interplay of two deep dramas, the client's *and* the therapist's. There is no option about whether the dramas *exist*. The choice is whether we *pay attention* to both dramas or not. The therapist's drama cannot conveniently be bracketed under the rubric of "professional persona" and left out of the therapy room! A deeper personal scrutiny and a more profound personal reflection is demanded of the therapist. While we can begin with the notion of clinical collaboration, we quickly move on to a more intense and personal questioning. The therapist drama we are focusing on can elicit many currents for the therapist in *this* moment: family of origin, developmental stage of life, culture, current struggles, ethical stance, personal and political beliefs, moment-by-moment thoughts and feelings, all combining into that changing constellation, "the whole person".

Kahn (1991) puts it well:

> In the consulting room there would be two complex dramas played out, and one of them was going to occur in the unconscious of the therapist. It seemed clear that the more aware the therapist was of this fact, the safer the client would be, and the richer the therapist's sources of information. [p. 118]

It becomes important, then, that the therapist be aware of what he or she brings to the therapeutic encounter. If not, the richness of the encounter is lessened both for the therapist and for the client. When any therapist walks into the room he or she immediately affects and is affected by the family or system dynamic. If what we try to change doesn't change us, we are playing with blocks.

AN ETHIC OF PARTICIPATION: CLINICAL IMPLICATIONS

Lynn Hoffman's (1993) elegant phrase "an ethic of participation" heads this section as the foreground of our clinical philosophy. Our question is: how does "an ethic of participation" within an evolving collaborative therapeutic relationship, an interactive moment, translate into the down-to-earth reality of clinical practice? We have struggled with how best to illustrate our theory with casework. Our first temptation was to appear clever and smart, but we feared we would soon be unmasked!!! Then we remembered the Zen teaching: true wisdom makes its presence felt in simple events. So we have chosen extraordinarily *ordinary* vignettes. We wish to show how this collaborative attitude can begin with who comes to the session, who determines the direction of therapy, how mysterious need therapy be, how important the human person of the therapist is quite apart from therapeutic expertise. Simple yet subtle shifts of expertise and language can enhance collaboration and require a more profound therapist presence.

Client expertise

Goolishian and Anderson (1992) remind us that true collaboration requires the recognition of the expertise of the client. How can we develop and extend client expertise? This can occur in a very simple way from the moment of the first telephone contact.

Who comes to the session?

Clients can be respectfully asked who they think should come to the session. It was once a custom that family therapists demanded that all the family attend the session irrespective of the issue. We now understand that the different groupings that come for the therapy session offer a rich variety. The way the invitation to therapy is handled on the telephone can set a collaborative tone even before the first session.

Case study 1

A 40-year-old woman, Norma, phoned to say that she was having marriage problems and would like an appointment for marital counselling. When asked if her husband, Bill, intended to come, she said she would like him to come but doubted that he would as he had never attended any previous counselling sessions. The issue, from her point of view, was whether the marriage could survive, and she felt that he was essential to the conversation. The therapist affirmed the wisdom of her thinking. Feeling supported in her own expertise, she put a strong case to her husband to attend, and both came to the first session. The therapist could have short-circuited the discussion by insisting that both spouses attend, and consequently snuffing out some initial client expertise. The style of the initial negotiation set a more collaborative tone for the whole of the therapy, and both parties continued to feel that their *own* capabilities contributed significantly to the therapeutic conversation and outcome.

During the session

Therapists sometimes carry to an unnecessary extent the responsibility of determining appropriate therapeutic directions during the session. This burden is a residue from more traditional strategic practice in which the therapist was seen as the one who not only carefully determined therapeutic directions, but was also the sole source of interventions. That is not to deny that there are times when therapists need to take clear and unapologetic control, especially in times of crisis. But it is just as true that clients offer profound insights into the best directions to go in a session and so become collaborative partners in the journey.

> *Therapist:* "Bill and Norma, you have named three major issues affecting your lives right now. Firstly, your marital relationship has been highly conflictual for the last ten years, to the stage where you are both wondering whether you wish to stay or not. Secondly, you are having major difficulties with the two eldest children. Thirdly, Norma, you have to make a decision almost immediately about whether to return to work or not. I am wondering where we should start, with the most urgent issue or the easiest one or what?"

The couple chose to explore the marital relationship, since in their estimation it impinged on the other two issues and would create some sense of support for the rest of the work ahead. Their choice and prediction turned out to be most accurate and created a clear direction for, and commitment to, therapy. They also felt affirmed and respected in being consulted about the choice.

*Making available to clients
what the therapist is thinking*

The world of therapy is often quite mysterious to the client. Many clients believe that the therapist is secretly "psychoanalysing" them or engaging in some profound thoughts that would be far beyond their grasp. Andersen's process of reflecting encourages the therapist to "think aloud", to make known to the client the therapist's hunches, musings, ideas, misgivings, and possible directions, and to ask the client for her or his reactions to these shared thoughts. Such exchanges amplify collaboration, remove mystery, and encourage a partnership of exploration.

> *Therapist:* "Norma and Bill, my silence indicates that I feel stuck and I would like to let you know my dilemma. I have been watching you relate to each other for some time now. One thing I notice is that you very easily slip into mutual nagging about grievances of the past. I am not sure whether this nagging is merely something that happens to most couples from time to time or whether it indicates a more profound dissatisfaction with your relationship. Could you help me clarify my confusion?"

Therapists have often been educated to believe that *they* should make these assessments from their position of supposed superior knowledge. Such decision-making procedures can be an unwarranted imposition of expertise, do not allow for the possibility of therapist error, and disrespect client contributions.

Homework tasks

Homework tasks offer great possibilities for collaborative work. On those rare occasions when the therapist has the benefit of a reflecting team, the session can be concluded in a mutually responsible way: "Of all the ideas you heard from the team, and of the ideas that came up during the session, which ones do *you* feel would be useful to keep in mind when you leave here?" Alternatively, when a therapist leaves the room to consult a team, a suggestion before departing can go something like this: "The team will no doubt have some ideas about possible changes, but we will first of all be curious about your ideas for future directions."

Without a team, a collaborative approach to homework can go something like this: "I have been having a few thoughts during the session about what might be useful. But, firstly, I am particularly interested in what *you* think will be some good strategies to keep in mind when you leave here."

Understanding the client system

Goolishian and Anderson (1992) make the task of understanding a cooperative venture. They often use the collaborative statement: "I need you to help me understand something!" It is a useful sentence to have tucked away in any therapist's repertoire. But it is definitely *not* to be used by the therapist who feels that he or she should be a guru and a source of all wisdom!

Case study 2

A couple came for marital therapy: an Australian husband who had lived for many years in Japan, and his Japanese wife. Early in the session, the therapist said: "While we work together I will need your help. My culture is Australian, and my training in therapy is from a Western viewpoint. I will need you to tell me if I make comments or suggestions which clash with Japanese culture, and I would like you to be very open about that." Because of this permission, the family was able to correct the therapist when he made the inevitable cultural slip, from a simple error like mispronouncing important names to the appropriate hierarchy in seeking information from the family. At the termination of therapy the family commented that they appreciated the therapist's openness and willingness to learn.

The immediate therapeutic relationship as a medium for client growth

The very act of being present with a client in the intensity of a truly collaborative therapeutic relationship generates enormous potential for growth. Research by Truax and Carkhuff (1967) on therapeutic outcomes shows that the therapeutic process is not a neutral one: it is for better or for worse, and the tone of the relationship has a major effect on positive or negative outcome. Because systemic therapists have often been trained with a keen eye to watching for "who does what to whom, when, where, and under what circumstances", they might be blind to another level of therapeutic process: how they as people, with their particular personality, their struggles, their smiles and hopes, their respect, and their empathy affect the client; how they as human beings relate to this other human being. Not infrequently, the therapeutic relationship provides the first occasion for a client to speak of painful issues, to feel understood and respected, with consequent raising of self-esteem and self-respect. The therapist can easily underestimate the healing capacity of the therapeutic relationship and miss the delight and demand of being truly present to another person.

Case study 3

June came for therapy because all the men in her life either had abused her or, in the case of her husband, were presently abusing her. She told her story for the first time, and as the sessions went by she sorted out issues with her father, separated from her husband, settled the children into a new school, and began to discover that life could have sunshine as well as rain! At the end of the therapy, she and the therapist were reviewing their time together. The therapist commented that he felt she had made many gains, had courageously faced difficult decisions about her marriage, had resolved family conflicts, and rightly felt good about herself. When it came time for June to reflect on her experience of therapy, her statement was different: "I realize that I have made many changes and that I deserve credit for them. But the most significant change for me is that during our time together I have learned that I can respect and be respected by a man!" Her major learning had been the unspoken experience of a relationship with a male in which respect for each other was the currency. Such respect requires openness and vulnerability on the part of the therapist, a willingness to truly relate to this person, to offer a different kind of relationship than previously experienced.

Therapist narratives

The collaborative therapy we are proposing calls for ongoing self-scrutiny by the therapist beyond the immediacy of the therapeutic encounter. Herein lies a deeper demand for the therapist: with our clients we cannot be other than who we are in our ordinary lives. We cannot "turn on" collaboration, respect, or compassion for the therapeutic moment if these qualities are not part of our day-to-day selves. It is not a matter of "if you can fake sincerity, you've got it made". It doesn't work like that. To be present therapeutically requires awareness of the baggage, the pre-formed narratives and the texts we bring with us into the therapy room. We find it useful to make an arbitrary split into two kinds (recognizing this split is the very one we are critiquing—no one said we have to be consistent!): professional and (even more demanding) personal.

Professional

"The talk of any theorist is never a matter of innocent description" (Shotter, 1994). We all walk into the room, as Hoffman puts it, with our eyes bandaged with professional texts: the texts of our training and preferred ways of working, and so on. These texts are a help or a hindrance, largely depending on how aware we are of them and how flexible we can be in their use. They set up grids that can be cooperative and expand resources for our clients, or grids that can shrink resources and further mystify the therapeutic process. It can be very appropriate for a therapist to make his working parameters explicit, to explain why he works the way he does, and to invite questions. This self-disclosure can put clients at ease and implicitly invites them to be collaborators in the therapeutic process.

Case study 4

A mother, father, and two children came for therapy, sent by their children's school. Early in the first session, the mother tentatively said that they had been for family therapy on a previous occasion and had not liked the experience or found it particularly useful. "We felt the therapists didn't take us seriously, we felt disrespected, and the homework didn't make sense. They seemed to speak to us with tongue in cheek." The therapist invited the family to speak at length of the experience. He then volunteered to tell them how he worked. He invited them to say what they hoped would happen during the therapy sessions and to ask him questions either then or at any stage of the therapy.

We find a useful question to ask our client is whether she or he has any questions or worries about how therapy will proceed.

Personal

"We confront life's situations with code in hand" (McNamee & Gergen, 1992, p. 1). We are all prone to the grave illusion that the way we see and describe what happens in the room is the way things are. We find it difficult to own our "premises, points of view, biases", our family texts, and so on. While it is impossible not to have our personal premises, points of view, and biases, a challenge for our therapist growth is to become more aware of these lenses, especially when they may affect the client–therapist relationship. Our own unfinished business can dribble into the therapy room and become an unhelpful and unaware grid.

Case study 5

A student therapist was reflecting with the training group on her therapeutic style in a live session which all had just viewed. She became puzzled as to why she seemed to spend a lot of time on the client's "lame dog" part. As the discussion progressed she was able to see that she was still struggling with part of her own "lame dog" from her family of origin, and that some resolution of this personal issue would be of benefit to the clarity of her relationship with this client. This is but a small example of how our own baggage is inevitably part of our therapeutic relating, and our growth as therapists demands the never-ending journey of self-discovery.

These brief and very ordinary clinical vignettes point the way to the art of truly collaborative therapy. To the unobservant it may seem of small moment to work *with* clients about who comes to the session, what direction therapy should take, what they think of therapist ideas. It may seem inconsequential for clients to help in teasing out therapist understanding, to experience genuine therapist care, or be party to therapist parameters. But such tiny shifts of therapist language and expertise begin to fold back upon each other and weave a climate of respect, of trust, of common humanity, where the client can begin to unravel a story never told before and know that she or he will be safe. This demand for a deeper personal investment on the part of the therapist is more than rewarded by the excitement of the mutual journey of client and therapist. If taken seriously, collaborative therapeutic work opens us therapists to a more challenging and ongoing self-questioning, a challenge we would now like to address.

THE POSTMODERN THERAPIST: ONE WHO LIVES IN A "DISQUIETED PLACE" (GOLDNER, 1994)

"Any true relationship requires . . . a certain vulnerability, and openness to being affected and changed." [Moore, 1992, p. 404]

As we read through our chapter, we are left with a certain disquiet. Have we exempted ourselves too much from our own questions and uncertainties? Do we, if ever so subtly, exempt ourselves from the loop of change, from uncertainty and doubt and the need for continual re-positioning? If the therapeutic relationship is to be a real one, the therapist can only prevent personal change by a defensive posture. As we struggle with our clients on their journey, we hear echoes of our own struggles; as we see them resolve difficult relationship tangles, we will be reminded of relational issues in our own lives which need attention; as we rejoice in their successes we can recall some of our own. By trying to shut off from the reciprocity of the client–therapist relationship, we refuse a gift for ourselves, and to that extent we come away diminished people. And that diminishment can lead to therapist burnout in which, instead of the client–therapist relationship being nourishing for *both* parties, the therapist can relive the Sartrean fear that "hell is other people".

Goldner (1994) reminds us that one of the commonest deceptions of humankind is to imagine that, while change and uncertainty apply to all those *other* people, *I* am outside the loop of change. Change is for other people. How do we as therapists, in the current jargon, de-construct and re-construct ourselves? How do we hold on to our personal and professional positions and at the same time entertain the ambiguity that calls us to move on from them? How do we sustain the tension between our present beliefs and ideas and be open to the next disturbance on our journey? Have we invited our clients to launch into the rapids while we sit quietly—and disquietedly—on the bank? What about *our* rapids? Are we just leading our clients up the creek!?

We began our therapist journeys from different places. One of us was initially trained in the biomedical and instrumental approaches to clinical work. The role of spirit, hope, and healing was less valued. The other began his studies in an ancient philosophical and theological tradition in which cure was seen solely as the domain of the spirit. Preoccupation with the "human" and the "medical" and the "body" was viewed with suspicion and disdain.

Virginia Goldner (1994) rightly says that no one can see his biases on his own. He has to allow other voices into the arena to shake his complacency and keep his disquiet active. Our clients and our colleagues can open cracks in our rock-solid and too-entrenched positions. An offering can be to allow enough disquiet into our settled ideas and convictions to provoke change. As we worked together over time, our journeys have crossed: the psychiatrist has been touched by "psyche" and "soul"; the priest has been grounded in the "human", the "body", the "earth". We have not given up our former selves (though we continually joke about holding our former positions), but these selves are enriched by the continual discourse between where we are and where we still need to go. We are slowly giving up our "master narratives" (Goldner, 1994). While we take a position with respect and care, another part of ourselves will always work against it to produce another synthesis—till it in turn becomes grist for the mill! If we as therapists try to absorb the challenge of postmodernism into our work, we can never rest too presumptuously on our therapeutic oars. The moment we believe we have reached the master narrative is the moment of our demise. No "lens" (Hoffman, 1990) ever provides the ultimate vision but is always to be questioned by other lenses. Our most profound challenge, then, is to be willing to continue this personal and professional journey, and not to shy away from the as-yet-unasked questions. And so this paper does not reach a neat conclusion. Instead, it finishes with a quote from a letter.

When Rilke was asked by a student how to become as good a poet as Rilke, he answered

> ... have patience with everything unresolved in your heart and try to love *the questions themselves* as if they were locked rooms or books written in a foreign language. Don't search for the answers, which could not be given to you now, because you would not be able to live them. And the point is, to live everything. *Live* the questions now. Perhaps then, someday far in the future, you will gradually, without even noticing it, live your way into the answer. [Rilke, 1986, pp. 34–35]

REFERENCES

Andersen, Tom (1992). Relationship, language and pre-understanding in the reflecting process. *The Australian and New Zealand Journal of Family Therapy, 13* (2), 87–91.

Bader, Michael J., & Chernin, Kim (1993). Current trends in psychoanalysis: social constructivism. *Tikkun, 8* (1), 36–37, 75.

Baur, Susan (1991). *The Dinosaur Man*. New York: Harper Collins.

Cantwell, Peter, & Holmes, Sophie (1994). Social construction: a paradigm shift for systemic therapy and training. *The Australian and New Zealand Journal of Family Therapy*, 15 (1), 17–26.
Cecchin, G., Lane, G., & Ray, W. (1992). *Irreverence: A Strategy For Therapist Survival*. London: Karnac Books.
Goldner, Virginia (1994). *Geoff Goding Memorial Lecture*. Parkville, Victoria: Bouverie Family Therapy Centre.
Goolishian, H. A., & Anderson, H. (1992). Strategy and intervention versus nonintervention: a matter of theory? *Journal of Marital and Family Therapy*, 18 (1), 5–14.
Hoffman, L. (1990). Constructing realities: an art of lenses. *Family Process*, 29 (1) (March), 1–12. Also in *Exchanging Voices: A Collaborative Approach to Family Therapy*. London: Karnac Books.
Hoffman, L. (1991). *Relational Systems Work: Family Therapy in a Different Voice*. Unpublished manuscript.
Hoffman, L. (1993). *Exchanging Voices: A Collaborative Approach to Family Therapy*. London: Karnac Books.
Kahn, Michael (1991). *Between Therapist and Client*. New York, W. H. Freeman.
McNamee, Sheila, & Gergen, Kenneth J. (1992). *Therapy as Social Construction*. London: Sage.
Madanes, Clöe (1993). Strategic humanism. *Journal of Systemic Therapies*, 12 (4), 69–75.
Moore, Thomas (1992). *Care of the Soul*. New York: Walker.
Rilke, Rainer Maria (1986). *Letters to a Young Poet*. New York: Vintage Books, 1986.
Rogers, Carl R. (1967). *On Becoming a Person*. London: Constable.
Shotter, John (1994). Conversational realities. Paper presented at the Conference on *The Discursive Construction of Knowledge*, Adelaide, Australia (text taken from audiotape).
Skynner, R. (1987). *Explorations with Families: Group Analysis and Family Therapy*, edited by John Schlapobersky. London: Methuen.
Smith, Thomas Edward, Yoshioka, Marianne, & Winton, Mark (1993). A qualitative understanding of reflecting teams, I. Client perspectives. *Journal of Systemic Therapies*, 12 (1), 28–43.
Thorne, B. (1992). *Carl Rogers*. London: Sage.
Truax, Charles B., & Carkhuff, Robert R. (1967). *Towards Effective Counselling and Psychotherapy*. Chicago: Aldine.

CHAPTER 7

A systemic therapy unravelled: in through the out door

Amaryll Perlesz, Mark Furlong, and the "D" family

INTRODUCTION

How could one ever write about a therapy in a way that comprehensively reflected the therapeutic relationship, involved the family in those reflections in a truly collaborative manner, did not treat the therapy and the family as "a case", explored the co-therapy relationship, and was honest enough to describe the vicissitudes in the complex set of relationships between therapists and family over a period of more than eighteen months? These were some of the issues that we, the therapists, pondered over as we once again contemplated this project, drinking Guinness on one of those winter Melbourne days that silently, without notice, turn into night. The glass of Guinness was not as creamy and as rich as we would have liked, just as we knew that an account of a therapy can never "accurately" reflect the experience of the participants. The map cannot be the territory. Only 5,000 words, two therapists, five family members, eighteen months of therapy, twenty-three sessions, and a paper to be written within three months.

Although the family had willingly agreed to participate in the project, we knew that it was our own interest, focus on the therapy, and desire to complete the paper that would outweigh the family's involvement. Imbalance to begin with. The second pot of Guinness was almost finished. The task seemed, as always, daunting. At least we both recognized that there was not an imbalance in our own relationship. Peers in the truest sense of the word; more than a decade spent working, writing, arguing, drinking, co-therapying, and being good friends. A fine place to begin.

The process gradually began to unfold. We decided that the family and therapists would have access to tape transcripts from seven of the twenty-three sessions. Although a limited sample (only the first, second, sixth, seventh, eighth, fifteenth and sixteenth sessions had been taped), these transcripts would facilitate recollections about the therapy. Therapists and family members would also review file notes written by the therapists after each session. All participants would then independently make notes about the therapeutic relationships from their own perspective. A couple of weeks later, we would meet with Elizabeth and Stephen, the parents, and Timothy and Michael, the sons, at the family home. At this meeting, there would be an audiotaped review/discussion. Whether or not Kate, Elizabeth's twin sister who had attended two sessions, was to be present at the gathering was up to the family to decide.

The most radical decision made at the pub on that first evening was that the focus of the writing about the therapy would be on the therapeutic relationships rather than the content of the sessions or the therapeutic interventions. We also decided to describe the personal interactions and affect just as they were experienced by the participants, rather than making a theoretical analysis of the interactional processes. Moreover, the family members' views of the therapeutic relationships would be interwoven with the therapists' views throughout the discussion, rather than tacked on at the end.

We met with the family as planned, the family choosing not to include Kate. The following account is derived from notes written in the family's file between September 1991 and March 1993 (reviewed by therapists and family); retrospective accounts of each individual's perspective of the therapeutic relationships, written prior to the review session; and the review session—a combined family/therapist discussion fifteen months after the completion of therapy.

This chapter combines descriptions by therapists and family members of different views of a shared experience of participating in a systemic therapy. The challenge to undertake such a project effectively is reflected in the problem of parsimoniously translating and integrating multiple perspectives. There can be both a richness and a daunting complexity generated by differing descriptions and affect arising from a shared experience. The current project attempts to interweave perspectives from all participants whilst maintaining an "illusional" meta-perspective.

ENGAGEMENT

Engagement—the making of relationships within therapy—is a complex process of interactions not only between the therapists, family, and wider network but also amongst family members themselves as they negotiate the rules for interacting within the therapy. Relationships and how they are perceived and affectively experienced also change over time and are unlikely to be static during the course of therapy.

The initial contact

Elizabeth had been advised by a rehabilitation physician to contact the Acquired Brain Injury Team at Bouverie Family Therapy Centre (BFTC—a publicly funded family-therapy clinical/training agency) when she had expressed concerns about the behaviour of her head-injured son and the stress this was causing within the family. When Elizabeth first contacted BFTC, she spoke at length with Mark and gave him a considerable amount of personal information at an initial intake interview. Mark learnt that Elizabeth was 53 years old and married to Stephen, who was fourteen years older. Also living at home were two sons, Michael, 27, and Timothy, 22. Michael was an unemployed artist, and Timothy had worked for the State Electricity Commission prior to having a motor-bike accident three years earlier. Timothy had become more rigid in his thinking, unable to express himself, epileptic, inactive, and bored at home, highly frustrated, and prone to very angry temper outbursts, particularly towards his father. Nine years earlier, Elizabeth's then eldest son, David aged 20 years, had shot and killed himself in his bedroom at home. Stephen had retired shortly after David's suicide, and Elizabeth felt that the suicide had prevented her from separating from her husband as she had previously planned. She also expressed a frank desire to "kill" her husband because she blamed him for David's death, but had refrained from doing so as it might "hurt" her children. Elizabeth had been in weekly individual psychotherapy with a psychiatrist for 15 years. Elizabeth now felt very burdened caring for a disabled son and retired husband and was particularly distressed by the conflict at home, which was the reason she was seeking help for her family. She expressed relief at being able to leave the house each day for her part-time work as a legal secretary.

The initial intake interview had an enduring impact upon both Mark and Elizabeth. Reflecting on beginning therapy, Elizabeth remembered that her first contact had been with Mark, and, having shared so much with him during that time, she felt apprehensive about starting again with a new therapist. Mark was also significantly affected by the initial conversation with Elizabeth. He felt shocked and concerned about the family and uncertain as to how volatile the family situation actually was. Mark wrote more details than he normally would on the intake form, and the family was allocated "urgently" to two experienced therapists.

As Stephen, the father, pointed out in the review session, the family had suffered significant trauma and therefore had a "story" that was both worth telling and needed to be told:

Stephen: "After the trauma we've been through we deserve to make a big story about it"

Amaryll: "You had plenty to say."

Stephen: "Exactly! We were not messing around. We had the facts behind us. When we came along we had something to talk about. We weren't fooling around. We had to get in there and get rid of it."

Amaryll: "That's a gutsy thing to do. We were just a couple of strangers."

Stephen: "We took you on your merits."

Elizabeth: "On instinct. We liked you."

Amaryll: "You didn't like us all the time." (*Everybody laughs*)

Empathy: a challenge

The effect of this initial contact on the subsequent cementing of the relationship between Elizabeth and Mark cannot be underestimated. Mark remained responsive to the family throughout the therapy, and Elizabeth was particularly sensitive to, and appreciative of, his empathy.

> ". . . what you had to say was very accurate. I couldn't get over how you . . . you were very tender. You really felt these things. How can you bear this? But you seemed to get such a feeling for us."

Implicit here too in Elizabeth's comments is her understanding that the therapists bear a burden in the containment of affect-laden information.

However, despite the therapists' most concerted efforts to understand, it was never really possible to fully "feel into" the family's experience (see Harari's discussion on empathy, in Chapter 3). Amaryll and Mark described a disquieting and profound sense of disorientation that was prompted by family feedback as well as the therapists' direct experience of how far-out at times their assumptions were about each of the family members' inner experience. Attaining a coordination of meaning between participants would often seem a realizable aim but without notice would suddenly appear to be a thousand miles away.

The situation described, or the story told by the family, was sometimes so overwhelmingly awful, shocking, or painful to hear that the relationships inadvertently became moulded by the content. A pattern in this therapy emerged whereby the family, in a way that they had never had an opportunity to in the past, openly talked about some of their intimate fears, desires, and unfulfilled dreams about life and death in what appeared to be a very matter-of-fact, apparently unperturbed manner. Although it was nine years since David's death, they had never had any family discussions or shared how they had felt at the time or even how they felt currently. Despite being connected through living in the one house, family members ate separately and had their own televisions or sound systems in their own separate bedrooms. They never gathered together in any room in the house at any time of the day or night. It was as though the tragic moment had sent the family into a centrifugal spin.

David's death and life were described in the starkest, most forthright detail down to remaining bone fragments, blood on the carpet, hole in the wall, toothbrush in the bathroom, and fingerprint on the bedroom lamp. These descriptions and disclosures at times left the therapists feeling so paralysed that they failed to pick up quite how gut-wrenching and terrifying the process of the "telling" was for Elizabeth and Michael in particular. For example, Elizabeth's openly expressed fears that her husband would murder her in the night startled the therapists because this seemed such an unlikely possibility. Although the therapists were able to make explicit underlying feelings of guilt, blame, hostility, rage, and so forth that may have been plaguing the family since David's death, it was possible that they inadvertently displayed their shock rather than a curiosity and compassion that would have permitted further exploration of this fear. To the therapists, Stephen appeared to be gentle, harmless, and non-intimidating. However, for Elizabeth, Stephen was a particularly threatening character who she genuinely believed might attack her. Elizabeth felt she had, with great difficulty and trepidation, raised her innermost fears, and she was therefore disappointed and angry with the therapists, whom she viewed as siding with Stephen and not taking her fears seriously. Elizabeth was courageous enough to write to the therapists after the third session and admonish them both for their lack of empathy:

"I may be wrong but I feel you did not take this seriously and made light of it. To me it was a terrifying time. I get the impression you think I am a monster and poor, quiet, easy-going Stephen is getting a raw deal having to live with me."

Following this letter, both Mark and Amaryll felt suitably chastened and somewhat distanced from their preferred self-image as caring and perceptive practitioners. From the therapists' perspective, within this context of fluctuating co-ordination of meaning, it appeared to be the family's good will and motivation for change that underwrote the therapeutic process and allowed the therapists to be so clumsy with the private worlds of each family member. The therapists were given so many chances. It seemed as though the family members moved themselves about with so much good grace that they were in a position to answer whatever they were asked. From the family's perspective, however, had the therapists not ultimately been as compassionate and as caring as they were, family members would not have been able to share their innermost thoughts and feelings.

MULTIPLE PERSPECTIVES

Implicit and explicit understandings surrounding the purpose of meeting together can dramatically impede or facilitate the making of a relationship. Not surprisingly, family members and therapists all had different views about the therapeutic agenda. Family members also had different views about their history or the meaning of significant events in their lives.

Multiple agendas

At one level, all family members shared a belief that therapy was not necessary; they were getting on with their own lives, they were accustomed to their personal separateness and felt comfortable rather than isolated. The therapists, on the other hand, were more openly preoccupied with death, love, and life. They both experienced a sense of urgency and perhaps even some sense of responsibility to release the family from their post-suicide time-capsule.

Despite expressing comfort with the status-quo, at another level family members had various reasons for attending therapy. Timothy's view of the purpose of the sessions was always the one most clearly stated. As the family had come to therapy because of his temper problems, once his frustration tolerance increased and he had stopped fighting with his father, from Timothy's perspective there was no longer any need to attend. Although he came because his mother suggested it, the therapists suspected that he looked upon them as benign and irrelevant.

Stephen did not appear to have a strong view about the purpose of therapy. As long as it was helpful to Tim, that was what he most cared about. As he personally appeared to enjoy the sessions, he was quite happy to attend, irrespective of the content. Stephen's comfort with the sessions translated into an easy and mutually respectful relationship with both Amaryll and Mark. However, Stephen's passivity and peripheral position within the family bemused the therapists, and they were unwittingly seduced into supporting him as the "underdog". The therapists openly admired Stephen's apparently high level of acceptance and adjustment to his traumatic past, yet it was just this attitude of acceptance that the rest of the family most envied and were most irritated and angered by.

Michael, like Timothy, had assumed that the purpose of the sessions was to deal with the fights between his brother and father. However, he very easily engaged in wide-ranging discussions about the past as well as his own future plans. Michael's style of relating was more intense and demanding than his brother's, and in that sense he engaged more of the therapists' and his parents' attention. He argued, displayed his angst, and railed against injustice in general. Of all family members, he found it easiest to tell the therapists most directly that they had got it wrong.

Elizabeth was the most therapy-wise in the family, and for this reason she felt very comfortable in the evolution of the content away from Timothy towards some resolution of past grieving, particularly her own numerous losses which began at the age of

3, when she was sent to boarding school when an older brother died. Although not as directly as Michael, Elizabeth was able to confront Mark and Amaryll at times when she felt that they had not understood her view or had misread her feelings. Elizabeth was pivotal to the therapy because there was little doubt that, without her urging, the therapy would not have taken place. Although she encouraged a playful and open relationship with both therapists, her central position within the family made her the gatekeeper of both the family's emotions and, to some degree, the content of the sessions. Her vulnerability and attachment to the therapists was complemented by the therapists' desire to please her and to fix up the family as she had ordered.

Deconstructing the event

Although Elizabeth initially sought help to deal with Tim's behavioural management, it appeared that David's suicide had cast a spell over the family and that the implicit agenda for seeking help was, rather, to attempt to make some sense out of David's death and, in so doing, release the spell that had cast family members into their own separate worlds, rarely connecting with each other. Family members did not appear to be grief-stricken per se, but they all had a personalized version or explanation of the suicide event, its aetiology, and its aftermath.

Each parent had pursued separate pathways in coming to terms with their eldest son's death. Stephen felt that he had fully resolved his grieving through regular attendance at meetings of Compassionate Friends (a self-help group to facilitate mourning). Elizabeth, on the other hand, had retained a long-standing belief that her husband was partially responsible for David's death, and for this reason she continued to be hostile towards Stephen and unresolved in her grief.

The brothers also had different views. Tim's reckless behaviour, which led to the motor-bike accident, was deemed to be an attempt to live out a life (or a death) as David would have done. Timothy felt that he had been too young at the time to form an opinion about his brother's suicide, although he did have a very practical and non-blaming view that David had merely been testing out the gun. For Michael, Timothy's near-death had made

David's suicide recede into the background. In his view, an "as if" death and its sequelae were more distressing and difficult to come to terms with than an "actual" death. Michael's anger was the most palpable; he was angry with David for killing himself, angry with David's girl-friend and himself for not being able to save him, angry with Tim for ruining his own life and leaving the pressure and the expectations on Michael as the able-bodied son, angry with his father for not being able to support and protect his mother, and he was furious with the therapists for revealing his anger to himself. In his own words:

"And alas, my repressed anger always seemed to spill out on Mum—the one who means most to me."

FORMING MULTIPLE FAMILY–THERAPIST RELATIONSHIPS

The family was aware of the complex task of forming more than one relationship:

Elizabeth: "I'd met Mark before I'd met you. When he said that Amaryll would be there, I wondered what you'd be like. It's strange. You're telling your innermost thoughts to people. Also, when you're with a psychiatrist, it's just you and him. But when you're with a family and you're saying all this, it's even harder. You're wondering . . . if I say this, maybe . . ."

Mark: "You've got to think about not just Amaryll or me but how it's going to affect others in the family."

Elizabeth: "That's right. He might say . . . (*diplomatically, broadly indicating all other family members*) 'How could she say such a thing as that?!'"

Despite the caution expressed here about the difficulties in taking into account the personal politics, coalitions, and alliances within the family, the therapists were always impressed by the family's ability to share their views about very difficult issues openly:

Mark: "It wasn't just that you were honest. It was kind of gutsy. Ruthlessly straight about incredibly difficult things, and I was very moved."

Elizabeth: "I'm not used to people reacting. You go to a psychiatrist, and they just sit there. You let out a lot of garbage but you're not getting a reaction. It's nice to get a reaction. You feel like you're getting somewhere."

In the review session, the therapists and family members were able to discuss openly the different types of relationships that each of the therapists formed with each of the family members and how these relationships changed over time. Stephen got on well with both Amaryll and Mark, probably because they were the only people in the room who initially displayed unreserved respect for him. As there was a clear alliance between Elizabeth and her sons, Stephen relished the therapists' positive response towards him.

From Timothy's point of view, when his behaviour was no longer the focus of therapy, he felt more of an observer who would take part when invited. If the sessions went on too long, he would become quite fatigued. Although slow to speak, Tim's comments were always insightful, relevant, and revealing of family dynamics. The therapists experienced Tim as likeable, friendly, forebearing, and very straight with them, and it is possible that his cognitive difficulties created a sense of a more reserved relationship with the therapists than actually was the case.

Michael initially felt reluctant to attend family sessions in which his brother and father were present because he was concerned that he might offend them. When he did eventually attend family sessions (after four individual sessions and eight months into therapy), Michael talked openly and perceptively, and the therapists enjoyed his company. His passion clearly energized both the family and the therapists. Michael was ambivalent about the family sessions. He described the therapy as "like talking to a friend, really. They'd ask a question and you'd say whatever you wanted to." Yet in contrast to this, at times he experienced the family sessions as an "interrogation" in which he was never sure that he was getting to the "right answer". Although he understood that he was being given permission to be angry, he often experienced family meetings as an unsettling experience. After each family session he felt drained and "wrung out".

As noted earlier, Elizabeth and Mark made an early and strong connection. Their high level of mutual respect was not seriously undermined by the lapse in empathy by the therapists. Elizabeth and Amaryll's relationship, however, was less straightforward. At first, Elizabeth felt daunted by Amaryll's challenging directness:

"I thought, '. . . my God, if I do say something that's not honest!' . . . That's why you had to be sure that everything you said was right. Because I knew you'd pick it up if I didn't."

Towards the end of therapy, in a thank-you letter to Amaryll, Elizabeth wrote:

"You have such a caring, gentle manner and always seemed to be able to pick up on the various reasons for our different behavioural problems. I was amazed that Michael would even agree to come, let alone as part of a family group. . ."

The shift in this relationship is explored later in this account. The family clearly differentiated between the two therapists and recognized that they had quite different styles. A more candid discussion about the differences between the therapists than is normally possible in thank-you letters from clients revealed that the family found Amaryll to be more direct, open, and confronting than Mark, whom Elizabeth viewed as tender and full of feeling:

"If you got sort of scared with Amaryll you knew Mark was there!"

It was easy to admire Elizabeth's devotion to her sons, her loyalty towards the family, her honesty and reliability, and her courage in surviving an earlier, serious depression, an unhappy marriage, the suicide of one son, and the head-injury of another. However, both therapists feared that contact with the family would be interminable because of the timeless web of grief that hung over the family. Moreover, Amaryll had begun to share Elizabeth's irrational and superstitious belief that Elizabeth had the capacity to have a harmful impact on those around her. To be accepted by the family was deemed by the therapists to be a risk that involved the prospect of imprisonment: through a door to a chamber with a door to another chamber. Each of the steps in were experienced as steps down to further levels of disorientation and dismay that were, for the family, not at all shocking or even strange but were just where they lived. This state may not have been the best of all possible worlds—it was the only world. As Mark noted:

"... the ghosts in my own nursery were unsettled ... The more I entered the private world of each family member, the more my own experience of the loss of a brother and, I guess, of even earlier fault-lines raised my anxiety and simultaneously allowed me to know more of the ecology of feelings and meaning within which the family existed."

For Amaryll and Mark together it was like holding hands in the mire and leaning closely but subliminally on each other. They shared an unspoken but strong sense of reliance on each other throughout the therapy.

RITUAL OF ACCEPTANCE

The turning point between Amaryll and Elizabeth was in part due to Elizabeth's acknowledgement of Amaryll's achievement in being able to talk with Michael on four occasions without alienating him from therapy. Michael's attendance at family sessions was a significant personal sacrifice in that his anxiety was so great. His meeting with the family was an important symbolic gesture of "regrouping the tribe", which allowed the family for the first time to share their experiences of the significance of events such as: Elizabeth's psychiatric hospitalization, when the boys were 14, 12, and 8 years old; David's death; Timothy's near-death; and more positive experiences, such as the boys' happy memories of their early childhood and doing activities with their father in their adolescence.

Amaryll's increasingly open acceptance of, and empathy towards, Elizabeth also contributed to the warmer connection between the two women. It became more obvious that it was only "apparent ease" with which Elizabeth spoke of her suicide pacts with her sons and her desire for her husband to die; she was in fact genuinely troubled and fraught by her own preoccupation with death. Amaryll, too, felt extremely saddened and moved by Elizabeth's reaching out to her twin sister and timidly asking for more of her time. However, it was a home visit—in which each member of the family shared their own private worlds with the therapists, and Elizabeth generously shared David's personal memorabilia in the room in which he had shot himself—that had the greatest impact on the cementing of the therapeutic relationships.

This first home visit, which occurred ten months into therapy, was a very special event for all participants. Following a discussion in the lounge (with the pet bulldog on Amaryll's lap), each of the family members showed Mark and Amaryll their rooms—their own personal space where they lived their own separate lives. Stephen showed the therapists striking photographs of a recent trip to Central Australia. Tim displayed his motor-bike posters and his musical instruments. Michael showed the therapists his paintings and the work he had just begun on the garden, whilst Elizabeth allowed the therapists a privileged viewing of David's memories in a way she had never shared with outsiders before. The details of his death, shocking as they had been initially, became the focus of a very moving home visit which transformed the horror into loving memories connecting David with his family and the therapists in the most powerful way possible. As Amaryll noted:

"At that time I felt like they were just ordinary, friendly folk, to whom something grim had happened and that they *were* getting on with their lives very well. I felt much more optimistic because I felt we had been shown how the glue was working, and for that very reason it had lost its grip."

The home visit was the beginning of the end of therapy, because once the therapists had been initiated into the family's private domain, both the family and the therapists were reassured that they could survive without each other. It became clear that family members were getting on with their own lives, and, by sharing David's life and death with outsiders, the family had successfully diffused the boundaries of their grief.

The last meeting with the family took place at the family home and was explicitly bitter-sweet. This session, like the review meeting that took place fifteen months later, evoked mixed feelings for family members and therapists. Mark and Amaryll felt awkward in saying goodbye; they felt close to family members and deeply affected by their pain, resilience, pride, and generosity. The journey together had been an intimate experience, and it was sad to part. As Elizabeth wrote:

> "... I will miss seeing you—a little like losing part of the family."

On the other hand, it was exciting and affirming to have come so far together. The therapists felt as though they had been allowed in through what had been a closed back-door and invited to leave openly from the entrance hall.

EPILOGUE

Throughout therapy, Stephen had been aware of a worsening of his memory which signalled an early dementia. His deterioration in cognitive and physical functioning has continued following the completion of therapy. Elizabeth and the boys have been more tolerant, compassionate, and accepting of his "funny habits" as they are more clearly seen now in the context of an organic illness. Timothy is engaged in almost full-time social and leisure activities, which has greatly increased the quality of his life. He is therefore happier and less bored, and he views his life as more productive. The family is proud of what he has been able to achieve since his accident. Elizabeth is more tolerant and accepting of her husband and her role as a care-giver. She also has a very different world-view regarding life and death:

"I used to think how good it would be to die. Now I always tell the boys I'll be around till I'm in my 90's."

Michael has transformed the garden into an exotic, creative, and very much alive masterpiece.

On reflection, the process of writing this account was made considerably less daunting by the family's collaboration and genuine interest in the project. Family members found several aspects of the process of reviewing the therapy important to them. They had not expected the therapeutic relationships to have such an impact upon the therapists, and they had initially feared that the therapists would find them boring. That they, as individuals, had mattered to the therapists confirmed their sense that the process was worthwhile. Reading the transcripts and file notes provided an unusual opportunity to reflect on the openness of what had been said during therapy. As Elizabeth said:

"I was honoured and flattered that you trusted us to read the file."

We, the therapists, have been deeply affected by our relationship with all family members. We feel that we have received a very special gift—an opportunity to connect with people we may otherwise not have had an opportunity to spend time with—and we have accepted their invitation to confront our own fears and discomfort about death, intimacy, dependency, and disability. Our understanding of the complexity of the empathic process and the therapeutic relationship has been extended, through both embarrassing and comforting experiences. We are now more optimistic that longer-term systemic therapies can and do end!

Acknowledgements

We would like to acknowledge and thank the Victorian Association of Family Therapy for research funds which contributed to transcribing the tapes of the sessions.

CHAPTER 8

From both sides now: the therapeutic relationship from the viewpoint of therapist and client

Catherine Sanders

INTRODUCTION

Systemic therapy has been responsible for the production of thousands of words and has absorbed the time and energy of theoreticians and practitioners the world over. Yet despite the more recent rhetoric of conversation and goals of equality and respect, the bulk of this material has reflected the practitioner's understanding and experience of the therapeutic process. As Conran and Love (1993, p. 2) reflect:

> it is not typical for therapists to ask clients for their opinions about therapy. Most therapists . . . have listened to other therapists for their opinions about therapy.

When considering the nature of the relationship between client and therapist, this balance seems particularly inappropriate. By definition, systemic therapists view the relationship as shaped and guided by circular and reciprocal processes, which influence both the person asking the questions and the person answering the questions. It seems ironic, therefore, that there has been so little description of the client's experience of this reciprocal process of therapy.

This chapter begins to address this imbalance, and in doing so it aims to follow the growing trend in systemic therapy to honour clients' knowledge and to respect this in more equal dialogues. The chapter addresses themes that are typically raised by systemic therapists about the therapeutic relationship, and it explores the experience of a small group of clients with respect to these themes. The clients' descriptions are placed alongside the literature discussion of these themes and the thoughts of their therapist, who is also the writer of this chapter.

EXPLORING BOTH SIDES— THE FORMAT FOR THIS PROJECT

The themes about the therapeutic relationship which are used in this project were culled from a comprehensive review of the literature. Initially, twelve themes were selected and became the subject of open-ended questions in the interview process with the clients. Subsequently, six major themes were chosen as the focus of this study: (1) power and control, (2) therapist responsibility, (3) neutrality and the therapist's view, (4) the process of change and the most important elements of the therapy, (5) respect by the therapist of the client and her system, and (6) affect and intimacy. Four clients participated in the project, and they were interviewed by a colleague of the therapist, who also uses a systemic approach. Each interview lasted approximately two hours.

The clients who participated in the project have many things in common. They were all seen in individual therapy over a substantial period by the same therapist—the length of therapy varied from eighteen months to six years, with an average of four years. All the clients interviewed were women, and they ranged in age from 41 to 50 years. Each woman had entered therapy with serious concerns that compromised her ability to work, have satisfactory relationships, and at times to stay alive. Each had experienced abuse as a child: for three of the women this had been sexual abuse, and the fourth had experienced emotional abuse and neglect. Each had one or more children, including a daughter. One was married to her first husband, while the others had experienced a number of painful separations from male or female partners. This was not the first therapy for any of the women, and they had all experienced the previous work as difficult. During the course of systemic work, two of the women took anti-depressant medication with the encouragement of their therapist.

As a group, these clients are clearly not meant to be representative of the diverse category of "clients" who are the consumers of systemic therapies, for systemic therapies may be short-term or long-term, and the work may be with individuals, couples, families, or other social groupings in the client's world. Moreover, clients come to therapy with a range of different struggles, and therapists' personal styles very much affect the therapy process. Indeed, in considering this diversity, it is important to note at the outset that these clients are in fact part of a very specific group. Thus, the aim of the project was not to attempt universal conclusions about clients' views, but rather to consider the insights that these women were able to offer about the application of systemic ideas in the very particular contexts of their own therapies.

It may also be important to give some information about the therapist and writer of this paper. She is slightly younger than these clients, is married, and at the time of the therapies had no children of her own. She has a strong liking and profound respect for the courage and character of each woman. She espouses a second-order approach (Hoffman, 1985), has been influenced by the Milan team and feminist writers, and has practised as a therapist for sixteen years.

In presenting this project, each chosen theme is simply taken in turn. The format is to begin with a review of the discussion in the literature around this theme, followed by a sample of the clients' thoughts about the issue, and then a discussion of these thoughts and the thoughts of the therapist/writer. In presenting the material in this way, a deliberate choice has been made to allow space for the women's comments to stand in their own right, and to clearly demarcate the therapist/writer's summaries and interpretations of their comments.

POWER AND CONTROL

The debate about the efficacy and ethics of the exercise of power in the therapeutic relationship has a long history in family therapy. Bateson and Haley engaged in the famous debate about whether power was an "epistemological abomination" (Dell, 1989, p. 3), while more recently therapists have explored the implications of second-order cybernetics for the exercise of power. Hoffman draws a distinction between approaches that "truly respect second-order cybernetics and those approaches that distort it by emphasizing therapist power and control" (quoted in Golann, 1988, p. 51). Atkinson and Heath (1990) suggest that the measure of a therapy based on second-order principles is not necessarily how directive or nondirective, active or passive, instrumental or non-instrumental, judgemental or nonjudgemental the therapist appears to be, but is more related to the extent the therapist is determined to have clients accept ideas or suggestions that the therapist proposes. They go on to state that the therapist will continually acknowledge that their view is not "true" but is constructed from a limited perspective and that clients should be free to disagree. The question of giving advice is addressed by Silver (1991, p. 307), who notes that while many systemic therapists consider the giving of advice to be a "major therapeutic error to be avoided", clients experience its absence as unhelpful or uncaring. He concludes that it is most helpful to give advice in such a way that the family can "take it or leave it, depending on whether it is relevant or helpful". From this perspective, advice is just one of many ways of interacting within the therapeutic conversation. Other writers have considered the exercise of power and control in terms of who chooses the topics to focus upon (Atkinson & Heath 1990), who dictates the meaning of the problem (Weingarten, 1992), and who structures the timing of sessions (Friedman, 1985).

James and Kirkland (1993, p. 178) give power a central place in their schema and state that there is "a decided place for legitimate power in a therapeutic relationship". This brief review would suggest that systemic therapists can and should exercise power, but in a way that fits comfortably within the dialogue and allows for disagreement. The clients perceived the issue in these ways:

> ". . . it was very useful to have somebody who would listen carefully and then clearly summarize what the options were, then I usually chose which ones I wanted to do."

> "In the initial stages she provided more instructions, but then it became more of a joint act and I was in control."

> "She had the power but she gave it away."

> "Mostly I agreed with the issues focused on because they were things that I was focusing on and we would work that out at the beginning."

> "I think it was important to her that we had collaboration . . . we tackled the issues side by side and sometimes we had different ideas about how to go about attacking it."

> "It was easy to disagree with her."

> "Power? when I was feeling very fragile . . . she didn't really stand over me but it was like she had control."

> "A few times I might try to get off the track if I didn't want to talk about certain things and she'd keep pulling it back and I knew she was doing it and I used to get a bit annoyed but as it turns out it was what needed to be done . . . I would have done anything to avoid whatever she wanted to get to."

> "Sometimes she gave me advice . . . she always, always asked permission to give me advice."

> "Therapy was more about finding my own solution rather than being given advice."

> "Well, the power relationship is not equal because I don't think that a counsellor/client relationship can be equal . . . I never felt as though Catherine had answers that I didn't . . .

and I never felt as though the process was out of my control
... I always felt from the very beginning that if something
wasn't right, I would be able to say that ... and that we could
discuss it."

"I don't think she had any investment in me seeing things one
way or the other ... I mean, maybe she did want me to see
through her eyes the extent of the abuse."

"I think there have been occasions when she not so much
imposed meanings as said what she thought at the start and I
would disagree if I didn't think that she was right on track ...
and as I became more familiar with her in terms of the conversations that we had, that probably happened more because
she knew a lot more about my background and family and all
those character things."

Clearly, these clients do not share systemic therapists' fear and
distrust of power and control, but approach it in a more straightforward fashion. A respectful and responsive use of power was
viewed as facilitating problem resolution rather than as an exercise of "power over" the client and her difficulty. The therapist is
viewed as appropriately exercising a leadership role, which involved selecting issues for discussion, mapping options, and
fashioning an understanding of the problem. Within these set
limits, clients expressed a freedom to disagree and challenge
the therapist and to involve her construction of the problem or
advice critically. Differences were more in terms of the point
at which control was exercised, with some women finding a
loosening of the therapist's grip as time progressed, and others
feeling that she exercised more overt control as the two became
better acquainted. Giving advice was also experienced differently, with some being clear that advice was given, while others
viewed the therapeutic process as helping to find their own
solutions.

From my own perspective, the client's experience closely
matched my own of providing a safe, secure context in which
difficult and frightening matters could be tackled. My belief is
that the therapist, as one who supposedly has expertise in hu-

man difficulties, has a responsibility to provide a framework in which solutions do emerge and to guide the conversation into territory where the client may not willingly venture alone. The differences are instructive as they point to the very personal nature of the relationship and the fit that develops between two people working in such an intimate fashion. Reflecting on each person's responses led me to recognize that my appreciation of them as individuals shaped my readiness to exercise more or less control and advice as the process evolved.

THERAPIST RESPONSIBILITY

A related area to power and control is that of the responsibility exercised by the therapist. Friedman (1985), in a paper exploring the prevention of burnout in therapists, suggests that those who take undue responsibility are putting themselves at risk, and that clinicians should remain clear that the problem and major responsibility for positive change belongs with the client. Specific questions about who took responsibility for the problem and its resolution and the more general topic of the areas in which the therapist did take responsibility were canvassed.

> "She took responsibility to know where we'd been and where I was up to."

> "She didn't take responsibility for my choices because basically they were my choices ... She didn't take responsibility for my life ... I still felt that I was in control of my life, whether I lived or died."

> "We took different sorts of responsibility I think ... I don't think she really took any responsibility for the problem because the work was mine ... She took responsibility for some of the structure and some of the suggestions that were made ... She was the umbrella under which we worked."

> "Catherine was responsible for timing within the session."

> "My responsibility was just listening ... tell her as accurately as I could what happened or how I felt."

"My responsibility was to be honest ... and always to be respectful of Catherine and what she had to say ... I think that it's possible to disrespect people and that's a two-way thing. That was part of her responsibility, to be respectful."

These clients' views about responsibility are congruent with both the literature and each other. It is clear that the therapist is responsible for monitoring the process in terms of listening, planning, maintaining a focus, and time-keeping. However, these women are very clear that the work of change is their own, with a particular responsibility to listen carefully and speak honestly.

As the therapist, the clear division made by the clients closely parallels my own. I am particularly interested in the emphasis on the need for honesty and mutual respect, values that I would place highly in the process.

NEUTRALITY AND THE THERAPIST'S VIEW

Hoffman (1985) identifies a number of qualities that characterize approaches respecting a second-order approach, including "a view of the problem that is not judgemental or pejorative" (Golann, 1988, p. 51). This is one aspect of neutrality that avoids blame of any one person in order to avoid linear explanations, refrains from proposing solutions, and entails a quiet non-reactive stance from the therapist: "The neutral therapist is a follower, moving with clients but remaining unmoved" (Nichols, 1987, p. 59). Closely related to neutrality is the client's perception of the therapist's view of the problem: whether she attempted to impose her meaning on the dialogue, and how attached she became to outcomes. The clients' experience of these matters were reported in these terms:

"A lot of Catherine's view was similar and a lot of it was very filmy."

"Well, at the end of those interviews, she would explain how she saw the situation ... Drawing together of things into a cordial relationship ... Which wasn't a judgement thing."

"I don't know . . . I'm not sure how she viewed the problem, she probably could see it differently from me."

"Yeah, she seemed to share her view . . . She seemed to always be on my side . . . To sort of empathize."

"She viewed the problem very seriously."

"She made it very clear from the beginning that she wasn't neutral . . . about me suiciding . . . She said that she would be really pissed off and that it wasn't on . . . for her and myself . . . but in terms of other aspects of our conversation, I think in the beginning she was neutral . . . Well, she was even-handed."

"I guess when she asked questions . . . she would explore the perspective like my parents' perspective or other people's perspectives and my perspective . . . She never said anything like 'what a bastard your father is' . . . She said things like 'you've been hurt . . . by your parents' rather than 'god, your father's an arsehole' . . . So I suppose in that way, she was being fair."

Systemic therapists have long struggled with both defining and implementing the concept of neutrality, and these clients' responses reflect a similar diversity and perhaps uncertainty about the questions asked. Interestingly, the women experienced the therapist as sharing their view, yet they seemed to express some uncertainty about what that opinion was. Rather, they spoke in terms of being empathized with, taken seriously, and treated fairly. The question of suicide was a matter that one client and I were both clear is not a subject for neutrality, and a very strong stance was taken. My own approach to neutrality is one that emphasizes the fair "even-handed" stance that allows the finest possible exploration of difficulties and emergence of solutions.

THE PROCESS OF CHANGE AND THE MOST IMPORTANT ELEMENTS

Another feature of a second-order therapy is its emphasis on the provision of a context for change as opposed to suggesting specific changes. Keeney and Ross (1985) suggest that change occurs when clients encounter "meaningful noise" whereby meaning is constructed from the explanation offered by the therapist. The therapist sets out "explanations for prescribing a particular pattern of stability and change" (Golann, 1988) which may be drawn from the client's history, cultural myths, and true or invented stories about other clients. This aspect was explored by asking interviewees about the extent to which the therapist provided solutions as opposed to providing a context for change. The question of change was also approached through enquiry about the clients' experience of the most important and memorable aspects of the relationship.

The process of change

"I think it was both context and specific changes . . . The context for change was my view about myself and my confidence to be who I am and to show the world."

"Well, mostly it was about context for change but there were occasions when there have been suggestions that were specific changes."

The most important elements

"I thought the most important part was those initial weeks . . . that somebody was prepared to acknowledge, . . . to care . . . to allow me to call at any time . . . to help me work out what I wanted to do, and basically she stood very strongly by me at a time when I was really a wreck and gradually helped me to gain more control back over my life."

"The most memorable thing was remembering when I was a small child . . . I had an older sister and I fell very much in her shadow and I had this belief that people would only like me if I was as good or better than her or did the same thing . . . There was an incident at school where the teacher told me off because I wasn't like my sister, and Catherine asked me how I felt about what they had said to me . . . I couldn't remember and she asked me what I would say to my daughter and I couldn't think of anything and so what she actually said was what she would say to her daughter . . . that thing about loving that person just for who they were because it would be really boring to have people exactly the same, and loving that person just for their own position . . . and I think that was . . . part of coming to value yourself more as an individual different from other people with your own special qualities."

"She approved of me, and a lot of things flowed from that . . . It meant that she respected me and it meant that if something had happened to me and I was upset about it then it was something that was worthy of her time and her energy and her interest."

"One of the really important things she did was redefining my behaviour as misdemeanours rather than crimes . . . Another important thing was you don't have to do it all now, so if somebody's putting you under pressure always reserve the right to take twenty-four hours."

"Probably just knowing I could come here and explain and not having her jump on me."

"I think her insistence on my courage was the most memorable thing . . . I can look at things now and I can see where it was."

"I think the most important thing was the boundaries . . . Because she was so clear that helped me to maintain the clarity."

"I said that I was suicidal, and she asked when was the first time I wanted to die? And I'd never ever thought of it but it was really significant because the first time I'd wanted to die was when I was about seven . . . It was like therapy exposing patterns of things . . . It was the first time I'd felt like I was going to get to the bottom of it."

The clients interviewed were generally in agreement that the context for change was primary, a view that I also shared. More interesting were the comments about the most important elements in the process towards change. Many of the elements they report are strongly reminiscent of Carl Rogers' (1967) early work on counselling, which seems to have been misplaced by systemic therapists. A broad range of very "human" experiences is canvassed: being cared for and respected, not being criticized, having someone who is perceived to be available, reliable, and strong. These experiences are placed beside what therapists term "intervention" and focus upon as the source of change: making connections, reframing, and giving advice. Differences seemed to relate more to the individual's particular difficulties and history than to the therapist's model. While most respondents spoke of a sense of being safe and respected, one woman emphasized the importance of clear boundaries between herself and the therapist. She related this directly to previous unsatisfactory experiences with therapy and her own family of origin. The most meaningful utterances were not necessarily the carefully constructed interventions that the therapist would have identified as crucial. Rather, they were observations and opinions given in the course of the session that to me were less consequential.

This mix reflects my own belief that the best "formal" intervention possible will have less impact where the relationship elements have not been addressed. This is particularly so with clients who have experienced unreliable, hurtful early relationships, and it appears that the therapeutic relationship being essentially different is crucial to the process of change.

RESPECT BY THE THERAPIST
FOR THE CLIENT AND HIS OR HER SYSTEM

Respect for the client and his or her system has been identified as crucial to success in the therapeutic endeavour. Atkinson and Heath (1990, p. 147) assert that "great gardeners, political leaders and psychotherapists are successful not because they know all the detail of the systems within which they operate, but because wisdom leads them to respect the conditions necessary for the functioning of these systems". One way that respect can be communicated is through the therapist's willingness genuinely to explore the recipients' expectations of the process. When this topic was raised, the following responses were made:

> "I always found her very respectful of me and my world..."

> "I got the feeling that my expectations of therapy were the sort of things that actually happen."

> "She's very respectful to me and respectful about my surviving... She hasn't been respectful of what people who have made things hard for me have done at all, but she's been respectful of my need to keep some relationship with them."

> "We explored my expectations of therapy all the time, but we explored them fairly formally in our first sessions and I was clear."

> "She was respectful, not ignoring or trivializing what I said ... If I said something she believed me and took it seriously no matter how absurd it may have been."

> "Always very respectful... It was probably more what she didn't do than what she did do."

> "My expectations of therapy were that it didn't work and that nothing would ever help... I said I think all counsellors are fucked and I basically said 'well, what are you going to do that's going to be different?'... So I guess to that extent we did explore my expectations or lack of them."

While the women interviewed agreed that they experienced respect from the therapist, personally and in relation to others in their world, they did not appear to perceive the exploration of expectations as a particular mark of respect. Again, respect was experienced in different ways depending on the client's own circumstances. These responses accord with my own beliefs. While it is true that it is respectful to explore a client's expectations of therapy, it is more the manner in which it is done than the act itself which accords respect. Respect is more an attitude that is conveyed by the therapist to the client, significant people in their world, and the choices and decisions that they have made in the past and canvass for the future.

AFFECT AND INTIMACY

A number of writers in recent years have recognized the failure of second-order theoreticians to include the emotional interac-tion of client and therapist in their calculations (Flaskas, 1989; Smith, Osman, & Goding, 1990). As the latter authors note, "much effort has been expended in trying to "do away with" or mini-mize the emotional impact of the family on the conceptual and interventive capacity of the therapist" (Smith et al., 1990, p. 140). Yet a recognition of the central place of the affective dimension is key to the work of Virginia Satir, who wrote of care, trust, and affection and placed compassion and the creation of a healing relationship as primary. Those systemic writers who have aimed to reintroduce the emotional dimension have also stressed its central place. James and Kirkland (1993) speak of one task of therapy as being "to replicate a healthy attachment experience; to provide clients with a secure base from which they can explore; to develop their capacity for empathy and for tolerating repre-sentation of intense and painful emotions. They include intimacy as one of three motives which are key to therapy" (p. 179). Flaskas (1989) urges the recognition of both client and therapist affect as a way of generating hypotheses and as a monitor of the process between them. This dimension was explored with each client.

> "I knew it was okay because she offered tissues, she accepted that emotion was okay."

> "I felt that she was in control, she acted ... very profession-ally, you know, she didn't burst into tears on me ... She didn't get really angry."

> "There was a lot of sadness and probably a lot of anger, too."

"She didn't say how she felt other than she would say things like it wasn't fair, was it, or I could see by her face ... I could see she was concerned that I was crying but we didn't stop work."

"Not crying, she didn't show her feelings ... She approved of me so much and I know that she likes me so and I could see it in her eyes, her demeanour when we were talking."

"Catherine just passed me the tissues ... Sometimes she just stopped for a while and let me have a little cry or take a break."

"I just couldn't have kept crying if she did, but I think she probably felt something ... Maybe she did feel quite joyful at times."

"Sometimes it was very distressing but I never felt like it was just cathartic bullshit."

"I think there were periods when for me it was very emotional and then there were other periods where it was more intellectual and that seemed like a reasonable balance."

"I don't want responsibility for someone else's stuff when I'm trying to sort out my stuff. I want them to be really clear and stay clear ... I think that as a therapist she has a responsibility not to show, even though it could be very hard, and I don't want my therapist to be crying and sobbing all over the place and lying on the floor ... She can go home and do that."

Questions around affect and its expression produced coherent responses. Each woman agreed that, for them, therapy had been a highly emotional experience and that the therapist had sanctioned their powerful affect. They were equally clear that while they believed the therapist had an appropriate emotional response to their experience, it was important that she did not express it. Each was adamant that the therapeutic domain was appropriately their own for emotional expression, and they did not want it complicated.

My own experience of this work was of a highly emotional and intimate interchange. My feelings ranged through deep compassion, sadness, distress, distaste, anger, and admiration. At times, I struggled with my own desire not to believe the extent of the horror presented to me or to cushion myself from the pain it had produced. However, my own belief is that these feelings were not appropriately displayed in the context of therapy, and it is my responsibility as therapist to contain them. This is not a view shared by all systemic therapists or enshrined in the literature, but reflects a personal belief.

CONCLUSIONS

As a practising therapist, it is heartening to note the high level of congruence between what therapists claim they do from a theoretical perspective and how these same principles are experienced by their clients. Each category explored produced a high level of congruence between the writer and therapist and the women with whom she worked. The exception was power and control, where these clients had a much less convoluted and fearful view than many therapists.

While these observations are of interest, they fail to recognize the central and indefinable place of the person who is the therapist, which seems to be beyond theory. Nichols (1987), in reviewing a conference with Gianfranco Cecchin and Maurizio Andolfi, reflects on the huge differences in practice of two therapists who would both be labelled as systemic. Atkinson and Heath (1990, p. 154) believe that "the personal habits of the therapist are more relevant than the particular model of therapy or class of techniques". A project similar to this one undertaken by Treadway (1991, p. 76) resulted in the observation that "what seems to be important is that we tried things, we cared deeply, and we never gave up". In reading the full transcript of the interviews, these are the elements that stand out. Clients are less impressed by intellectual brilliance and theoretical purity than by dogged persistence, patience, compassion, and optimism. They value a wider perspective than their own which can be safely and respectfully debated. The final word should go to one woman who after completing the interview returned to the therapist saying that she had been thinking about the conversation and wanted to add to it. On a separate piece of paper, she wrote that the therapist was "an ordinary person who asks clever questions and makes me feel safe to answer them."

Acknowledgements

I wish to acknowledge the skilful and sensitive interviewing of my colleague, Robyn Boord, and the women who so generously and freely spoke of their experiences. They each taught me a great deal.

REFERENCES AND BIBLIOGRAPHY

Atkinson, B., & Heath, A. (1990). Further thoughts on second-order family therapy—this time it's personal. *Family Process*, 29 (June), 145–155.

Conran, T., & Love, J. (1993). Client voices: unspeakable theories and unknowable experiences. *Journal of Strategic and Systemic Therapies* (Summer), 1–18.

Dell, P. (1989). Violence and the systemic view. *Family Process*, 28 (1), 1–14.

Flaskas, C. (1989). Thinking about the emotional interaction of therapist and family. *Australian & New Zealand Journal of Family Therapy*, 10 (1), 1–6.

Friedman, R. (1985). Making family therapy easier for the therapist: burnout prevention. *Family Process*, 24 (December), 549–553.

Golann, S. (1988). On second-order family therapy. *Family Process*, 27 (March), 51–71.

Hoffman, L. (1985). Beyond power and control: towards a second-order family systems theory. *Family Systems Medicine*, 3, 381–396. Also in *Exchanging Voices: A Collaborative Approach to Family Therapy*. London: Karnac Books, 1993.

James, L., & Kirkland, J. (1993). Beyond empathy—seasons of affiliation, intimacy and power in therapeutic relationships. *Australian & New Zealand Journal of Family Therapy*, 14 (4), 177–180.

Keeney, B., & Ross, J. (1985). *Mind in Therapy: Constructing Systemic Family Therapies*. New York: Basic Books.

Nichols, M. (1987). Neutrality or provocation: a conference with Gianfranco Cecchin and Maurizio Andolfi. *Networker* (January–February), 59–62.

Rogers, C. R. (1967). *On Becoming a Person*. London: Constable.

Silver, E. (1991). Should I give advice? A systemic view. *Journal of Family Therapy, 13,* 295–309.

Smith, J., Osman, C., & Goding, M. (1990). Reclaiming the emotional aspects of the therapist–family system. *Australian & New Zealand Journal of Family Therapy, 11* (3), 140–146.

Treadway, D. (1991). From Arete to Crow. *Journal of Strategic and Systemic Therapies, 10* (1), 66–77.

Weingarten, K. (1992). A consideration of intimate and non-intimate interactions in therapy. *Family Process, 31* (March), 45–59.

CHAPTER 9

Cross-purposes: relationship patterns in public welfare

Mark Furlong

INTRODUCTION

One hallmark of systemic theory, particularly second-order systemic theory, is its attention to the contextual relationships within which "personal" relationships occur. This attention has made it possible to move from the narrower lens of simply considering intra-familial relationships, to the wider lenses of considering the family in the context of the family–therapist relationship, the family–therapist system in the context of the network of "helping relationships" in which the therapy may be taking place, the structuring of relationships within the social domains of (for example) the health and welfare fields, and the dominant cultural ideas that govern how family relationships and, indeed, the activity of "therapy" are able to be constructed and enacted.

This chapter chooses to use these wider lenses in locating the patterns of difficulties that commonly emerge in public welfare practice. Rather than focusing on the therapist/family relationship *per se*, the focus is on the wider context, which is the venue for therapist/family relationships in this arena. In this way, public welfare practice becomes a "case study" for mapping a particular set of contextual relationships for the therapist/family system.

The chapter begins with a brief description of the "problematics" of public welfare, and a vignette is used to illustrate a set of tensions that people often face when working in this field. It then moves to an analysis of the context of these dilemmas, by considering the social position of "the family" and "the child", the ideological conflicts inherent in the field, and the common patterns of blame and volatility and confusion that ensue. It ends with a discussion of the person of the practitioner, and the leeway that is still possible for constructive therapeutic relationships in this field.

THE "PROBLEMATICS" OF PUBLIC WELFARE

In public welfare practice, it is rare that relationships between clients and practitioners are straightforward, regardless of whether the practitioner is a statutory child-protection worker or a "therapist".[1] Unlike the benign image of the therapeutic relationship depicted in counselling psychology texts, where a voluntary client meets with a benevolent expert towards the achievement of a mutual goal (Barber, 1991), public welfare clients do not usually put their hands up and request intervention. Because the contact between practitioners and clients in public welfare has a statutory basis, relationships develop within a particular and often antagonistic legal, cultural, and phenomenological context. This context tends to shape the meanings, emotions, and relationships that arise, even though clients and practitioners tend to perceive the problems that occur as being the result of the personal qualities of the individuals involved, rather than as the results of the context and the respective roles.

Using a systemic perspective to view the emotional experience of, and the relationships occurring between, participants in this field involves recognizing that there are likely to be particular perspectives and emotions associated with specific roles, agency mandates, and the like. It will be assumed that the intense emotions that occur will be "communicated" between professional participants as they are between children, their parents, substitute carers, and the community at large. The position of therapists is considered as one, but not the only, reference in what follows. If the generic term "practitioner" is used, this signals that statements are being made that are believed to be true for protective and therapeutic personnel alike.

Of necessity, work in public welfare is emotionally intense. It can be "vicariously traumatizing" (McCann & Pearlman, 1990) and over time may challenge one's basic assumptions. Not only do individual practitioners find themselves highly stressed, but relationships with clients, supervisors, immediate colleagues, and the range of practitioners with whom one works are emotionally loaded. Frequently, an atmosphere of crisis, of impotence and anger, seems to accompany the impossibility of everyday tasks. In this affective hothouse there can, at times, be a quality of contagion that neither adherence to procedures nor personal dedication can contain.

The families that practitioners meet are often as likeable as they are flawed, as admirable as they are damaged. Yet workers also see, and must respond to, the thoughtless insensitivity of some parents, as well as to occasional acts of cruelty committed against children by adults. One knows that parents do not set out to fail or intend to be unhelpful, but this belief seems to be contradicted by the everyday evidence of family failure, or even dangerousness. An awareness of this contradiction is intrinsic to understanding the subjectivity of practitioners and of the interprofessional relationships that develop. A brief vignette illustrates several of these tensions.

Case study 1:
Where you stand depends on where you sit

Kylie is a 10-year-old girl who has suffered consistent neglect with occasional episodes of violence from Meg—her head-injured and, occasionally, substance-abusing single mother. Kylie had twice previously been placed on a supervision order whilst remaining at home. After a third notification, Tom was assigned as the investigative worker. In court, Tom strongly advocated that Kylie be placed away from her mother Meg.

The children's court ignored this recommendation and decided that Kylie should remain with her mother and made this contingent on certain conditions being met—for example, individual counselling for Kylie and family therapy for the mother and daughter. Meg was relieved at this result yet also felt that she needed help but was not really going to get it. In his position Tom felt both angry and disconfirmed by this result: "I'll be the bunny who gets the blame if Kylie is hurt, but they don't even listen to what I say."

After a great deal of advocacy, Tom was able successfully to refer the family to Jane, a private therapist who did some work with families. Jane had mixed feelings about the referral but was committed to doing what she could for women and families. Two months later, and now three months after court, Tom heard from Meg, who told him that "I've got no help from the therapist". Tom again rang Jane, deeply concerned about Kylie's welfare and the fact that the court's orders were not being met, a fact of which his own supervisor kept reminding him. In this contact, Tom's frustration with Jane was not well disguised. Jane, whose time was extremely precious, felt attacked and unacknowledged. She had made a number of appointments with the family that they had not kept, and she believed she had just had a "breakthrough" with Meg when, over the telephone, Meg had told her that "I can't come in unless you make appointments just after pension day". When Jane communicated this hopefulness to Tom, a difficult discussion occurred about who had been "sucked in" and who was really acting in Kylie's long-term interest.

At this point, Tom was experiencing his own supervisor as punishing (just as Meg experienced him) and the family therapist as "precious" and "uncooperative"; Jane perceived Tom as punitive, even vindictive, whilst she saw Meg as a disempowered woman needing another chance. The mother saw the caseworker as dangerous because he might take her daughter away but, at least, as a straight talker, whilst she saw the family therapist as, at least for the moment, irrelevant. Each participant's perception was largely determined by their respective role position. Each of the relationships was emotionally charged, blaming yet somehow volatile, given that alliances might quickly shift—for example, if Meg were to align with Tom in blaming the family therapist.

These kinds of "cross-purposes" tend to structure relationships found within public welfare. A theme that is developed throughout this analysis is the emphasis that needs to be given to the worker's internal experience. I will argue that unless this experience is identified and affirmed, therapists and protective workers alike may inadvertently internalize or mirror the conflicts and contradictions they work within, to the detriment of their clients, of their own selves, and of the client–practitioner relationship.[2]

THE SOCIAL POSITION OF "THE FAMILY" AND "THE CHILD"

To understand child abuse and its meanings, it is necessary to consider the ambiguous social position occupied by families. On the one hand "the family" is broadly revered as an ideal of nurturing and selflessness, as a generator of opportunity and as a provider of financial and emotional security. The family is also seen to provide much of the raw material by defining one's identity and as an engine for the production of life-purpose, especially for parents. Yet it is the expectation that the family is a safe place. As a popular song, *Summertime,* by George Gershwhin says:

> "One of these mornin's, you goin' to rise up singin',
> Then you'll spread yo' wings an' you'll take to the sky.
> But til that mornin', there's a nothin' can harm you
> With daddy an' mammy standin' by."

This positive symbolic image of what the family should be is, at least when individual families are seen as less than perfect, complemented by a community impulse to look critically at those families who are not up to the (impossible to realize) standard.[3] For the same reason that guilt, as well as pride, is a feature of parenthood, the condemnation of families is always just around the corner. Popular culture attributes a wide variety of phenomena to family insufficiency—for example, an individual child's bad behaviours, lack of confidence, poor academic results, negative self-image. In addition, broad social problems are often considered by the media and others to be the result of collective "family dysfunction"—for example, delinquency, poor work habits, alienation, violence (Carpenter, 1993). "The family" is an intensely positive icon in society, yet "the family" is also an often-used default option for the allocation of blame.

Almost twenty years ago, Lasch suggested that the family was a "haven in a heartless world" (Lasch, 1977). Without wishing to support the patriarchal nostalgia for which this work has been criticized, for a majority of citizens it is true that "the family" is broadly perceived as a wellspring in a desert. If this fount is found to be a kind of poisoned well which sickens rather than nourishes, then a sense of disturbance and outrage will be evoked. Moreover, if families are supposed to be safe and nourishing, the young child is regarded as the embodiment of what is good. Children, and particularly "the child", are viewed in a positive, perhaps even iconic light. Children are that which is vulnerable, innocent, and of new and unspoilt possibility. Children who are defiled by battering or sexual abuse, especially if this is perpetrated by those who are entrusted to be the child's care-givers, cannot help but produce intense indignation and a belief that urgent and decisive action must be taken.

If the position, so far, is clear for the community, it is far less clear for parents and child victims—and from a parent's point of view, it is hard to overestimate the trauma that is felt if the label of "neglectful" or "abusive" is pointed at you by a community representative. Before moving to an analysis of how parents might react to such a shaming accusation, several further ideological conflicts of Western society need to be noted.

THE ENVIRONMENT OF CROSS-PURPOSES: SOME FURTHER IDEOLOGICAL CONFLICTS

As well as noting the symbolic social position given to "the child" and "the family", there are also some fundamental ideological conflicts invoked by child abuse which play a key role in forming the environment within which public welfare practice takes place. As well as ambiguities in relation to definition (Hutchison, 1990), broader conflicts include:

1. *Incongruent community beliefs about the integrity of families:* Many conservative spokespersons believe that families have an inviolate right to privacy and that "big brother" should stay out. Others believe that this is the first generation that has the opportunity to really tackle child abuse and that this must be done to ensure the rights of children.
2. *Changing community premises about what is best for children:* It was only recently that public policy authorized the transportation of orphaned children to Australia from the United Kingdom and removed Australian aboriginal children from their families. At present, public opinion and public policy tends towards a greater respect for "family preservation", yet there is also a clear community discomfort with the idea that some parents do injure or even kill their children.
3. *Incompatible community impulses to assist and to censor parents:* For example, our media godparents often advocate that "bad" parents should be punished by having their children removed. However, other experts say the opposite.
4. *Community confusion as to what constitutes child abuse:* "If you spare the rod, you'll spoil the child" is still a common belief, yet corporal punishment can be grounds for state investigation. At the extreme end, child abuse is self-evident, yet judgements about what is less "extreme" abuse is very much in the eye of the beholder. Critics of current public policy say that these "judgements" have become the province of a patronizing middle class and, as such, public welfare practice amounts to a kind of class warfare.

Of necessity, agencies established to respond to child abuse operate within the tensions that arise from the conflicts noted above. Somehow workers have to both support families and correct them if they are wrong. The conflicting imperatives for action that follow from these different premises cannot be logically clarified; they are not the product of muddled thinking, or of unprofessional and unfocused agency planning. It has been argued that the collective impact of these incongruent premises constitutes a practice environment that is essentially contradictory rather than "just" unclear (Healy, 1985, 1988; Healy & Springfall, 1988).

Other characteristics of public welfare compound these difficulties. Statutes and court procedures generally lag behind, or are in considerable tension with, currently held specialist practitioner and pressure group opinion in relation to, for example, the laws of evidence in sexual abuse cases. Public welfare is also daily fare for the sensationalist media, which bay for blood when public welfare staff are supposedly irresponsible in marching in to an innocent family with their jackboots, and bay for blood when an innocent child has been irresponsibly left unprotected (Valentine, 1994). Sadly, it is inevitable that public welfare staff cannot ensure the safety, let alone the longer-term welfare, of each child who comes to their attention.

Moreover, the uncertainty of current practice methods is such that effective help for children and their families cannot be guaranteed even if goals could be clarified and adequate resources were available (Hasenfeld & English, 1974; Jones & May, 1992). What organizational theorists have termed the "indeterminacy" of public welfare practice is highlighted here for its relevance to the aim of making understandable the conflicted emotions and relationships found in public welfare, not as an argument for non-intervention. What would it do to your equilibrium if, as a protective worker or therapist, your primary client said "you have just made it worse", despite your best efforts to be caring and committed? The vexed nature of public welfare establishes an environment within which attributions of blame flourish.

CROSS-PURPOSES: PATTERNS OF BLAME

The casting of blame is a key feature within public welfare. Disagreement, or even dispute, may occur about who is "really at fault", but it is almost always true that practitioners and clients will be blaming someone, as will the courts, the media, and the public.

To turn first to the practitioner's perspective in the patterning of blame. The thought that a child's parent(s) might have allowed, let alone have directly committed, an act of abuse when a parent's role is to nurture and protect is bound to disturb. Mixed reactions of anger (perhaps even hate), impotence, horror and shock, revulsion, and numbness are entirely natural. As workers are operating within particular roles that require them to pursue defined (albeit often contradictory) goals, it is necessary to "do something" with these feelings. Given this imperative, practitioners need a stance that can both distance what is so emotionally distressing and which can also introduce a sense of conceptual closure. In these circumstances, the option of blaming is always attractive (Furlong & Young, 1995).

Blame is at once a feeling, a thought, and a behaviour. If a practitioner is at some level blaming of a child's parents, this is likely to affect the initial relationship. As contact with the child's parents develops, a practitioner may begin to feel an empathy for the "unfit" parent which may be substituted for the blame or, more confusingly, may stand with the blame. In contact with parents one often develops a deeper relationship within which it is untenable simply to blame. In most situations, it is intellectually obvious that simply blaming the neglectful, or even offending, parent is neither appropriate nor helpful. In this situation it is still true that the child's pain and vulnerability is disturbing and must be the focus of attention. Yet the child may wish to be with the "abuser", the "abuser" may insist that the child be returned, or, perhaps more poignantly, the "guilty" parent(s) may not want or feel able to have the child returned.

These emotionally difficult scenarios take place against a background in which the public in general, and protective service hierarchies in particular, insist that something should be done and that mistakes must not be made. Also, the practitioner is likely to be in an environment where linkages between service components are structurally and ideologically poor, and where protective and publicly funded therapeutic services are chronically under-resourced. Thus, as Tom found in the earlier vignette, if a protective worker tries to refer to community-based supportive and therapeutic services, she or he may find it difficult to be patient if these services do not immediately accept a referral. Therapeutic staff, like Jane in the vignette, tend to talk in terms of "therapeutic engagement", "currently our waiting list is eight weeks", and so forth. From the statutory agent's point of view, such responses are likely to be interpreted as "precious", "elitist", "uncooperative", or even "irresponsible"—that is, as blameworthy.

Therapeutic staff, in turn, often feel pressured and misunderstood by statutory workers. Differences in organizational and professional culture between therapists and protective workers can result in these groups acting as apparently antagonistic tribes (Furlong, 1989). Rather than affirming the need for interdependence, colleagueship, and collaboration (Hallett & Stevenson, 1980; Robinson, 1986), a pattern of mutual denigration between protective and therapeutic staff can occur. As Tom and Jane found in the vignette, there are many "invitations" to be blaming.

The question of blame is also central to the experience of parents involved in public welfare. Issues around blame can remain disputed throughout the stages of initial investigation, court hearings (which can extend over a protracted time with adjournments, appeals, and the like), into the period of post-court supervision. At the level of "lived experience" (Schutz, 1972), parents become fundamentally concerned with questioning their own adequacy and culpability: "Have I been a bad father/mother?" "Should we be judged wrong?" As Meg found in the vignette, being a parent before a children's court risks what is so important to retain. It is even worse if there is a court declaration of the parent(s) as "neglectful" or "unfit", as this kind of declaration is a formal and highly significant disqualification.

Disqualification leaves only two broad stances available to those parents:

1. A parent can become adversary and "resistant", and dispute the decision by blaming the court or (more likely) the relevant protective services staff for causing the problem. This "blame-them" reaction inhibits change and the development of an alliance with practitioners as parents righteously dig in

2. Alternatively, a parent can be "compliant" by accepting the

court decision in terms of blaming her/himself. This "blame me" reaction also inhibits change, as it suggests hopelessness and dependence.

Thus, the dynamics of an adversarial court process tend to suffuse all participants in a tangle of blame that is prescriptive of the kinds of relationships that are established post-court.

CROSS-PURPOSES: PATTERNS OF VOLATILITY AND CONFUSION

In addition to the patterns of blame, a feature of public welfare practice is the quality of volatility. The ground sometimes just seems to shift beneath one's feet. Several papers have noted that radical re-definitions of role can occur in public welfare (Carr, 1989; Ney, 1988). "Victims", such as sexually abused children, can suddenly be understood as "rescuers" when they re-unite the family; "rescuers", such as therapists, can find themselves treated as "persecutors" when therapy is experienced by the client as intrusive and overpowering (Durrant & Kowalski, 1990); "investigators", such as pre-court caseworkers, can find themselves investigated by the media; and so on. Carr (1989) and Ney (1988) favour particular conceptualizations for explaining this phenomenon, yet the fact that such events can take place at all is itself disturbing and tends to distribute a sense of "provisionality" to relationships (Boulet, 1989). Dramatic re-appraisals of meaning lead participants to doubt what is ordinarily assumed—that there is consensus and stability in definitions of reality. Participants who have previously been through the "looking-glass" and experienced these "crazy" events do not seem to regard these inversions of meanings as intrinsically bizarre. Rather, such radical shifts are accepted as inevitable if not as comfortable.

Fragility in terms of definitions of meaning and relationship is particularly prominent in work with the sexually abused. The practitioner's disgust for the perpetrator, combined with anguish regarding the effects of such behaviours, can make it hard for practitioners to make space for the survivor to express the many "lost positives", rather than simply the anger, which is so much part of the recovery process.[4] The emotional connectedness that often persists between the survivor and the perpetrator in the subjectivity of the victim can be too terrible for the helper to countenance.

In the disturbed and disturbing territory of sexual abuse, practitioners can also feel compromised because means and ends can become confused. Which side of the moral fence are we really on when the grooming of a victim could be seen to find a (part) parallel in the sensitive leading of the "denying" man towards the acknowledgement of his abuse? This, in turn, is a parallel with the sensitive work done towards maintaining a disclosure that a victim understandably may now wish to take back. Collaboration is a term with a positive professional valence, yet collaboration in times of war is a crime: you lie down with dogs and you wake up with fleas.[5]

What are the consequences of these blaming, unpredictable, and compromising phenomena on the patterns of relationships found in public welfare? One consequence is a tendency for practitioners to default to "black-and-white" relationships. Battles and battle-lines occur with regularity between, for example, parents and public welfare staff, and between therapists and protective staff. In these symmetrical relationships, participants exchange the same affects, behaviours, and experiences: the more I feel blamed, the more I blame; the more I see that I have been disqualified, the more I disqualify (Bateson, 1972). Once such vicious cycles are established, polarizations may become entrenched (Wenders, 1968). "Good" is seen to be embodied in one and in one's tribe, "bad" is embodied in the other. Feelings of righteousness and a constriction of the capacity to empathize accompany these feud-like patterns. "Complex thinking" retreats, as "dichotomous thinking" takes charge (Berlin, 1990).

THE LEEWAY FOR CONSTRUCTIVE RELATIONSHIPS AND THE PERSON OF THE PRACTITIONER

Despite the difficulties outlined above, participants can develop a positive alliance enabling constructive work to be done. The "co-ordinated management of meaning" framework outlined by

Pearce and Cronen (1980) provides one "lens" for understanding how this might occur. This framework suggests that the implicatory force of what is said and done between participants in the here-and-now may, over time, redefine the meanings derived from higher-level connotative expectations. For example, if parents have viewed the state and its representatives as adversaries, they will tend to interpret suspiciously what is said ("I want to help you") and what is done ("we meet in their office") in a way that is consistent with the connotations of an adversarial relationship. Over time, it is possible that what is said and done may challenge this adversarial definition to the point where the relationship might be redefined as "partnership" or even "friendship".[6] Fortunately, there are many examples of this kind of re-creation of meaning and relationship definition in public welfare, and the following vignette gives a flavour of this kind of change in the practice environment.

Case study 2:
Promoting confidence in the relationship
without promising confidentiality

June, a mother of three, and her current partner were explicitly hostile to each statutory worker and therapist they had encountered in the three years since they first attended the children's court. When a new caseworker met the couple to discuss the possibility of the two youngest children returning home, she offered the family (another) referral to a family counselling centre. "It will just be the same as before—you'll all talk behind our backs, I can't trust any of you" was June's dismissive retort. "Yes, we will talk", said the caseworker, "but I will ensure that you two know what will be said by me to the therapist before it is said. I'll also make sure the therapist does the same."

In a series of meetings, letters, and telephone calls that continued throughout the "support" that was forced upon the family, the caseworker and the therapist persisted with their plan to regulate information exchange painstakingly. Particularly through a notification that the therapist made to the caseworker, which was discussed in detail with the mother and step-father before it was made, the expectation of untrustworthiness was challenged and eventually redefined. June said to the caseworker a month after the notification episode: "I still reckon you're all bastards, but you two might be a bit different."

Examples of the re-creation of the practice environment may appear simple, yet they are achieved with difficulty and require both therapeutic and protective workers to "hold against" the negative patterns so easily engendered in the atmosphere of cross-purposes. It has been noted that the child care/child protection system can inadvertently "replicate functional and dysfunctional family patterns in their interactions (between service components) and with the children and families whom they service" (Swartzman & Kneifel, 1985, p. 87). As in "dysfunctional" families, the system can be punitive, can be casually violent, seems at times capricious in its decision making, makes decisions and does not enforce them, and can even be neglectful. One can also observe that practitioners can experience a kind of critical scrutiny from their superiors that distinctly parallels the experience of parents involved with the mandated supervision of their performance by statutory staff. These kinds of "parallel processes" (Smith, Osman, & Goding, 1990) are familiar to those who work in or around public welfare.

It has been argued that public welfare is inevitably embedded in contradictions, and as such it is impossible to avoid parallel processes completely. Perhaps this tends to occur as the contradictions found in public welfare seem to mirror uncannily the antagonistic forces inherent in family life—that is, the concurrent impulses to nurture and to control, the need to care and to discipline, the desire to be an individual and also to belong, and the presence of good intentions and negative results. If this is so, mindful of the broader contradictions noted earlier, it seems likely that professional practice within public welfare will evoke primary and conflictual aspects of family life within the subjectivity of the practitioner.

What is it that determines whether a practitioner internalizes or behaviourally mirrors this emotionally intense work? What determines whether the relationships established by practitioners with clients and colleagues will be effective or uncontained, collaborative or adversary? An important factor relevant to these questions is the person of the practitioner. When one works with a particular public welfare client, there may only be one child in the spotlight but many children on the stage. Workers are constantly faced with their own feelings and identifications with particular children and families. This may be overtly clear to workers in some situations, but it may also be at play in an implicit way.

There is almost always an aspect (or aspects) of a presenting situation that causes one to land on one's hip, that knocks on one's emotional glass jaw. It is not a question of whether this occurs, but rather the question for the practitioner is: "How will I identify and deal with these associations as they inevitably occur?" Organizational issues will significantly mediate the practitioner's capacity to attend to this question—for example, is supportive, rather than casual or punitive, supervision and case consultation available?

There are many opportunities for personal and professional growth that training and supervision in public welfare practice can facilitate. It is important, if under-acknowledged, work and taking it seriously is necessarily also taking it personally. Being aware that panic (like enthusiasm) is contagious, and that to be immune to it is to be inhuman, is to become better qualified professionally. One cannot keep one's head when all around are losing theirs, yet, paradoxically, once one becomes practised at noticing these phenomena, one's equilibrium is less at risk.

CONCLUSION

Rather than considering the therapeutic relationship in isolation from the network of other professional relationships in welfare, this chapter has given attention to the common cultural beliefs and ideological conflicts that create the environment of cross-purposes in public welfare. The dynamic of blame, and the qualities of volatility and confusion, are inevitable in the patterning of the relationships that come to exist between clients and practitioners, and in the wider organizational and social responses to public welfare work. In considering the leeway that exists for constructive therapeutic relationships, the person of the practitioner stands as one of the crucial mediators. Indeed, the person who is the practitioner stands to experience both the trauma of this area of work and the personal and professional growth that comes from being able to step outside the destructive parallel processes that so often shape relationships in this field. The chapter began by signalling the space that systemic theory gives to the wider social and relational contexts of the therapeutic relationship. The discussion and analysis of public welfare practice which has been developed here is an attempt to begin to fill in that space.

Acknowledgements

The material presented in this chapter is taken from direct experiences and from a recently completed postgraduate thesis. Particular ideas have been developed by the author and two colleagues, Pam Rycroft and Jenny Dwyer, who worked as a team for several years. Ideas expressed in relation to sexual abuse are very significantly influenced by a group of colleagues who work as a specialist team in this area. Jeff Young deserves special thanks for the material on blame. Sarah Jones and the editors were of great assistance with the final text.

NOTES

1. The term "public welfare" is used to encompass the field of statutory/mandated child welfare practice; that is, all investigative, protective, case management, judicial, and administrative activities undertaken on behalf of the relevant child safety acts, including circumstances where such acts might be invoked. Intra-national, as well as international, differences between public welfare settings need to be acknowledged as it is incorrect to assume that "like" settings are in fact identical when cultural, legislative, organizational, and practice specifics significantly affect what differentially occurs. Nonetheless, for the purposes of this exercise, it will be suggested that first-world public welfare practice demonstrates commonalities across distinct environments in terms of the emotional and interactional patterns encountered.

2. The author is not attempting to explore the mechanisms via which emotions are "communicated" between persons. Flaskas (1989, 1994) and Smith et al. (1990) theorize in relation to this question. For the current

purpose it is proposed simply to accept that emotional exchanges do in fact occur.

3. This conflicted attitude to families at least partly reflects, if not is actually constituted by, the social position of women. For example, motherhood is idealized, yet if something has gone wrong with a child, or even the husband, the mother somehow ends up bearing the blame. James and McKinnon (1990) have discussed this idea in relation to incest, and Chess (1982) and Caplan and Hall-McCorquodale (1985) in relation to mental illness.

4. Doka (1988) talks of "disenfranchised grief" in relation to situations where (for a variety of reasons) the identification and legitimacy of grief is negated. The "loss" of the relationship with the (abusing) father, the "loss" of the feeling of normality that disclosure often entails, and the "loss" of the idealization of family unity are important feelings for survivors, as are their feelings of rage and betrayal. (Miller, 1995)

5. Within the possibilities of the current exercise it is not feasible to examine the many specific themes that arise in the "sub-fields" of public welfare: for example, that gender issues are intensified in work with, even in discussion about, sexual abuse; that acting-out, self-destructive adolescents make both parents and professionals feel useless.

6. I am not advocating that "friendship" is desirable, or even possible, between practitioners and their clients. Rather, I wish to note that feelings of affection and closeness can arise and need to be reflected upon, as do feelings of anger and blame.

REFERENCES

Barber, J. (1991). *Beyond Casework*. Basingstoke: Macmillan.

Bateson, G. (1972). *Steps Toward An Ecology of Mind*. New York: Ballantyne Books.

Berlin, S. (1990). Dichotomous and complex thinking. *Social Service Review* (March), 46–59.

Boulet, J. (1989). Societal aspects of child abuse: politics, the media and public opinion, or how NOT to deal with responsibility. *Ninth Annual Congress of the Australian and New Zealand Association of Psychiatry, Psychology and the Law* (unpublished paper).

Caplan, P., & Hall-McCorquodale, I. (1985). Mother blaming in major clinical journals. *American Journal of Orthopsychiatry*, 55, 345–353.

Carpenter, J. (1992). What's the use of family therapy? *Australian and New Zealand Journal of Family Therapy*, 13 (1), 26–32.

Carr, A. (1989). Countertransference to families where child abuse has occurred. *Journal of Family Therapy, 11,* 87–97.

Chess, S. (1982). The "blame the mother" ideology. *International Journal of Mental Health, 11,* 95–107.

Doka, K. (1988). *Disenfranchised Grief: Recognising Hidden Sorrow.* Lexington, MA: Lexington Books.

Durrant, M., Durrant, I., & Kowalski, K. (1990). Overcoming the effects of sexual abuse: developing a self-perception of competence. In: M. Durrant & C. White (Eds.), *Ideas for Therapy with Sexual Abuse.* Adelaide: Dulwich Centre Publications.

Flaskas, C. (1989). Thinking about the emotional interaction of therapist and family. *Australian and New Zealand Journal of Family Therapy, 10* (1), 1–6.

Flaskas, C. (1994). Exploring the therapeutic relationship: a case study. *Australian and New Zealand Journal of Family Therapy, 15* (4), 185–190.

Furlong, M. (1989). Can a family therapist do statutory work? *Australian and New Zealand Journal of Family Therapy, 10* (4), 211–218.

Furlong, M., & Young, J. (1995). *Blame it on Cain.* Unpublished manuscript, Melbourne.

Hallett, C., & Stevenson, O. (1980). *Child Abuse: Aspects of Interprofessional Co-operation.* London: Allen and Unwin.

Hasenfeld, Y., & English, R. (1974). *Human Service Organizations.* Ann Arbor, MI: University of Michigan Press.

Healy, W. (1985). Social work in public welfare: contradictions in practice. In: D. McIntyre (Ed.), *Delivering the Goods: Promoting Practice Standards in Social Work (Proceedings of Nineteenth Conference of the AASW),* pp. 103–108.

Healy, W. (1988). Confronting disadvantage through social justice: the case of public welfare. In: E. Chamberlain (Ed.), *Change and Continuity in Social Work Practice* (pp. 81–90). Melbourne: Longman Cheshire.

Healy, W., & Springfall, J. (1988). The forgotten fieldworker: a challenge for social work education. In: R. Berreen, D. Grace, D. James, & T. Vinson (Eds.), *Advances in Social Welfare Education.* Sydney: University of N.S.W. Press.

Hutchison, E. (1990). Child maltreatment: can it be defined? *Social Service Review* (March), 60–78.

James, K., & MacKinnon, L. (1990). The "incestuous" family revisited: a critical analysis of family therapy myths. *Journal of Marital and Family Therapy, 16* (1), 71–88.

Jones, A., & May, J. (1992). *Working in Human Service Organisations*. Melbourne: Longman Cheshire.

Lasch, C. (1977). *Haven in a Heartless World*. New York: Basic Books.

McCann, L., & Pearlman, L. (1990). Vicarious traumatization: a framework for understanding the psychological effects of working with victims. *Journal of Traumatic Stress, 3* (1), 131–138.

Miller, R. (1995). *Recognising the Trauma Experienced by Sexual Abuse Survivors Post Disclosure: A "Both–And" Response*. Unpublished manuscript, Melbourne.

Ney, P. (1988). Triangles of abuse: a model of maltreatment. *Child Abuse and Neglect, 12*, 363–373.

Pearce, W., & Cronen, V. (1980). *Communication, Action and Meaning*. New York: Praeger.

Robinson, M. (1986). *Working with the Broader System*. Workshop presentation, Melbourne.

Schutz, A. (1972). *The Phenomenology of the Social World*. London: Heinemann.

Schwartzman, H., & Kneifel, A. (1985). Familiar institutions: how the child care system replicates family patterns. In: J. Schwartzman (Ed.), *Families and Other Systems: The Macrosystemic Context of Family Therapy* (pp. 87–107). New York: Guilford.

Smith, J., Osman, C., & Goding, M. (1990). Reclaiming the emotional aspects of the therapist–family system. *Australian and New Zealand Journal of Family Therapy, 11* (3): 140–146.

Valentine, M. (1994). The social worker as "bad object". *British Journal of Social Work, 24*, 71–86.

Wenders, P. (1968). Vicious and virtuous circles: the role of deviance amplifying feedback in the origin and perpetuation of behaviour. *Psychiatry, 31*, 312–313.

CHAPTER 10

Personal relationships in systemic supervision

Banu Moloney and Lawrie Moloney

INTRODUCTION

In this chapter, we consider systemic supervision and the importance of an understanding of the personal nature of the experience for both supervisor and supervisee. The chapter begins with a general discussion of the interpersonal nature of supervision and then moves to a description of four cases of supervision. These descriptions invoke the issues of the personal involvement of the therapist and supervisor in meeting the clients' situations, and raise the accompanying issues of emotions, parallel process, transference, trust and respect, self-awareness, and self-disclosure. The cases become the springboard for a wider discussion of the personal in systemic therapy and of concepts that have been used to describe systemic patterns and personal interaction.

THE INTERPERSONAL NATURE OF SUPERVISION

Most definitions of supervision emphasize its interpersonal nature. Hess (1980), for example, defines supervision as:

> a quintessential interpersonal interaction with the general goal that one person, the supervisor meets with another person, the supervisee in an effort to make the latter more effective in helping people. [p. 25]

Loganbill, Hardy, and Dellworth (1982) include within their definition the terms "intensive", "interpersonally focused", "one-to-one relationship".

Hawkins and Shohet (1989) suggest that all supervisory activity can be divided in the first instance into two areas—"two interlocking systems". The first is the *therapy system* in which the supervisee and supervisor pay attention to therapist and client(s), reflecting together on reports, notes, tape recordings, and so on. The second is the *supervisory system* in which consideration is given to how therapy is reflected in the here-and-now experiences of the supervisory process.

Hawkins and Shohet divide each of these areas into a further three sub-categories. The *therapy system* contains reflection on content, exploration of strategies, and exploration of the therapeutic relationship. The *supervisory system* focuses on the therapist's "transference", the here-and-now issues between supervisor and supervisee, and the supervisor's "countertransference". Like many other writers in the supervision field, Hawkins and Shohet assume a developmental stance in which the relationship between supervisee and supervisor progresses through stages of increasing sophistication. Though they believe that all six stages should be present in high-quality supervision, they liken the achievement of this (presumably for both supervisor and supervisee) to learning piano scales of increasing complexity before putting together the final piece.

Systemic theories have the capacity to offer a challenging critique of the incremental/developmental notions that dominate the supervision literature. However, in a critical review of family therapy supervision, Everett and Koerpel (1986) conclude that the level of theoretical enquiry and research has not kept pace with broader developments in the field. They believe that, in general, family therapy supervision is fragmented and lacking in an integrative theory. Earlier reviews (Everett, 1979, 1980; Liddle & Halpin, 1978) make similar points.

Everett and Koerpel suggest that the majority of family therapy supervision literature falls within the category of techniques and procedures. Of particular interest with respect to the present enquiry is the obverse of this conclusion—an almost complete absence of reference to the supervisory relationship in family therapy supervision. It is as if the second half of supervisory models such as that of Hawkins and Shohet is almost completely missing.

In the four cases presented below, we invite the reader to consider the usefulness of holding in tension the need to attend to systemic supervisory tasks whilst simultaneously monitoring the development of an open and respectful supervisor–supervisee relationship. In the first three cases, the supervisees, each of whom is working with the first author, are at quite different stages of sophistication in their understanding of systemic therapy. In the fourth case, the first author is being supervised "live" by one of her peers.

We agree with Ronnestad and Skovholt's (1993) suggestion that supervision should involve a process of "facilitative reflection", which generates concurrent creativity, curiosity, exploration, and integration. But we note that their own research into supervision practice suggests that the experience of novice counsellors fell far short of this ideal. Instead, the supervisees studied by Ronnestad and Skovholt became increasingly rigid, clinging to an external skills focus as a method of survival. Earlier research in Australia by Stolk and Perlesz (1990) uncovered a similar pattern in trainee therapists.

A study by Geer (1994) also reports that novice therapists expressed a desire for structure and instruction. In Geer's study, however, the most popular supervisory activity was work as a member of a reflecting team. It is clear from Geer's study that the reflecting team afforded these novice therapists the opportunity to attend to the relationship between supervisor and supervisee. It reinforced an important notion that personal and therapeutic power derives from the generation of options and that the generation of options is facilitated by trusting, interpersonal relationships. Geer speaks of one supervisee who, within the context of a reflecting team, was able to hear feedback for the first time without appearing to feel threatened: "I focused on listening", she said. "There was no need to explain or defend myself."

As in therapy, a central task in supervision is to find ways of helping supervisees to listen to themselves—to find in themselves things that, at one level, they already know. But in the anxiety and considerable complexity of family work, this task is constantly in danger of being obscured. We suggest that amongst other things, the cases described below demonstrate that systemic sophistication offers no guarantee for either supervisor or supervisee against historically and emotionally driven blocks and blind spots. For the success of the enterprise, much depends on the experience of the supervisor in combination with her capacity to create an environment of mutual trust, curiosity, and respect.

FOUR PRACTICE EXAMPLES FROM SYSTEMIC SUPERVISION

Case study 1:
Sally

Sally, a new supervisee, seeks systemic supervision for her clinical work. She has psychology qualifications but no formal training in working with couples or families.

She brings to supervision a couple with whom she has just commenced working and speaks of their presenting issues. Dianne has been married previously and has two teenage daughters. Omar, a refugee from the Middle East, has not been married before and comes from a large, traditionally patriarchal family. He is in the process of getting his qualifications recognized in Australia.

The issues they bring to therapy are around the non-acceptance of Omar's fathering by Diane's older teenage daughter. Omar, in turn, has difficulty in allowing children so much room in the family to negotiate. These issues are affecting the couple's relationship. Omar is reluctant to bring the children to therapy as he feels they should not be involved in adult affairs. The children are also reluctant to attend.

It is clear that from Sally's formulation and conceptualization of the issues, the supervisor needs to coach her to ask questions that are consistent with a systemic theoretical framework. At the same time, Sally and the supervisor must work together within a developing relationship. A failure to acknowledge and monitor the relationship is not only indicative of poor teaching, but would also imply in this case that the relationship between Sally and her clients is not important.

Within supervision, the feelings Sally is identifying in herself as a therapist are incompetence, frustration, and anxiety. It is, of course, consistent with her own inexperience that she sees the family as stuck, difficult, and continually looking to the therapist for answers that she does not have. Moreover, she feels certain that were she more experienced and clever, she would surely have the right solutions for this family. For their part, the newly formed, cross-cultural step-family feel that they lack the necessary expertise and need to be told what to do by the therapist.

Sally would listen to her supervisor and leave each supervision session as if armed with a well-loaded gun. Despite this, she was feeling increasingly dissatisfied and did not seem to progress to a point of being able to think about the case for herself. She was not getting closer to the couple. Indeed, her dread of sessions with them became more pronounced. The couple would faithfully return with the message that nothing had changed. "Could Sally give them better ideas?" Inevitably, the couple also moved towards the experience of frustration, stuckness, and incompetence in both the therapeutic relationship and in their own lives. The stage was now set for a potentially problematic dynamic. Just as Sally felt that the family was looking to her for the answers, the supervisor also experienced Sally as looking to her to simply instruct her with respect to the right interventions for the family.

Gradually, Sally's feelings about her therapeutic efforts became feelings about herself in the wider domain. Towards the end of a supervisory session, she declared, "I'm not doing so well myself as a step-parent. I sometimes think I shouldn't be making any suggestions to this couple when I'm so stuck in my own life."

Sally herself is a parent in a step-family situation, and the supervisor encouraged her to speak of the joys and frustrations of relating to her step-child. For Sally to respond to this invitation, the supervisor recognized that it was critical for a relationship of trust to have been established between herself and the supervisee. Though personal in nature, these were not issues for which Sally required or was seeking therapy. On the other hand, had they not been recognized and given a voice within a genuinely supportive environment, Sally's feelings of incompetence and frustration would have eventually sabotaged the learning process. As she spoke, the supervisor was able to connect emotionally with Sally's world by recalling and sharing aspects of her own family of origin, also a step-family. Like her supervisor, Sally began to become un-stuck as the feelings were recognized, commented upon, and mutually explored.

In this case, the feelings of frustration reflected in both directions within the supervisory space paralleled feelings of frustration in Sally's life, in the therapy process, and, in turn, in the relationship between the couple. In a classic Rogerian manner, giving voice to the feelings allowed space for the rediscovery of past and present competencies. Only then could Sally see and address the strengths the couple was bringing to therapy. This, we would suggest, represents a critical meeting point between systems and feelings.

A case such as this is complicated by the fact that the supervisor *does* know considerably more about the theory and practice of systemic work than does her supervisee. An important question in such a case becomes one of how to teach respectfully. The tension that the supervisor must hold is the simultaneous recognition that she has knowledge in the domain of systemic theory which her supervisee does not possess. At the same time, like the family brought to supervision, she and her supervisee bring their own equally valid competencies and experiences with respect to relationships and families.

Like classic Rogerian therapy, much contemporary systemic work aims to put clients back in touch with competencies they had failed to recognize or had forgotten. We believe that this can never be a mechanical exercise. Our view is that when stuckness in therapy is reflected in stuckness within supervision (or vice versa), the supervisor–supervisee relationship is always worthy of attention. In this case, the constraints to discovering the already existing competencies that would free the supervisee/therapist and her clients are embedded in unspoken or unrecognized fears and projections between supervisor and supervisee.

Step by step (if the reader will permit the pun), Sally was now able to invite her clients to work collaboratively as problem-solvers rather than set herself up as the expert in relation to their predicament. She was able to share with Diane and Omar some of her own frustrations as a step-parent. This was a much better point from which to engage them in a discussion about cultural differences and the difficult issue of a traditional patriarchal stance. Re-engaged with her own personal creativity, Sally could invite her clients to see the strength of their own achievements. Sally was now herself more open to exploring areas in which she would need to read more and gain more practical experience.

Case study 2:
Shirley

Shirley has been in supervision for almost eighteen months. She has a good working knowledge of systemic frameworks and uses these in her work with individuals, couples, and families. Although she likes working with families, she finds them somewhat overwhelming. Nonetheless, she decided to take on a job as a family therapist in a community health centre. She is excited by the families she is presented with in her agency. The majority of her clients are single-parent families with adolescent children.

In supervision, Shirley begins to adopt a somewhat dejected and defeated manner. She likes her clients, but lately she has started to feel that she is not getting anywhere with them. The families keep coming but at the same time report no change. The adolescents are running away from home, and the mothers are in despair. Shirley has begun to question her effectiveness as a therapist.

At about this time, Shirley was two weeks away from returning to England to meet up with her family of origin. She had had a troubled relationship with her parents, particularly with her mother. In the past few years she had made several attempts to "make peace" with her mother and had supported her at a time of conflict with her father. Shirley's mother nonetheless continued to feel rejected and abandoned by her. This time, when Shirley had written home to announce her visit, her mother had written back to say that there may not be enough room in their home for her to stay.

In speaking of her experiences with her family of origin and her sense of hopelessness that she will ever be accepted for having "run away" to Australia, Shirley became overwhelmed by a sense of futility at trying to effect change. In acknowledging this, she could also see that her own pleasure and enjoyment at having brought up two adolescents as a single parent made her feel more aligned with the adolescents and more frustrated with the mothers' complaints. She was resistant to being reminded of tough times.

During this period, the supervisor was aware that she wanted to hold Shirley and nurture her. In the language of transference and countertransference, Shirley was projecting wished-for maternal qualities onto her supervisor, and her supervisor was responding. In Searles' (1955) formulation, it would be expected that the information contained in this recognition would be directly explored within the supervisee–supervisor relationship. In this case, however, the supervisor used it as a cue for further exploration of Shirley's family of origin—an exploration that led to an acknowledgement of Shirley's deep-seated wish that, during her visit to England, her mother would literally and emotionally find room for her. She would acknowledge her by recognizing her life choices, her migration to Australia, and her skills as a counsellor. Most importantly, she would love and nurture her.

Once again, the recognition and revelation of this material can, in our view, only take place within an atmosphere of a trusting relationship between supervisor and supervisee. Once again, the systemic difficulties are inextricably linked to emotional issues and transgenerational patterns, which are in turn reflected, as Searles and many since have discussed, in the relationship between supervisor and supervisee. Unrecognized emotional truths, often outside the supervisee's awareness at the time of being stuck, set limitations on what a particular systemic therapist can achieve with a particular client or group of clients. Recognition and acceptance create the possibility for the therapist to expand her range of both personal and systemic options.

Such emotional truths can be more powerfully illuminated within the supervisory relationship when the supervisor is willing to share how the experiences resonate with her. In this case, the supervisor was genuinely moved by Shirley's story and revealed that she, too, had left her home country as an adolescent and had become a therapist in Australia.

Case study 3:
Sonja

Sonja works for an agency whose general starting position is that the resolution of problematic relationships requires commitment to personal change. It had been clearly established during supervision that Sonja has a thorough understanding of systemic frameworks. Despite her strength and resources, she finds herself confounded by a particular couple who have been coming for therapy regularly, but they consistently report no change in their relationship. She feels stuck, irritated, and puzzled.

The couple have been together for nearly ten years. They report having always had a conflicted relationship in which Lisa feels unloved, misunderstood, and unsupported by David. Both have strong conflicted and ambivalent connections to their own families of origin. They believe their own parents stayed together throughout marriage despite problematic and unsatisfactory relationships. Recently, David's father died, leaving David sad and angry. David was regretful, believing that his father had deserved better love and care from his mother. He considers his father did not receive it from her, even as he was dying. David's anger would often manifest itself in snide sarcasm directed at Lisa.

Sonja's supervisor was curious about how a competent therapist was becoming increasingly invested in helping this couple stay together. The harder she tried, the more the couple remained the same. The harder the supervisor tried, the greater were Sonja's feelings of futility and ineptitude. At the same time, the supervisor was aware of feelings of anxiety in herself at her failure to assist in breaking the apparent deadlock.

Expression of these feelings permitted the supervisor to become aware that, not only did Sonja have high standards for herself as a therapist, but that as a supervisor she too was constrained by similar beliefs. It became clearer that the fear each was carrying was that any admission of a decrease in these standards might damage the supervisor–supervisee relationship. Could this mutually valued and mutually respectful relationship survive such a reduction?

Sooner or later, such questions must be faced within all significant relationships. The fear and disappointment of discovering defects may be too much to cope with. There is a risk that the other will withdraw—that a more exciting or more competent supervisor or supervisee will be found.

In this case, once the fear within supervision was in the open, Sonja became aware that her concern was being projected onto David and Lisa. Her desire for what she saw as high-quality relationships meant that for her, successful therapy could only be couched in terms of significant changes in the way David and Lisa related to each other. It became clear that the agency, the therapist, *and* the supervisor were "colluding" in assumptions about a need for meaningful and rewarding relationships as defined by *them*. For David and Lisa, however, attending therapy was in itself a measure of differentiation from their own parents' relationships. What difference this difference was creating had not, until that point, attracted sufficient curiosity from supervisor or supervisee.

Case study 4:
Sebastian

In this case study, the first author had been working with Sebastian, a young man who, at the time that therapy began, had been diagnosed with a terminal illness. Sebastian had made it clear that the reason for seeking therapy was not because of his illness, but because of his wish to understand better both himself and his approach to relationships.

Sebastian saw himself as extremely exacting and unwilling to tolerate personal insincerity. With the exception of his lover, Peter, he had been extremely disappointed with the relationships he had formed. Nobody other than Peter had ever been able fully to understand, appreciate, and love him. He declared that he would not stay in therapy if he found the therapist to be either incompetent or insincere.

During therapy, which proceeded over approximately eighteen months, a colleague, Dominic, acted as peer supervisor. Dominic remained in the room rather than behind the screen because Sebastian had insisted that any discussions about the therapy process be conducted in his presence. He had in effect instructed his therapist and her peer supervisor to act as a reflecting team.

As therapy progressed, so did the debilitating aspects of Sebastian's illness. Though this inevitably became a focus of therapy, Sebastian felt satisfied that the issues he had brought to therapy had been attended to. The therapist was simultaneously mindful of the need to end therapy and reluctant to finish. She was strongly connected to Sebastian and knew also that his death was imminent. The thought of breaking the relationship before Sebastian died was a painful one.

Sebastian for his part became angry with the therapist for both passionately and coolly addressing questions of completion of therapy. He protested against the difficulty of ending a relationship that had come to mean so much to him and had been such a catalyst for his better understanding of himself. How, he exclaimed, could this therapist be so calculating and precise about finishing when she was so clearly moved by him? During one such encounter the therapist could not hold back tears, agonizing in the knowledge that termination of therapy was necessary and in the full awareness that no other form of relationship was either appropriate or ethical.

The therapist became immobilized, torn between the dilemma of acting responsibly and professionally in her need to address termination issues and her personal pain at having become so attached to her client. She needed her peer supervisor to remind her and to remind Sebastian in that moment that the crux of therapy had been about forming relationships in which Sebastian could feel he was loved and accepted for who he was.

From within the room, Dominic had shared the experience of this therapy in a very personal way. Yet his meta-perspective brought client and therapist to the realization that what had transpired was precisely what Sebastian had worked for. The therapist's acceptance was simultaneously professional and utterly genuine. At the same time, the therapist recognized that she had allowed herself space to attend to Sebastian's deepest concerns, precisely because the work had been conducted in the presence of a colleague for whom both she and Sebastian had trust and respect.

THE PERSONAL IN SYSTEMIC THERAPY: THE BROADER PICTURE

We suggest that in the privacy of systemically oriented supervisors' and therapists' rooms, encounters such as those described may not be uncommon. But rarely are they written about or otherwise formally acknowledged. The reluctance of systemic writers formally to legitimize an analysis of the therapeutic relationship in discussions of theory and practice has been noted by Flaskas (1989), Smith, Osman, and Goding (1990), and by a number of the contributors to the present volume. Flaskas (1993) also echoes Gibney (1991), Luepnitz (1988), Nichols (1987), and an earlier volume edited by Pearce and Friedman (1980) in suggesting that one set of tools that may serve an exploration of interpersonal issues in systemic work is to be found within the psychoanalytic tradition.

Whether contemporary psychoanalytic approaches will be seen to be sufficiently respectful and reflexive to fill an acceptable gap for systemically oriented workers is likely to be the subject of ongoing debate. From a historical perspective, there is both hopefulness and irony in the fact that the question is even being asked. We recall a series of seminars in Australia in 1975, for example, when Salvador Minuchin was asked to address the question of whether or not family therapy trainees needed to have psychoanalytical training. Minuchin, who like many family therapy pioneers at the time had received a solid grounding in psychoanalytic theory, suggested that such experience probably was not necessary. His response was precisely what most of us in the audience *wanted* to hear. Not only had the psychoanalytic dragon been slain, it seemed that any future dragons could now be ignored with impunity.

Conceptually, systems theory continues to stand somewhere between sociological approaches, which emphasize broad external forces, and individual psychotherapies, most of which encourage the exploration of inner conflicts, "defences", and perceptions. At its best, systems theory sometimes provides a rickety bridge between the two. But like other conceptual frameworks, it too has struggled and largely failed to transcend the false dualism of inner and outer worlds. The problem is a central one in philosophy and psychology as well as in attempts to articulate religious and spiritual experience. We feel ourselves to be unique individuals living within private worlds of our own construction; at the same time, we are social beings who must have relationships outside our relationship with ourselves. We cannot seem to function adequately without a viable sense of our individual selves; at the same time, we cannot flourish without the experience of intimacy with others.

Smith et al. (1990) suggest that openness to the emotional experience of working as a family therapist assumes a willingness to re-engage with the sometimes painful emotions associated with our own families of origin. Publications on supervision that emphasize issues such as family of origin (e.g. List, 1986) are very much in the minority. Indeed, as we have noted, most of the family therapy supervision literature is focused instead on questions of technique. We now better understand that the promise of technique in both therapy and supervision was a promise that could never be delivered. Family therapists had to learn to respect the reality that they, too, are part of the system within which change is sought. Within this framework, the therapeutic relationship is not simply something that is fostered at the front end in order to oil the wheels of the real therapeutic work. It is a living, ongoing dynamic which cannot be divorced from the emotional responses of each person in the system and which is integral to the whole business of therapy.

Smith et al. (1990) offer a feminist-oriented explanation for family therapy's devaluing of emotion and interpersonal relationships. They see much of the difficulty as stemming from male-dominated models of therapy and "the error of equating male experience with human experience" (Smith et al., 1990, p. 143). The explanation has immediate appeal. It is tempting, for example, to speculate about what the field of family therapy would look like if Virginia Satir in the United States or Margaret Topham in Australia had been even more influential during the 1970s and 1980s. However, though space does not permit, it would also be interesting to speculate on why other therapeutic orientations such as psychodrama, gestalt, and most models within the humanist tradition, all of which have maintained a significant male presence, have continued to value emotion (including the therapist's emotional response) as valid expressions of truth.

ISOMORPHISM AND PARALLEL PROCESS: SYSTEMIC PATTERNS AND PERSONAL INTERACTION

Everett and Koerpel (1986) note the multiple references in the family therapy supervision literature to the notion of isomorphism (the tendency of forms or patterns in one setting to be repeated in another).[1] For a systemic therapist, the notion of repeating patterns has a ring of familiarity. It seems reasonable to assume that patterns that emerge from the therapeutic dance, co-created and co-evolved by therapist and family, are assumed to be re-enacted in the patterns created when the supervisee/therapist brings his or her work to the supervisor. Perhaps less familiar to family therapy supervisors is the more intrapsychic and interpersonal notion of reflective process, or parallel process, as it became better known[2], first outlined by Searles (1955). Searles suggested that when difficulties occur in supervision, the supervisor should consider the possibility that the supervisee has struck a problem in therapy which parallels a problem in personal development. Because the difficulty is assumed to be unconscious, the supervisee cannot give clear voice to it. Instead, he or she "acts out" the difficulty in supervision, creating a further parallel stuckness in that arena also.

In various ways these ideas feature strongly in the supervision of therapists in the humanist and psychodynamically oriented traditions. They are given support by a study of Doehrman (1976), who for more than six months collected data on the work of two supervisors, their four supervisees, and the supervisees' eight clients. Using the psychoanalytic language of transference and countertransference, Doehrman found that whenever transference issues were resolved with a supervisor, the supervisee/therapist was also freed up in his or her work with the client. Conversely, supervisee resistance to help offered by the supervisor had strong parallels with the difficulties that supervisee/therapists were experiencing in helping their clients.

"Isomorphism" is a word in the grand tradition of systemic terms. To our knowledge, however, there is no research-based evidence equivalent to that of Doehrman's work which convincingly establishes the existence of isomorphic patterns across discrete settings. Though as a concept it makes intuitive sense, we believe it should at this stage be treated with caution. (It is perhaps worth recalling that there was a time in the development of family therapy when the concept of homeostasis, though not formally researched, was also intuitively felt to be correct.)

Parallel process, at least as understood and studied by Doehrman, is a more narrowly constructed notion. It is more directly interpersonal, and, we believe, the assumptions upon which it rests can be demonstrated more convincingly. Parallel process creates the possibility of seeing the personal issues, which are part of all therapy, mirrored within supervision. It provides a rationale for bringing therapy right into the supervisor's room and into the supervisor–supervisee relationship. An important question then is why the concept of parallel process, which is at the heart of so much of the supervision literature, has been all but ignored in the supervision of family therapists.

Does part of the answer lie in the old enmities between systemic and psychoanalytic theory? As noted, the language of Hawkins and Shohet's "supervisory system" is the language of transference and countertransference, a language that, historically at least, is steeped in hierarchical and developmental assumptions with which most family therapists would have difficulty. Ironically perhaps, although Searles took a psychoanalytic perspective, he was a neo-Freudian who was quite clear that the parallel processes of which he spoke move in both directions. In Williams' (1995) terms, parallel process should not be assumed to be like some sort of cancerous growth that comes up from the lower reaches. It could equally be seen as a fog that descends from above.[3]

A further reason why family therapy supervisors have neglected any exploration of parallel process may lie in Everett and Koerpel's observation that the term isomorphism has, to a large extent, come to mean that supervision should be theoretically congruent with the model of therapy being employed. Once again, there would be some irony here if the proposition were true—especially given that a number of writers such as Williams (1995), though clearly preferring the term parallel process, use this and the word isomorphism interchangeably. If the therapy itself places little or no value on the client–therapist relationship, it would indeed be somewhat incongruent to emphasize relationships in supervision. But a major problem with falling back on the notion of isomorphism as a rationale for attending to relationships in systemic supervision is that it contains an assumption that two systems or patterns *must be* compatible. It becomes, in other words, a self-fulfilling prophecy.

If we accept that meaning is context-specific and that context must include the relationship, it follows that there simply must be a place for exploration of the relationship issues between supervisor and supervisee. An understanding of parallel process merely makes this exploration much more immediately relevant. But the idea of parallel process in both directions makes the potential richness of that exploration almost immeasurable.

In addition, if we accept a two-directional (perhaps even circular) parallel process, we avoid the problem inherent in "studying down"[4] the supervisee or the family members. Our stance can remain recursive, respectful, and systemic. Our work will more closely resemble that of postmodern ethnographers who, Hoffman (1992) claims, are interested in dialogue rather than standard textual analysis. Like therapists who remain true to the insights of second-order cybernetics, these ethnographers reject the ideology of observer and observed.

CONCLUDING COMMENTS

In each of the cases described, the development of the relationship at various stages of supervision is both acknowledged and enriched by holding both expert knowledge *and* individual experiences to be integral and interactive aspects of learning. We would suggest that this process also parallels good systemic therapy. Just as the personal and the political are ultimately inseparable, so the personal and the systemic are part of the same process.

The ramifications of giving serious consideration to such an approach are considerable. Systemic therapy and systemic supervision become both more complex and more satisfying. Self-awareness again becomes important—as it has been in the training of therapists and supervisors from a number of non-systemic orientations. The use of a self-knowledge, which is constantly enriched in the context of changing relationships with clients or supervisees, becomes an integral part of our systemic recursive stance. And, finally, like the postmodern ethnographers, we again find ourselves engaged in the practice and articulation of an ethic of connection supported—as human connection must always be—by an ethic of appropriate self disclosure.

NOTES

1. Wiffen and Byng-Hall (1982) and Liddle and Saba (1982) are amongst the references cited by these authors. Imber-Black (1988) and Elizur (1990) are amongst the considerable number of more contemporary authors who have written on the subject.
2. There are some references to parallel process in family therapy supervision literature, such as Liddle and Schwartz (1983), Keller and Protinsky (1984), and List (1986).
3. Indeed, a truly systemic interpretation of parallel process might dispense with upward and downward analogies altogether.
4. Hoffman (1992) has called this the "colonialism of mental health".

REFERENCES

Doehrman, M. (1976). Parallel process in supervision and psychotherapy. *Bulletin of the Menninger Clinic, 40*, 3–104.

Elizur, J. (1990). Stuckness in live supervision. *Journal of Family Therapy, 12,* 267–280.

Everett, C. (1979). The masters degree in marriage and family therapy. *Journal of Marriage and Family Therapy, 5,* 7–13.

Everett, C. (1980). Supervision of marriage and family therapy. In: A. Hess (Ed.), *Handbook of Psychotherapy Supervision* (pp. 367–380). New York: Wiley.

Everett, C., & Koerpel, B. (1986). Family therapy supervision: a review and critique of the literature. *Contemporary Family Therapy, 8* (1) (Spring), 62–72.

Flaskas, C. (1989). Thinking about the emotional interaction of therapist and family. *Australian and New Zealand Journal of Family Therapy, 10* (1), 1–6.

Flaskas, C. (1993). On the project of using psychoanalytic ideas in systemic therapy: a discussion paper. *Australian and New Zealand Journal of Family Therapy*, 14 (2), 9–15.

Geer, R. (1994). *Incorporation of a Narrative Approach into a Supervision Group of Beginning Counsellors*. Master's degree minor thesis, Graduate School of Education, La Trobe University, Melbourne.

Gibney, P. (1991). Articulating the implicate: an invitation to openness. *Australian and New Zealand Journal of Family Therapy*, 12 (3), 133–136.

Hawkins, O., & Shohet, R. (1989) *Supervision in the Helping Professions: An Individual, Group and Organizational Approach*. Milton Keynes: Open University.

Hess, A. (Ed.) (1980). *Handbook of Psychotherapy Supervision*. New York: Wiley.

Hoffman, L. (1992). A reflexive stance for family therapy. In: S. McNamee & K. Gergen (Eds.), *Therapy as Social Construction*. London: Sage. Also in *Exchanging Voices: A Collaborative Approach to Family Therapy*. London: Karnac Books, 1993.

Imber-Black, E. (1988). *Families and Larger Systems*. New York: Guilford Press.

Keller, J., & Protinsky, H. (1984). A self management model for supervision. *Journal of Marital and Family Therapy*, 10 (3), 281–288.

Liddle, H., & Halpin, R. (1978). Family therapy training and supervision literature: a comparative review. *Journal of Marital and Family Counseling*, 4, 77–98.

Liddle, H., & Saba, G. (1982). Teaching family therapy at the introductory level: a conceptual model emphasising a pattern which connects training and therapy. *Journal of Marital and Family Therapy*, 8, 63–72.

Liddle, H., & Schwartz, R. (1983). Live supervision/consultation: conceptual and pragmatic guidelines for family therapy trainers. *Family Process*, 22, 477–490.

List, D. (1986). Bringing it all back home: individual and group supervision in family therapy training. *Australian and New Zealand Journal of Family Therapy*, 7, 7–12.

Loganbill, C., Hardy, E., & Dellworth, U. (1982). Supervision: a conceptual model. *Counselling Psychologist*, 10, 3–41.

Luepnitz, D. (1988). *The Family Interpreted*. New York: Basic Books.

Nichols, M.P. (1987). *The Self in the System*. New York: Brunner/Mazel.

Pearce, J., & Friedman, L. (Eds.) (1980). *Family Therapy: Combining Psychodynamic and Family Systems Approaches.* New York: Grune & Stratton.

Ronnestad, M., & Skovholt, T. (1993). Supervision of beginning and advanced graduate students of counselling and psychotherapy. *Journal of Counselling and Development, 71,* 396–405.

Searles, H. (1955). The information value of the supervisor's emotional experience. In: H. Searles, *Collected Papers on Schizophrenia and Related Subjects* (pp. 114–156), edited by J. Sutherland. London: Hogarth Press.

Smith, J., Osman, C., & Goding, M. (1990). Reclaiming the emotional aspects of the therapist family system. *Australian and New Zealand Journal of Family Therapy, 11* (3), 140–146.

Stolk, V., & Perlesz, A. (1990). Do better trainees make worse family therapists? A following study of client families. *Family Process, 28,* 59–65.

Wiffen, R., & Byng-Hall, T. (Eds.) (1982). *Family Therapy Supervision: Recent Developments in Practice.* New York: Academic Press, Grune & Stratton.

Williams, A. (1995). *Visual and Active Supervision: Roles, Focus, Technique.* New York: W. W. Norton.

DISCUSSION PAPER II

Changing systemic constructions of therapeutic relationships

Elsa Jones

Two factors, in particular, have allowed systemic therapists to pay attention to the therapeutic relationship. The first relates to changes in systemic theory. As Carmel Flaskas and Amaryll Perlesz point out in their Introduction, taking a second-order cybernetic stance, and incorporating feminist and social constructionist ideas, has obliged us to think about the presence and influence of the self of the therapist—and the relationships between therapists and clients—as significant elements in the process of therapeutic change. Secondly, as systemic therapy has become better established it has become possible to acknowledge the potential contribution of psychoanalytic thinking; the denial of its relevance which characterized the (largely psychoanalytically trained) family therapy pioneers can be replaced not only by the much-trumpeted "re-discovery of the individual", but by attention to the inner worlds of therapists and clients.

As someone working in Britain, it is stimulating to note the similarity in the evolution of thinking about practice between our work here and that of our colleagues in Australia. However, while many—or some—of us may be doing things differently, it is also true, as regards therapy in general (Flaskas and Perlesz, Introduction) and supervision in particular (Maloney and Maloney, Chapter 10), that not enough is being written on it. This wide-ranging collection will therefore prove a stimulus to the practice and the writing of other systemic practitioners. Certain themes recur in all the papers in Part II; I discuss these below, with reference also to my own ideas and those of other European authors.

POWER

Inevitably, most of the authors in this section touch on the nature and exercise of power within therapeutic relationships—that is, relationships between clients and therapists, and between professionals. "Simple" changes in the day-to-day practice of therapy attempt to bring an "ethic of participation" closer to realization (Cantwell and Stagoll, Chapter 6), ways of including client voices in the description and evaluation of therapy are sought (Perlesz et. al., Chapter 7; and Sanders, Chapter 8), and the multi-systemic ramifications of power and powerlessness are explored (Furlong, Chapter 9).

As systemic therapists we have not yet come to a resting place on the question of the nature of power in relationships: that is, we are still exploring the flexibility of our theory to test out whether or not it will accommodate our clinical experience of the responsible and abusive ways in which power may be exercised and attributed between participants in non-lineal systems. It may be that we cannot and should not ever become comfortable about this issue. It is well known—but perhaps never sufficiently acknowledged—that not only family members but also therapists do abuse the power given to them (cf. for example the excellent nationwide investigation done in the Netherlands by Aghassy and Noot, 1990, as well as a British and American perspective offered by Jehu, 1994).

Catherine Sanders (Chapter 8) discovers from the feedback of her clients that the women with whom she had been working had "a much less convoluted and fearful view [of power] than many therapists". This is reassuring, and a compliment to her therapeutic work, but I would suggest also that such feedback from clients is only likely following a therapeutic experience in which the therapist not only took responsibility for the appropriate exercise of her power, but was also appropriately "fearful" of the abuses of power. In order to ensure the safety, trust, self-confidence, and freedom of speech demonstrated by these clients, we may need to continue to examine our practice and our theory, via self-scrutiny, feedback, and consultation. The client's vulnerable state of mind when entering therapy, the social construction of the role of therapist and the therapeutic relationship, as well as aspects of the therapist's own motivation, can combine into a heady power package. A "therapist is less likely to abuse this power if she acknowledges its presence, than if she believes her own propaganda and considers that she has succeeded in shedding her power" (Jones, 1993, p. 156).

INCLUDING MARGINALIZED VOICES

Systemic therapists are at present exploring a wide range of mind-sets and techniques aimed at allowing client voices to achieve equivalence with those of therapists, and at making therapist functioning more transparent and available for discussion and critique. We invite clients to become part of the decision-making process at every step of the work, and we share our thinking in tentative ways designed to maximize client freedom of choice. We seek out their evaluation of ourselves, as part of standard auditing and feedback procedures, as commentary on the therapy, on ourselves as actors in the therapeutic drama, and on the ideas that inform our work. We devise formats designed to influence our continuing work by incorporating clients' views into the structuring of services, and create opportunities to discuss our responses to them and theirs to us. Therapists and clients join together to write accounts of mutual work (cf. the papers in Part II as well as McGuirk & Byrne, 1994, Gorell Barnes & Henessy, 1995, Roper-Hall, 1991).

In one sense, it is not surprising that these trends have become so powerful in systemic therapy—they could be said to flow inevitably from the decision to open up our practice to scrutiny by the use of the one-way screen. Once the visibility of systemic work met up with feminist and social constructionist critiques, it would have been difficult not to continue to carry the implications of transparency and accountability to their logical conclusion. However, it is also true that systemic therapists have been vulnerable, at times, to a particular type of hubris. We repeatedly act as if we have invented the wheel for the first time, as if we have no history, and as if each plateau achieved is the summit.

Thus, while wishing to associate myself fully with all the shifts in thinking and practice referred to here, I also want to say "yes ... but". How freely do clients consent to therapist requests? For whose benefit do clients consent to participate in retrospective evaluation of therapy? The main beneficiaries are likely to be the therapists (as Perlesz and Furlong wryly point out) and their future clients. Carl Whitaker once said something like: "You need to thank the family you're currently working with for the benefit your next client family is likely to derive from the mistakes you're making with them now!" Paradoxically, then, our ethical desire to involve clients in the discussion of the process and relationships of therapy must include the ethical question of how this process of mutual discussion may be beneficial to the clients themselves.

Whether therapy is ongoing or completed, the influence of the therapeutic relationship is likely to affect the client's perception of the therapist in a variety of ways. Thus, the therapist's construction of the client as a free agent and equal participant in a mutually created endeavour may be different from the client's construct of the therapist. Those to whom power is mandated easily underestimate the influence of even their subtlest indications of desire on others, while those who have experienced significant loss of choice and power may well continue to believe that, despite the best intentions, some remain more equal than others.

An increased awareness of the importance of creating space for client voices to be heard in the process of therapy, in the structuring of services, and in the subsequent description and evaluation of the work done has led to innovative and stimulating procedures. Amaryll Perlesz, Mark Furlong, and the "D" family (Chapter 7) devote time and resources to the frank examination of their experiences of the mutual relationship during therapy. Gill Gorell Barnes and Sharon Henessy (1995) write about the process of their work together as client and therapist, and they discuss their experiences of struggling with therapeutic content and with their relationship using their individual voices as well as the "we" that emerges from having grown together through their shared experience. Myra McGuirk and Nollaig Byrne (1994) find creative solutions to the obstacle presented by the client's dyslexia and poverty-mandated lack of access to written fluency, so that their eventual joint account represents a mutual creation with different tasks, in which the therapist takes responsibility for editing taped conversations, which the client then vets and comments on.

POWERLESSNESS

Mark Furlong's exploration in Chapter 9 of the replication of pattern in the interactions between professional public welfare systems and the families with whom they are mandated to work offers a vivid picture of the sense of paralysis, adversariality, and "burnout" that workers in such systems may experience. By using our systemic skills to construct a wide-ranging description of the systems within which we become entangled, we also become able to see the possible changes in ourselves—our prejudices, emotional responses, beliefs—which may act as invitations to change within the larger systems set up to deal with difficult and emotive client-issues. Jane Dutton Conn (1995) explores the ways in which gender patterns contribute to experiences of mistrust and alienation in the working of similar service systems. Imelda McCarthy (1994, p. 229) adds another level of context by examining the fact that "welfare families generally live on the margins of our societies and as such are vulnerable to all kinds of social and professional intrusion". Understanding the wider contextual influences that lead professionals to feel unhappy, stuck, abusive, or abused may facilitate minor or major change in their perceptions of their position in the system, so that, thus re-empowered, they may become capable of creating the sort of relational space in which clients, too, can empower themselves.

THE SELF OF THE THERAPIST

Perhaps, since family therapists are not required to undergo a training analysis, we have forgotten (or never discovered) what it feels like to be in the client position, and how the relationship of power may look from the perspective of those who perceive themselves as having been the recipients of help. In Britain, the formation of the United Kingdom Council for Psychotherapy (UKCP), a body set up to scrutinize the training of psychotherapists from a range of orientations and to offer registration to those duly qualified, has brought to the forefront of discussions the question of whether or not family therapy trainees should be required to enter into their own therapy. The UKCP requires therapists wishing to be registered to "be aware of their participation in the therapeutic relationship". Various training institutes have evolved training components that attend explicitly to the self-awareness and development of trainee therapists (Hedges & Lang, 1993; Hildebrand & Speed, 1995). Thus, therapists are increasingly being invited by their supervisors, their peer teams, and their own sense of professional responsibility to scrutinize the contribution made to the progress or stuckness of therapy by their own inner life, families of origin, current life circumstances, "prejudices", or culture, gender, and ethnicity (Moloney and Moloney, Chapter 10; Cantwell and Stagoll, Chapter 6: see also Cecchin, Lane, & Ray, 1994; Jones, 1995).

Since we have for so long chosen to function a-historically in relation to our own professional origins, we may be at risk here of valorizing the therapist's expression of feelings, and sharing of his or her own experiences with clients, in ways likely to be less than helpful to our clients. While appropriate presentation of the therapist's own preoccupations may be helpful (Moloney and Moloney, Chapter 10: see also Hildebrand & Speed, 1995), it is also important for us to remember the eloquent plea from one of Catherine Sanders' clients in Chapter 8:

"I don't want responsibility for someone else's stuff when I'm trying to sort out my stuff. . . . I think that as a therapist she has a responsibility not to show [her feelings], even though it could be very hard, and I don't want my therapist to be crying and sobbing all over the place and lying on the floor . . . she can go home and do that."

Thus, in addition to using psychoanalytic ideas about transference, countertransference, and parallel process, we also require a continuous evolution of our working structures and theories that will allow therapists to process their responses within the therapeutic relationship, and to decide whether and how these can relevantly be fed back to clients, in ways coherent with systemic thinking.

SYSTEMIC CONSTRUCTIONS OF THE SELF OF THE THERAPIST

In seeking to legitimize the exploration of the influence of the self of the therapist on the process of therapy, systemic therapists have reached for ideas, derived from psychoanalysis, about the influence of the therapist's own history, relationships, and internal world. At the same time, psychoanalytically oriented therapists have in turn been influenced by systemic ideas, feminist critiques of the psychotherapies, and social constructionism. Thus, for example, Renos Papadopoulos and Graham Saayman (1989–90) explore, from a Jungian perspective, how family patterns and actions may constitute an invitation to the therapist to occupy an "archetypal designation", e.g. as "saviour" or "shadow". Susie Orbach and Luise Eichenbaum (1993) consider the possibilities, within the therapy relationship, of re-enacting familiar patterns and of transcending familiar ways of being through new approaches to the therapist's countertransference, which will include her awareness of how both she and her client are organized not only by familial patterns but by internalizations of the culture as well. They are particularly interested in how the therapist's claiming of her own subjectivity as a woman may facilitate a new possibility of subjectivity for the client:

perhaps more important is my own struggle to maintain myself as a subject within the analytic relationship. I need to be able to do that for them (for if I am merged I am useless) and I need to be able to do that for me. [Orbach & Eichenbaum, 1993, p. 81]

Systemic therapists are in the fortunate position of being able to benefit from these and similar explorations in the psychoanalytic field, while also holding our own unique and valuable awareness of the pull that systems can exert on their members, the invitation to achieve a fit with pre-existing patterns, the ways in which influence and adaptation occur within systems over time (demonstrated, for example, in Chapter 9, by Mark Furlong). It may then be useful for therapists, especially when stuck, to look to what is happening in their own relational and emotional lives (internal, personal, and professional), but also to look at their emotional responses as a source of information about what it is like to be a member of this family–therapist system.

In addition, while we cannot know all the complexities of the client's unspoken (and perhaps unconscious) responses to us, it is important for us to remember that clients, too, are organized in the relationship with us by their own history, internal constructs, family experiences, social and cultural learning, prejudices, and beliefs. How do our clients perceive our gender, class, age, speech patterns, styles of presentation, etc. etc., and how do these influence the process of therapy? By making these topics available for discussion within the therapeutic relationship, we enhance the likelihood of cooperation instead of falling prey to mutual misunderstanding, prejudice, and attributions of blame.

CONCLUSION

Like all good books, this one left me feeling that the conversation had only begun, so that I am left with many questions:

- How, for the sake of our own professional growth, can we continue to invite client voices into the discourse during and about therapy without becoming precious or burdening them when they are ready to move on?

- How can workers in low or intermediate positions in large systems be helped to obtain a systemic perspective on their own positions, feelings, relationships, or actions, and how can they feed these insights back into the system so as to make a difference? Can organizational systems (particularly those employing the helping professionals) be helped to change so that those who feel disempowered within them may be allowed to comment on their experiences without being further pathologized and blamed? What role can be played in these processes by systemic teachers and consultants?
- What are the subtleties and minutiae of our therapeutic conversations that enable clients to accept the invitation to collaborate in fully participatory work? Can we find further ways of sharing these details and "ordinary" moments with each other? Can we, in order to do this, resist the temptation to present only the brilliant sound-bites when presenting our work, and can we all cooperate in evolving non-heroic styles, within the systemic field, of writing, speaking, and listening?

The training experience offers a template in which trainee therapists can learn, via the relationship with the supervisor, much that is also of relevance to their own relationships with clients. Can we make space, in the construction of supervisory models, to attend to the many interlinked and overlapping complexities that affect the supervisory relationship as much as they do the therapy relationship? To do so, without converting supervision into psychotherapy—and while bearing in mind the implications of training programmes, in which the supervisor is also usually required to evaluate the supervisee—requires clarity of structure and intention. However, we cannot expect the next generation of systemic trainees to pay due attention to the therapeutic relationship in therapy if they have not had the opportunity, in supervision or elsewhere, to attend to personal history, relationship experiences, emotional responses, dilemmas associated with dimensions of power, gender, culture, and ethnicity, and the influence of these on relationships between therapists and their clients, colleagues, and trainers.

REFERENCES

Aghassy, G., & Noot, M. (1990). *Seksuele Kontakten binnen Psychotherapeutische Hulpverleningsrelasies*. Gravenhage: VUGA. [First names not given.]

Cecchin, Gianfranco; Lane, Gerry; & Ray, Wendel A. (1994). *The Cybernetics of Prejudice in the Practice of Psychotherapy*. London: Karnac Books.

Dutton Conn, Jane (1995). Autonomy and connection: gendered thinking in a statutory agency dealing with child sexual abuse. In: Charlotte Burck & Bebe Speed (Eds.), *Gender, Power and Relationships*. London: Routledge.

Gorell Barnes, Gill, & Henessy, Sharon (1995). Reclaiming a female mind from the experience of child sexual abuse: a developing conversation between writers and editors. In: Charlotte Burck & Bebe Speed (Eds.), *Gender, Power and Relationships*. London: Routledge.

Hedges, Fran, & Lang, Susan (1993). Mapping personal and professional stories. *Human Systems: The Journal of Systemic Consultation and Management, 4*, 277–298.

Hildebrand, Judy, & Speed, Bebe (1995). The influence of therapists' personal experience on their work with couples. In: Justine Van Lawick & Marjet Sanders, *Family, Gender and Beyond*. Heemstede: LS Books.

Jehu, Derek (1994). *Patients as Victims: Sexual Abuse in Psychotherapy and Counselling*. Chichester: John Wiley.

Jones, Elsa (1993). *Family Systems Therapy: Developments in the Milan-Systemic Therapies*. Chichester: John Wiley.

Jones, Elsa (1995). The gender of the therapist as contribution to the construction of meaning in the supervision of therapy. In: Maurizio Andolfi, Claudio Angelo, & Marcella De Nichilo (Eds.), *Feelings and Systems*. Rome: Cortina.

McCarthy, Imelda Colgan (1994). Abusing norms: welfare families and a fifth-province stance. *Human Systems: The Journal of Systemic Consultation and Management, 5*, 229–239.

McGuirk, Myra, & Byrne, Nollaig (1994). Just now I'd like to be called Myra. *Human Systems: The Journal of Systemic Consultation and Management, 5*, 155–168.

Orbach, Susie, & Eichenbaum, Luise (1993). Feminine subjectivity, countertransference and the mother–daughter relationship. In:

Janneke Mens-Verhulst, Karlein Schreurs, & Liesbeth Woertman (Eds.), *Daughtering and Mothering*. London: Routledge.

Papadopoulos, Renos, & Saayman, Graham (1989–90). Towards a Jungian approach to family therapy. *Harvest: Journal for Jungian Studies, 35,* 95–120.

Roper-Hall, Alison (1991). *Evolution of a Model for Evaluation Applicable in Everyday Practice for the Evaluation of a Systemic Therapy Service*. Dissertation, Dip. Systemic Therapy, University of Birmingham.

INDEX

abuse, 93, 160
   child, 176–192
   and countertransference of
      therapist, 28
   sexual, 183, 186, 187
acceptance, ritual of, 154–156
Ackerman, N., 59–60, 68
affect, 171–173
Aghassy, G., 216, 224
Andersen, T., 6, 11, 67, 68, 93, 97, 99, 100, 105, 128, 133, 140
Anderson, H., 6, 11, 22, 30, 66, 68, 78, 88, 91, 93, 94, 95, 97, 99, 100, 106, 115, 120, 127, 131, 134, 141
Andolphi, M., 6, 11, 81, 88
Angelo, C., 6, 11, 81, 88
Armon-Jones, C., 30
Atkinson, B., 161, 169, 173, 174
autonomous self:
   culturally embedded patterns of, 22
   re-socializing, 22–24

Bacal, H. A., 57, 68

Bader, M. J., 126, 140
Barber, J., 177, 192
Bateson, G., 4, 18, 19, 21, 23, 30, 58, 68, 75, 88, 91, 103, 105, 121, 161, 187, 192
Baur, S., 129, 140
behaviour, problematic, 26
behavioural family therapy, 67
Benhabib, S., 74, 79, 88
Berg, I. K., 94, 106
Berlin, S., 187, 192
Biestek, F. P., 100, 105, 115, 120
blame:
   attributions of, 183
   patterns of, 183–186
Boscolo, L., 70, 72, 74, 77, 80, 82, 85, 87, 88, 112
Boszormenyi-Nagy, I., 16, 17, 30, 35, 50, 60, 68
Boulet, J., 186, 192
Bowen, M., 57, 61, 69
Bowlby, J., 57, 69
Box, S., 49, 50, 58, 69
Breunlin, D. C., 46, 47, 48, 50, 119, 120

INDEX

brief systemic therapy, 20–22, 27, 28
Brighton-Cleghorn, J., 58, 69
British Object-Relations therapy, 57
Broderick, C., 20, 30
Buber, M., 115
Buckley, W., 29, 30
Burger, T., 53, 69
Burke, W. F., 49, 52
Burnham, J., 120
burnout, 139, 164, 219
Byng-Hall, J., 35, 50, 68, 69, 115, 119, 120
Byng-Hall, T., 212, 214
Byrne, N., 217, 219, 224

Cade, B., 110, 113, 120, 122
Calhoun, C., 24, 31
Campbell, D., 72, 74, 85, 88
Campion, J., 35, 50
Cantwell, P., 7, 9, 125–141, 216, 220
Caplan, P., 192
Carkhuff, R. R., 135, 141
Carpenter, J., 114, 122, 181, 192
Carr, A., 186, 193
Carter, B., 92
Casement, P., 114, 121
Cecchin, G., 6, 11, 65, 69, 70, 74, 85, 86, 88, 112, 128, 141, 173, 174, 220, 224
Chable, D. G., 42, 51
change:
 context of in therapy, 16–17
 intrapsychic, 36, 38
 process of, 167–169
Chernin, K., 126, 140
Chess, S., 192, 193
child abuse, 176–192
 ideological conflicts invoked by, 181–183
circular questioning, 43, 110
circularity, 65, 82, 128
client:
 as collaborative partner, 132
 equality of in therapy, 217–219
 expectations of, 170
 self-determination of, 115

system, understanding, 134
 and therapist, emotional interaction of, 171
 therapist's respect for, 169–171
 viewpoint of, on therapy, 158–175
"coindividuation" [Stierlin], 73
communication, analogic, 80–81
Comte, Auguste, 54
conflicts, internalized or mirrored by professionals, 180
Conran, T., 158, 174
constructivism, 4, 91
context:
 as defining and positioning, 83–84
 factors creating, 83
 limiting, 84
 therapeutic, creating, 85
contextual therapy, 60
"control hierarchies" [Broderick & Smith], 20
Copley, B., 50, 69
counselling, 169
countertransference, 27, 35, 36, 38–41, 43, 44, 45, 47, 49, 102, 209, 210, 221
Cronen, V. E., 21, 32, 188, 194
Crowther, C., 35, 50
curiosity, 112
 limited, 82
 therapist's, 65
cybernetic theory, 15, 29, 59, 63

"D" family, 8, 10, 142–157
Darwin, Charles, 54
de Shazer, S., 93, 94, 96, 97, 99, 106
deconstructionism, 95
Dell, P., 18, 31, 91, 92, 161, 174
Dellworth, U., 196, 213
Dilthey, W., 54
Doehrman, M., 209, 210, 212
Doherty, W. J., 5, 11
Doka, K., 192, 193
drama, therapy as, 129–130
Draper, R., 72, 74, 85, 88
Droysen, J. G., 54
Durrant, M., 186, 193

Dutton Conn, J., 219, 224

Efran, J., 18, 31
Eichenbaum, L., 221, 222, 224
Elias, N., 117, 119, 121
Eliot, T. S., 100
Elizur, J., 212
"embedded" and "embodied", concepts of, 73–74
embeddedness, 73–85
　and embodiedness, link between, 80
"embedded suggestion questions" [Tomm], 22
embodiment, 75–76
emotional distress, and distancing of professionals, 184
emotional response, of therapist, 209, 222
　need to suppress, 172
empathy, 5, 100, 115, 116, 146–148, 184
　and aesthetics, 55
　lack of, 114
　therapist's, 66, 68
engagement, 144–148
　process of, 41–46
English, R., 183, 193
Epston, D., 23, 33, 66, 70, 78, 89, 94, 96, 97, 107
Erikson, E., 20
"ethic of participation" [Hoffman], 128, 130–138, 216
ethical stance [Anderson], 95
ethics, 29, 218
ethnographer, postmodern, 211
Everett, C., 196, 197, 209, 210, 212
expertise, of client, 131–134
extended family, importance of, 61

Falzer, P. R., 4, 11
family:
　ambiguous social position occupied by, 180
　positive symbolic image of, 180
　power hierarchy of, 63
　relationships, and the Enlightenment, 53–55

　–therapist relationships, multiple, 151–154
family therapy:
　analytically oriented, 28
　communication models of, 58
　emotional interaction in, 101–102
　ethics, 95
　failure of to consider feelings, 101
　Milan model of, 58
　missing link in, 119–120
　models of, 58–67
　paradox in, 104–105
　and power, 103–107
　psychoanalytic theories in, 26–27, 101
　rigid and mechanistic, 112
　shift in emphasis of, 96–97
　theoretical myopia of, 98, 102
　theorizing of, 98–104
feedback, 146
felt reality:
　and action and therapeutic positioning, 80–83
　concept of, 79
　embedded and embodied, 80
feminist critiques, 72, 103, 208, 218, 221
feminist discourse, 23
feminist framework, 102
first-order change, 29
Fisch, R., 32, 58, 70
Flaskas, C., 1–12, 15, 31, 34–52, 72, 85, 88, 102, 106, 110, 111, 118, 119, 171, 174, 191, 193, 207, 212, 213, 215, 216
Forgatch, M. S., 67, 69
Foucault, M., 22, 31, 98
framework, relational, 17
Freud, S., 38, 40, 55, 56, 59, 69, 102
Friedman, L. J., 35, 51, 207, 214
Friedman, R., 161, 164, 174
Fry, E., 35, 50
Furlong, M., 8, 10, 142–157, 176–194, 216, 218, 222

Geer, R., 197, 198, 213

Gergen, K. J., 11, 120, 137, 141, 213
Gibney, P., 6, 7, 9, 12, 35, 50, 80, 88, 90–107, 115, 116, 120, 207, 213
Goding, G., 29, 31
Goding, M., 5, 12, 15, 32, 35, 51, 55, 70, 102, 107, 171, 175, 189, 191, 194, 207, 214
Golann, S., 161, 165, 167, 174
Goldner, V., 92, 138, 139, 140, 141
Goolishian, H. A., 6, 11, 66, 68, 78, 88, 93, 94, 106, 115, 120, 127, 131, 134, 141
Gorell Barnes, G., 119, 121, 217, 219, 224
growth, potential for, 135
Grunebaum, H., 11, 12
Gurman, A. S., 30, 31, 58, 69

Haber, R., 81, 88, 114, 121
Haley, J., 63, 68, 69, 91, 103, 106, 110, 161
Hall-McCorquodale, I., 192
Hallett, C., 185, 193
Halpin, R., 197, 213
Harari, E., 7, 9, 53–70, 111, 116
Hardham, V., 7, 9, 71–89, 119
Hardy, E., 196, 213
Hare Mustin, R., 92
Harré, R., 24, 30, 31
Hasenfeld, Y., 183, 193
Hawkins, P., 196, 197, 210, 213
Healy, W., 183, 193
Heath, A., 161, 169, 173, 174
Hedges, F., 220, 224
Heimann, P., 57, 69
Henessy, S., 119, 121, 217, 219, 224
hermeneutics, 54
Hess, A., 196, 212, 213
Hildebrand, J., 114, 121, 220, 224
Hobson, R., 115, 121
Hoffman, L., 6, 11, 12, 22, 31, 38, 50, 72, 88, 91, 95, 96, 97, 99, 100, 106, 111, 114, 115, 117, 121, 128, 130, 136, 140, 141, 160, 161, 165, 174, 211, 212, 213
Hofstadter, D. R., 21, 30, 31

Hollis, F., 115, 121
Holmes, S., 95, 97, 99, 106, 125, 141
homeostasis, concept of, 210
homework tasks, 133–134
Horgan, J., 129
humanism, 127
humour, use of, 110
Hutchison, E., 182, 193
hypothesizing, 65, 128

I–Thou relationship [Buber], 114, 117
Imber-Black, E., 212, 213
impasses, use of analytic concepts to resolve, 119–120
Inger, I., 114, 121
insight:
  of client, 132–133
  concept of, 75–76
intimacy, 5, 171–173
"invariant prescription" [Selvini Palazzoli], 65
irreverence [Cecchin, Lane, & Ray], 86, 128
isomorphism, 209, 210–211

Jackson, D. D., 57, 58, 68
Jackson, S., 42, 51
James, K., 43, 51, 193
James, L., 5, 12, 161, 171, 174, 192
Jehu, D., 216, 224
Johnson, R. A., 104, 106
Jones, A., 183, 191, 194
Jones, E., 7, 10, 215–225
Jung, C. G., 104

Kahn, M., 125, 127, 129, 130, 141
Kantor, D., 27, 31
Keeney, B., 91, 92, 167
Keller, E. F., 29, 31
Keller, J., 212, 213
Kingston, P., 122
Kirkland, J., 5, 12, 161, 171, 174
Klein, M., 39, 57, 69, 102
Kneifel, A., 189, 194
Kniskern, D. P., 30, 58, 64, 69
Koerpel, B., 196, 197, 209, 212

Kohon, G., 39, 40, 41, 49, 51, 52
Kovel, J., 20, 31
Kowalski, K., 186, 193
Krause, I.-B., 5, 12, 79, 87, 88

Lacan, J., 99
Lane, G., 128, 141, 220, 224
Lane, J., 6, 11, 86, 88
Lang, S., 220, 224
language and expressive action, bridging the gap between, 77–78
Lasch, C., 181, 194
Liddle, H., 197, 212, 213
Lipps, T., 56
List, D., 208, 212, 213
Loganbill, C., 196, 213
Lomas, P., 115, 116, 121
love, psychotherapeutic, 91, 103–104
Love, J., 158, 174
Luepnitz, D. A., 4, 12, 35, 51, 58, 63, 69, 72, 88, 101, 102, 106, 207, 213
Lukens, M., 18, 31

MacKinnon, L. K., 6, 12, 22, 29, 32, 43, 51, 72, 83, 88, 89, 193
MacKune-Karrer, B., 47, 50, 119, 120
Madanes, C., 64, 69, 128, 141
Magagna, J., 69
marginalized voices, inclusion of in therapy, 217–219
Marx, Karl, 55
Mathews, F., 18, 32, 75, 89
Maturana, H. R., 4, 29
May, J., 183, 194
McCann, L., 178, 194
McCarthy, I. C., 219, 224
McGuirk, M., 217, 219, 224
McIntyre, D., 72, 89, 193
McNamee, S., 11, 120, 137, 141, 213
meaning:
    co-construction of, 90, 92–96
    co-creating, 24
Mental Research Institute (MRI), 58, 110

model, 65
therapy, 59
Milan systemic therapy, 65–66, 68
Mill, John Stuart, 54
Miller, D., 22, 29, 32, 72, 89
Miller, J., 23, 32
Miller, R., 192, 194
Miller, S., 49, 52
Minuchin, S., 57, 62, 69, 110, 111, 207
Moloney, B., 8, 9, 10, 195–214, 216, 220
Moloney, L., 8, 9, 10, 195–214, 216, 220
moment, interactive, 129
Money-Kyrle, R., 57, 69
Moore, T., 138, 141
Moustaki, E., 50, 69

Napier, A. Y., 64, 69
narrative therapy [White & Epston], 66–67, 94
narrative/conversational models, 98
narratives, of therapist, 136
Neill, J., 64, 69
neutrality, 65, 112, 165–166
Newman, K. M., 68
Ney, P., 186, 194
Nichols, M. P., 35, 51, 165, 173, 174, 207, 213
Nietzche, Friedrich, 55
Noot, M., 216, 224

object relations family therapy, 49
object relations theory, 60
Ogden, T. H., 49, 51
O'Hanlon, W. H., 94, 96, 97, 106
one-way mirror, 62, 128
Orbach, S., 221, 222, 224
Orr, D. W., 49, 51
Osman, C., 5, 12, 15, 32, 35, 51, 55, 70, 102, 107, 171, 175, 189, 194, 207, 214
outsight [Stagoll], concept of, 74

Papadopoulos, R., 221, 225
parallel process, 209, 210–211, 221
parent, disqualification as, 185

Paterson, T. R. J., 7, 9, 15–33, 101, 102, 106, 117, 118
Patterson, G. R., 67, 69
Pearce, J. K., 35, 51, 207, 214
Pearce, W. B., 21, 32, 188, 194
Pearlman, L., 178, 194
Penn, P., 88
Pentony, P., 30, 32
Perlesz, A., 1–12, 111, 142–157, 197, 214, 215, 216, 218
Perry, R., 5, 12, 42, 51, 68, 69, 116, 121
personal narratives, of therapist, 137
"philosophical stance" [Anderson; Hoffman], 97, 99
Pinsof, W., 118, 119, 121
playfulness, 86
Pocock, D., 119, 121
positioning:
    ethical, 85
    in therapeutic relationships, 81–83
    self-embodiment as, 84–85
positive connotation, 43
postmodernism, 5, 95
poststructuralism, 93, 95
power, 216–217
    balance of, between therapist and client, 117
    and control, 161–164, 173
        debate over, 91
    imbalance of, 28
    and neutrality, systemic notions of, 72
    problems of, 91
    use of, 120
powerlessness, 219–220
Prata, G., 70
process, parallel, 209, 210–211, 221
professional narratives, 136–137
projective identification, 35, 36, 38–41, 43, 44, 45, 47, 49
Protinsky, H., 212, 213
psychoanalysis, 55, 66, 102, 110, 118, 221
    and development of family therapy, 59
    family perspective in, 56–58
    models of, contribution of in dealing with emotions, 101–102
    use of concepts of in systemic context, 15–17, 34–52, 207–210, 215, 221, 222
psychodrama, 208
psychotherapy:
    feminist, 58
    value to therapist of having, 118
public welfare:
    practice
        "indeterminacy" of, 183
        relationship difficulties in, 177–180
    re-definitions of role in, 186–187
    relationship patterns in, 176–194

Quadrio, C., 35, 51

Rabkin, R., 91, 106
Rambo, A., 22, 30
rape, 93
Ray, W. A., 6, 11, 86, 88, 128, 141, 220, 224
Real, T., 5, 12, 71, 78, 81, 89
reflecting team [Andersen], 66, 93, 99, 114, 128, 197–198, 205
reflexive stance [Hoffman], 95
reflexivity, 21
reframing, 60
    strategic, 99
Reik, T., 66:
respect, 22, 42, 45, 65, 67, 82, 83, 86, 95, 97, 103, 112, 115, 133, 135, 136, 138, 149, 152, 153, 158, 159, 160, 165, 168, 169, 170, 171, 173
Rickert, H., 54
Riesenberg Malcolm, R., 39, 51
Rilke, R. M., 141
Robinson, M., 185, 194
Rogers, C. R., 115, 121, 127, 129, 141, 169, 174
Ronnestad, M., 197, 214
Roper-Hall, A., 217, 225

Ross, J., 167, 174
Rucker-Embden, I., 32

Saayman, G., 221, 225
Saba, G., 212, 213
Sander, F., 56, 69
Sanders, C., 8, 10, 158–175, 216
Sandler, J., 49, 51
Satir, V., 58, 101, 111, 171, 208
Sayers, J., 102, 106
Scharff, D. E., 39, 51, 58, 70, 101, 107
Scharff, J. S., 39, 51, 58, 70, 101, 107
Schutz, A., 185, 194
Schwartz, R. C., 46, 47, 48, 50, 119, 120, 212, 213
Schwartzman, H., 194
screen, detachment of team behind, 113
Searles, H., 202, 203, 209, 210, 214
second-order change, 29
second-order cybernetics, 72, 73, 102, 127, 128, 161, 167, 211, 215
Secord, P. F., 24, 31
self:
 autonomous, 17, 19–22
 ethical use of, 84
 as own "internal supervisor" or "consultant", 114
 personal, relevance of the development of therapist, 116
 relational and autonomous, 17–19
 of therapist, systemic constructions of, 221–222
 therapist's use of systemically, 71–89
self-determination, respect for client's, 100
self-psychology [Kohut], 57, 127
Seligman, P., 113, 120, 122
Selvini Palazzoli, M., 65, 70, 113, 122
sequences, 7, 35, 41, 59
 application to the therapeutic relationship, 46–48
 concept of, 35
 definition of, 46
 negative, 45

session, persons who should attend, 131
sexual abuse, 183, 186, 187
Sharma, R. M., 56, 70
Shohet, R., 196, 197, 210, 213
Shotter, J., 129, 136, 141
Silver, E., 161, 175
Skovholt, T., 197, 214
Skynner, A. C. R., 49, 51, 58, 70, 101, 102, 107, 119, 122, 125, 141
Slipp, S., 29, 32, 49, 51, 58, 70
Smith, J., 5, 12, 15, 20, 30, 32, 35, 55, 70, 87, 102, 107, 171, 175, 189, 191, 194, 207, 208, 214
Smith, T. E., 128, 141
social constructionism, 5, 125, 127–129, 221
social constructionist critiques, 218
Solomon, R. C., 24, 31, 79, 89
Spark, G. M., 35, 50, 60, 68
Speed, B., 6, 10, 108–122, 220, 224
Springfall, J., 183, 193
Stagoll, B., 7, 9, 74, 89, 125–141, 216, 220
Stevenson, O., 193
Stierlin, H., 16, 32, 35, 52, 73, 74, 85, 89
Stolk, V., 197, 214
"strange loop" [Hofstadter], 21, 30
strategic approach (MRI), 58, 59, 65, 110
strategic humanism, 128
strategic therapy [Haley], 63–64, 98, 99
stress, effect of on professionals, 178
structural approach, 110
structural family therapy [Minuchin], 62–63
Sullivan, H. S., 57, 70
supervision, interpersonal nature of, 196–198
symbolic–experiential family therapy [Whitaker], 64–65
Symington, N., 39, 49, 52
system, autopoietic [Maturana & Varela], 29

systemic context:
  empathy in, 42
  use of psychoanalytic ideas in, 15–17, 34–52, 207, 215
systemic supervision, personal relationships in, 195–214
systemic therapy (*passim*)
  current approaches in, 78
  feminist critique of, 86
  and process of engagement, 41–46
  and psychoanalysis, 215
  and psychoanalytic approaches, 207
Szur, R., 49, 52

Tansey, M. J., 49, 52
theory and practice, linking together, 79
therapeutic paradox, embracing, 90–107
therapeutic relationship (*passim*)
  account of, 142–157
  ambiguity in meaning of, 109
  as context of change, 85
  collaborative, 129
  different approaches to, 126
  embeddedness in, 71
  embodiment in, 71
  and empathy, 9, 53–70
  emphasis on, 125–126
  exercise of power within, 216
  failure in, 43
  multiple perspectives in, 148
  and narrative/conversational therapies, 90
  and reflecting team, 113–114
  relevance of clients' input to, 117
  systemic perspective on, 15–33
  in systemic therapy, 1–12
  type of offered to clients, 118
  understanding, 34
therapeutic staff, and statutory workers, professional relationships between, 185
therapies, analytic and systemic, distinction between, 36–38

therapist:
  as both embedded and embodied, 76
  client's perception of, 218
    of views of, 165–166
  effect on of issues brought by clients, 117
  emotional connectedness of, 111–113
  and family, relationships between, in systemic writings, 110–111
  –family relationship, 15
  overlooked as critical ingredient in therapy, 120
  postmodern, 138–140
  responsibility exercised by, 164–165
  self of, 220–221
therapy:
  analytic
    abuse in, 41
    intrapsychic focus of, 34, 36, 38
  behavioural family, 67
  brief solution-oriented [de Shazer], 93
  brief systemic, 20–22, 27, 28
  as a co-construction of meaning, 92–96
  completion of, 206
  contextual, 60
  core qualities of, 115–117
  as the influencing of context, 85
  narrative, 66–67, 94
  object relations, 49, 57, 60
  process of, 4
  psychoanalytic, 17
  reasons for attending, 149–150
  relationships in recent times, 114–115
  responsibility and positioning in, 85–86
  second-order, 37
  social constructionist model of [Anderson & Goolishian], 93
  as two interlocking dramas, 129–131
  see also family therapy

thinking aloud, by therapist, 133
Thorne, B., 129, 141
Tomm, K., 21, 22, 32
Topham, M., 208
transference, 27, 35, 36, 38–41, 43, 44, 45, 47, 49, 209, 210, 221
Treacher, A., 114, 122
Treadway, D., 173, 175
Truax, C. B., 135, 141

Ulrich, D. N., 16, 17, 30
understanding:
  empathic, 112
  model of, 24–27
  subjective nature of, 128

Valentine, M., 183, 194
Varela, F. J., 4, 29
von Franz, M. L., 91, 103, 104, 107

Watzlawick, P., 20, 32, 58, 70
Weakland, J. H., 20, 32, 58, 68, 70

Weber, Max, 54
Weiner-Davis, M., 97, 106
Weingarten, K., 5, 12, 24, 32, 161, 175
Wenders, P., 187, 194
Wetzel, N., 32
Whitaker, C., 64, 65, 67, 69, 111, 218
White, M., 23, 33, 43, 52, 66, 70, 78, 89, 91, 94, 96, 97, 98, 99, 107
Wiffen, R., 212, 214
Wilkinson, M., 5, 12, 42, 52, 68, 70
Willi, J., 17, 33
Williams, A., 210, 211, 214
Winnicott, D., 57, 70
Wirsching, M., 32
Wolf, E. S., 56, 70
Wolstein, B., 49, 51, 52
Wood, A., 94, 107
written descriptions, lack of immediacy in, 111–113

Young, J., 184, 191, 193